JOHNSTON PUBLIC LIBRARY
DUPL
W9-DFV-271

PROFILES *in* LEADERSHIP

THE SOCIETY OF AMERICAN HISTORIANS (SAH) WAS FOUNDED IN 1939 by Allan Nevins and several fellow historians for the purpose of promoting literary distinction in the writing of history and biography. Since 1957, when the SAH inaugurated the annual Francis Parkman Prize for the best-written American history, the society's chief activity has been to identify and celebrate distinguished historical writing. In 1961 the society established the annual Allan Nevins Prize for the publication of the best-written dissertation in American history, and, in 1993, the biennial James Fenimore Cooper Prize for American historical fiction. In 2008 the society joined with the Franklin and Eleanor Roosevelt Institute to inaugurate the annual Arthur M. Schlesinger Jr. Award for distinguished writing of enduring public significance.

PROFILES *in* LEADERSHIP

Historians on the Elusive Quality of Greatness

EDITED BY Walter Isaacson

W. W. NORTON & COMPANY
NEW YORK • LONDON

Chapter openers with permission by: *Page 18*: © The Metropolitan Museum of Art/ Art Resource, NY. *Page 34*: Allen Memorial Art Museum, Oberlin College, Ohio; Gift of Lewis Tappan to Oberlin College, 1858. *Pages 56, 104*: Courtesy of the Library of Congress. *Page 82*: © Schenectady Museum; Hall of Electrical History Foundation/ Corbis. *Page 126*: A 1979 Herblock Cartoon, copyright by *The Herb Block Foundation*. *Page 148*: MPI/Hulton Archive/Getty Images. *Page 164*: National Baseball Hall of Fame Library, Cooperstown, N.Y. *Pages 186, 208, 228, 282*: © Bettmann/Corbis. *Page 260*: The Schlesinger Library, Radcliffe Institute, Harvard University.

Printed in the United States of America
First Edition

For information about special discounts for bulk purchases, please contact
W. W. Norton Special Sales at specialsales@wwnorton.com or 800-233-4830

Manufacturing by Courier Westford
Book design by Barbara Bachman
Production manager: Julia Druskin

Library of Congress Cataloging-in-Publication Data

Profiles in leadership : historians on the elusive quality of greatness /
edited by Walter Isaacson. — 1st ed.
p. cm.
Includes bibliographical references and index.
ISBN 978-0-393-07655-4 (hbk.)
1. Leadership—United States—Case studies. 2. Political leadership—
United States—Case studies. 3. Political activists—United States—Case studies.
4. Social reformers—United States—Case studies. 5. Businessmen—
United States—Case studies. I. Isaacson, Walter.
E176.P95 2010
324.2'2—dc22
2010021459

W. W. Norton & Company, Inc.
500 Fifth Avenue, New York, N.Y. 10110
www.wwnorton.com

W. W. Norton & Company Ltd.
Castle House, 75/76 Wells Street, London W1T 3QT

1 2 3 4 5 6 7 8 9 0

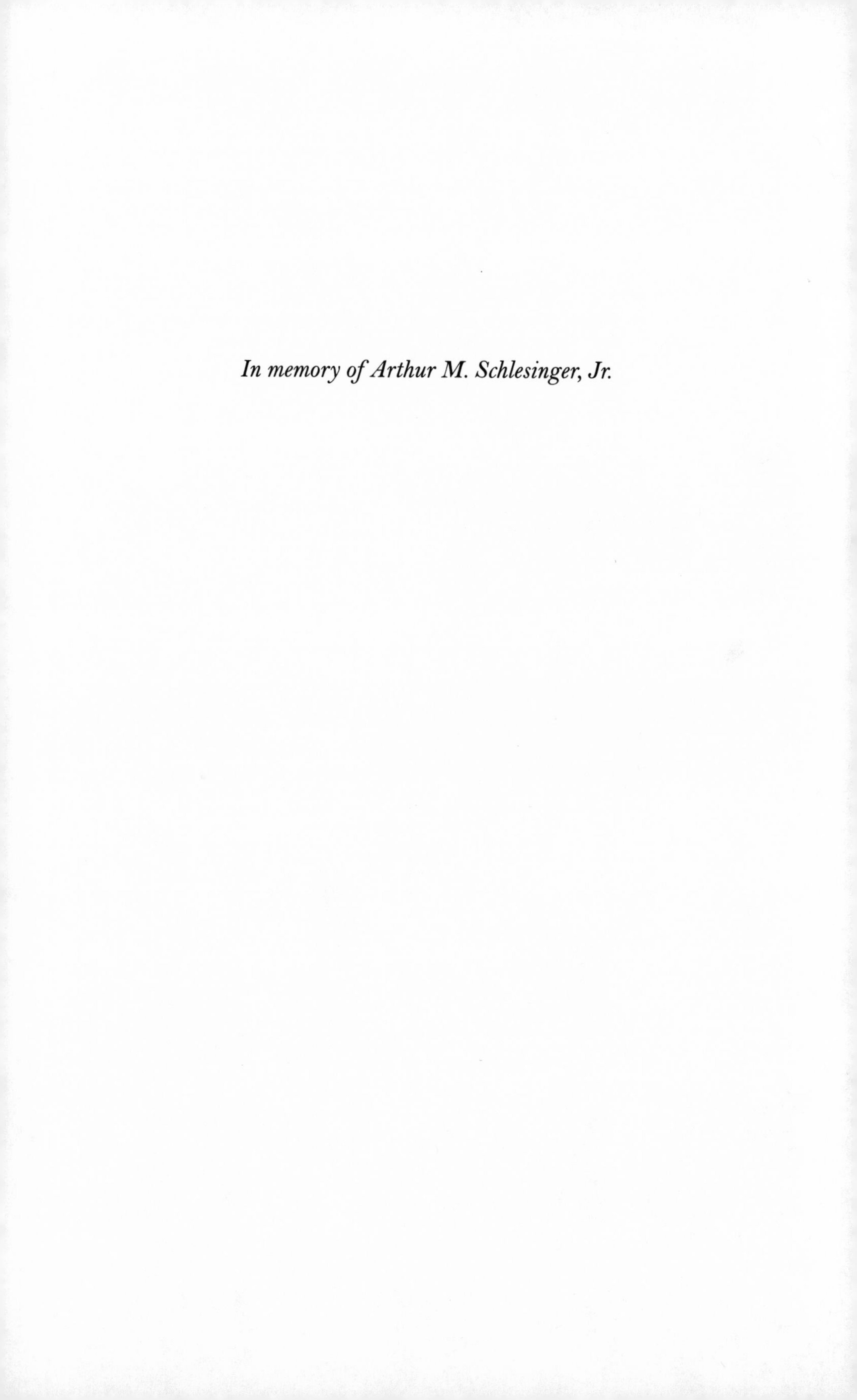

In memory of Arthur M. Schlesinger, Jr.

CONTENTS

—

INTRODUCTION

Walter Isaacson

—

THERE IS NO ONE RECIPE FOR GREAT LEADERSHIP. SOMETIMES THE men and women who emerge as leaders are the ones who are the most firmly wedded to their vision and principles. At other times it is the more flexible and practical who thrive. Even traits that might seem to be obvious assets to leadership are sometimes not as important as we assume. Take, for example, intelligence. Often the connection between it and successful leadership seems shaky at best; there are even times when it seems like an inverse correlation. Our most influential presidents—George Washington, Franklin Roosevelt, Ronald Reagan—were not necessarily our smartest ones, but rather the wisest at the tricky art of balancing pragmatism and principle.

That is one reason why crucial moments often call for a mix of leadership skills. That was true of America's birth. Each of America's founders displayed different yet complementary traits. George Washington possessed unassailable rectitude and stature. John Adams and his cousin Samuel showed great passion and fealty to principle. Thomas Jefferson and his protégé James Madison displayed elegant creative intelligence. Benjamin Franklin was inventive and pragmatic to the core and had a wry wit that warmed rather than wounded those around him. But most important in those tumultuous years, Franklin was sage enough to bring passionate people together, to lead them by listening to them.

Likewise, the history of a nation is probably best served by a mix of leadership styles over the years, sometimes creating a pattern of reactions and then counterreactions to what went before. There seems to be something charmed about America's political cycles that, along with an element of luck, serves up the people who are the right antidote or complement to the leaders who preceded them. The devious and darkly suspicious style of Richard Nixon, aided by the manipulative genius of Henry Kissinger, was suited to creating a triangular balance of power and détente with China and Russia. But Nixon's devious excesses at home and amoral realism abroad were countered by the fortuitous emergence of Gerald Ford and the election of Jimmy Carter, each of whom had a more solid moral grounding.

One of the themes of the essays in this book is that the greatest challenge of leadership is to know when to be flexible and pragmatic, on the one hand, and when it is, instead, a moment to stand firm on principle and clarity of vision. Even the best leaders get this wrong sometimes. I learned this when writing a biography of Franklin. His instinct was to try to balance the conflicting values that were at issue during moments of tough debate and to find common ground. At the Constitutional Convention he was, at eighty-one, the elder statesman. During that hot summer of 1787 the rivalry between the big and little states almost tore the convention apart over whether the legislative branch should be proportioned by population or with equal votes per state. Finally, Franklin rose to make a motion on behalf of a compromise that would have a House proportioned by population and a Senate with equal votes per state. "When a broad table is to be made, and the edges of planks do not fit, the artist takes a little from both, and makes a good joint," he said. "In like manner here, both sides must part with some of their demands." His point was crucial for understanding the art of true political leadership: Compromisers may not make great heroes, but they do make great democracies.

The toughest part of political leadership is knowing when to compromise versus when it is necessary to stand firm on principle. There is no easy formula for figuring that out, and Franklin got it wrong at times. At the Constitutional Convention he went along with a compromise that soon haunted him: permitting the continuation of slavery. But he was wise enough to try to rectify such mistakes. After the convention he became the president of a society for the abolition of slavery. He realized that humility required tolerance for other people's values, which at times required compromise of one's own; however, it was important to be uncompromising in opposing those who refused to show tolerance for others.

We usually admire, as Franklin noted, the leaders who stand firm on principle more than those who compromise. But as Alan Brinkley shows in his essay in this collection, Herbert Hoover's unshakable principles repeatedly shackled him as he tried to deal with the Great Depression. Franklin Roosevelt, on the other hand, was flexible, pragmatic, and willing to try all sorts of experiments, whether or not they seemed consistent with a set of principles. He had also learned, perhaps from trying to hide his polio, how to mislead, manipulate, and conceal his actions and purposes. But those traits—along with his incredible ability to project empathy—formed the right mix for the country at that time.

Wendell Willkie is an interesting, and overlooked, case of a leader who was both principled and willing to seek common ground with his political opponents. As David Levering Lewis explains in his essay, when Willkie won the 1940 nomination of the Republican Party, his best political strategy would have been to embrace the prevailing isolationist Republican sentiment and oppose any intervention in what was to become World War II. But Willkie followed his own principles and supported a consensus approach on foreign policy. After his loss Willkie helped devise, with great clarity of vision, a Republican internationalism.

Eisenhower was also good at eliciting consensus, as David Kennedy points out in his essay. When given a clear mission, he was able to bring people along and nurture a practical optimism. He did this not by being assertive. He never bought the notion that bullying and leadership were synonymous. But he was bold in his conduct of war because he was given a clear goal. Eisenhower was less effective, however, when he had to develop his own sense of mission and his own moral vision. That is why, Kennedy argues, he was timid on the race issue. He also valued comity over disruptive crusades for social justice. Added to that, I think, was that Eisenhower, like many people in the fifties, did not believe integration was something that should be rushed.

A similar calibration is described in the essay by Elliott West on the Native American leader Chief Joseph. He tried hard to balance the determination that comes from acting on principle with the diplomacy and adaptive skill that come from being realistic and pragmatic. As he guided his tribe through war and defeat and subjugation, Chief Joseph needed all these wiles and traits. He also realized that conveying an image of nobility and grandeur, as George Washington naturally did, was an important aspect of being a leader. After he lost on the battlefield, he won respect for himself and his people by showing himself as a man of integrity and as the ideal of the "noble savage."

There are of course many other themes and lessons in the following essays. Kevin Baker explores, in his piece on the great baseball manager John Joseph McGraw, how inner demons can fuel the drive that is sometimes necessary, sometimes problematic in a forceful leader. Evan Thomas, in his evocative essay on Robert Kennedy, likewise shows how fears and insecurities can be channeled into such leadership qualities as an impatient drive and empathy with the downtrodden.

Glenda Gilmore's riveting account of the inspiring struggles of Pauli Murray also struck me, because I knew so little about her. The essay, I hope, will catapult her into the canon of great civil rights and women's movement heroines. She was fearless, and she was persistent—two qualities of great leadership—as she took on segregation at the University of North Carolina. One of history's delightful ironies is that the great-great-grandfather of this spunky black woman was a genteel white slave owner who was a prominent trustee of UNC. It is particularly interesting to read this essay in combination with Annette Gordon-Reed's piece on the preeminent African American intellectual of the twentieth century, W. E. B. DuBois. By describing how DuBois reshaped attitudes of both blacks and whites, Professor Gordon-Reed shows how thoughtful leadership is sometimes as influential as commanding leadership.

Frances FitzGerald also analyzes a person who is now little known but who was, in the 1830s, the greatest evangelist of his times, Charles Finney. He was able to marry religious fervor with the spirit of Jacksonian democracy. The result was a social gospel based on individualism, faith in progress, and egalitarianism. His tale shows us how the frontier sometimes helped unmoor Americans from tradition, encouraging them to embrace iconoclastic, radical leadership.

Sean Wilentz's piece on Ulysses Grant will, I think, prompt a subtle reassessment of the man who has usually been portrayed as far better on a battlefield than in the White House. Yet here we see a president who was able both to push the principle of equal rights for freed slaves and to bring the American Union back together. After 150 years we still wrestle with the question of how much the Civil War was really about freeing the slaves; Wilentz shows that Grant, despite his background, deeply felt that it was indeed such a moral crusade.

As recent history has shown, financial leadership is sometimes as important as political leadership. That is why Jean Strouse's piece on J. P. Morgan seems so relevant today, a century after he rose to power as a banker and tycoon. Once again we see how important it is to be a decisive leader while knowing how to bring people together to act in concert. He also knew how to pursue his own interests while acknowledging that we are all stewards of the public interest. As Strouse notes, "imagine how different things might have been in the tech and housing bubbles at the turn of the next century if someone like Morgan had been watching closely over the managers of companies such as WorldCom, Enron, AIG, General Motors, and all the major banks, investment firms, and mortgage brokerage houses that made foolish loans and sold incomprehensible securities derivatives."

There is one essay here that goes counter to the grain. Robert Dallek looks at failures in presidential leadership. In these cases, Americans have little recourse. To remedy that, Dallek proposes an idea for a constitutional change that would permit failed leaders to be recalled.

This collection was conceived and compiled by the Society of American Historians, which was founded seventy years ago to encourage literary distinction in the writing of history and biography. Working with Steve Forman, the senior editor at W. W. Norton, we put together this book to help fund the continuing activities of the society. With the help of Mark Carnes, the Ann Whitney Olin Professor of History at Barnard College and until recently executive secretary at the society, we recruited a diverse group of authors in the society and invited them to write about whatever subject interested them from the perspective of leadership. The collection as a whole is not meant to be comprehensive or representative. We hope that the subjects chosen are interesting, effective, and occasionally surprising.

Reading these essays as a whole, we can see, once again, that no leader, no matter how great, has figured out the precise equations for being triumphant in a wide variety of dissimilar situations. That is fortunate because if the formula were easy, there would be less need for biographical essays or books like this one. As it is, I hope you will agree that the world is complex enough that it will always be edifying to look at the balance of traits and skills that sometimes work, and sometimes don't, in dealing with the shifting challenges that we continually confront.

PROFILES *in* LEADERSHIP

GEORGE WASHINGTON

The General

Thomas Fleming

—

HOW GOOD A GENERAL WAS GEORGE WASHINGTON? IF WE CONSULT the statistics as they might have been kept if he had been a boxer or a quarterback, the figures are not encouraging. In seven years of fighting the British, from 1775 to 1782, he won only three clear-cut victories—at Trenton, Princeton, and Yorktown. In seven other encounters—Long Island, Harlem Heights, White Plains, Fort Washington, Brandywine, Germantown, and Monmouth—he either was defeated or at best could claim a draw. He never won a major battle. Trenton was essentially a raid, Princeton was little more than a large skirmish, and Yorktown was a siege in which the blockading French fleet was an essential component of the victory.

Most contemporary Americans, even if unacquainted with these statistics, are inclined to see General Washington as a figurehead, an inspiring symbol whose dedication and perseverance enabled his starving men to endure the rigors of Valley Forge and Morristown winter quarters. He wore the British out by sheer persistence, with little reference to military skill, much less genius. There has been a spate of books devoted to how Washington's image was invented either by himself or by skillful propagandists. Almost as misleading is the post-Vietnam fascination with guerrilla warfare and comparisons of the U.S. defeat in Southeast Asia with the British failure in America. If American guerrillas defeated the British, Washington the general seems almost superfluous.

A general's ability to inspire his men is not of course to be discounted, and Washington unquestionably had this gift. But in the final analysis, the great captains of history are rated on their ability to conceive a winning strategy and devise tactics to execute it. Does Washington, the man the British called "a little paltry colonel of militia" in 1776, belong in this select group? The answer is complicated by Washington's character. He was, as the historian J. A. Carroll has pointed out, "not an architect in ideas; he was essentially a man of deeds." He never set down in a neat volume his military principles. The best way to grasp his superior qualities, Carroll maintains, is to examine his thoughts and actions at climactic moments of his career.

To judge his generalship this way requires a look at the strategy of the revolutionary army when Washington became its commander on July 3, 1775. By that time the Americans had fought two battles, Lexington-Concord and Bunker Hill, from which their politicians and soldiers drew ruinously wrong conclusions. At Lexington-Concord they saw proof that militia could spring to the defense of their homes and farms and rout British regulars on a day's notice. At Bunker Hill they thought they had found a secret weapon, the entrenching tool, that would enable them to inflict crippling casualties on the attacking British even if like the defenders of Bunker Hill, the Americans ran away at the end of the battle.

In fact the minutemen who fought at Lexington and Concord were a well-trained rudimentary army that had been drilling and marching for six months. They outnumbered the British five to one and knew it, a fact that added immensely to their élan. At Bunker Hill the overconfident British commander, William Howe, ordered a frontal assault on the entrenched colonials. Why the Americans assumed he would repeat this mistake in the future remains a mystery. As early as March 17, 1776, when the Americans outflanked the British defenses in Boston by seizing Dorchester Heights and fortified them with cannons dragged from Fort Ticonderoga in New York, Howe demonstrated he had learned his lesson by evacuating the city, something he had planned to do anyway.

A corollary to these bad ideas was the conviction that the war would be settled in one tremendous battle—in eighteenth-century parlance "a general action." Thus there was no need to sign men up for long enlistments; a year was considered more than enough time. There was even less need for a large regular army, which might endanger the liberties of the embryonic Republic. Militia could operate as well as regulars from behind Bunker Hill–like barricades. As Israel Putnam, the commander at Bunker Hill, summed it up, "Cover Americans to their chins and they will fight until doomsday."

Still another corollary of this strategy, though the term may be paying too much of a compliment to the Continental Congress's foggy military thinking, was the idea that if the Americans could push the British off the continent, the war would be won. So Washington obediently detached some of his best regiments and officers, such as Daniel Morgan and Benedict Arnold, to wrest Canada from royal control, a campaign that consumed close to half the twenty thousand regulars Congress had empowered him to enlist.

Washington did not question these strategic assumptions, or Congress's order to abide by a majority vote of his generals in councils of war, until mid-1776, when the main theater of conflict shifted to New York. Congress told him to defend the city; he did it Bunker Hill style. On Brooklyn Heights and at various points around Manhattan, his men expended immense amounts of energy building forts at which the British were expected to hurl themselves. One, on the corner of Grand and Greene streets, was appropriately named Bunker Hill.

Meanwhile, in mid-July, William Howe proceeded to land twenty-five thousand men unopposed on Staten Island, underscoring the idiocy of Congress's continental redoubt strategy in a war with the world's dominant sea power. Washington had only about ten thousand regulars to defend a city surrounded by rivers that permitted the enemy to land where and when they chose. The rest of his twenty-three-thousand-man army was militia.

In late August, Howe shifted his field army to Long Island and defeated the Americans in a battle of feint and maneuver. Faking a frontal assault in order to pin Washington's men in their entrenchments, Howe swung half his army in a night march around the exposed American left wing, creating rout and panic. Thanks to Howe's reluctance to make a final frontal assault, a shaken Washington was able to move his surviving troops to Manhattan by night.

A few weeks later Howe outflanked the American forts on lower Manhattan, landing at Kip's Bay (now Thirty-fourth Street) after a ferocious naval bombardment. The Connecticut militia guarding the shore fled without firing a shot. Washington, watching this stampede, cried out, "Are these the men with which I am to defend America?" Again, mostly thanks to British caution, Washington managed to extricate the bulk of his army, this time to strong positions on Harlem Heights, where a brisk skirmish with British patrols temporarily steadied their collapsing morale.

During "hours allotted to sleep," Washington began rethinking the strategy of the war in a series of letters to the president of Congress. Henceforth, he wrote, the Americans should "avoid a general action or put anything to the Risk, unless compelled by a necessity into which we ought never to be drawn." Their goal should be "to protract the war." In cutting terms, Washington demolished congressional prejudice against a large standing army. It was imperative to recruit regulars committed to serve for the duration and end the dependence on militia. "Men just dragged from the tender Scenes of domestick life, unaccustomed to the din of arms," had no confidence in themselves or their officers on a battlefield. They were impatient and impossible to discipline, and they infected the regulars with similar vices.

But Washington and his generals were themselves still infected with the Bunker Hill virus, which they now called "a war of posts." When Howe outflanked him again, landing on the Westchester shore of the Hudson troops who threatened to trap the Americans on Manhattan Island, Washington retreated to the hills around White Plains. Behind him he left almost three thousand regulars in Fort Washington, overlooking the Hudson at present-day 181st Street. These men were supposed to deny the British full use of Manhattan Island and the river.

At White Plains, Howe did little more than feint an attack, then detached a hefty portion of his army to assault Fort Washington. Masterfully combining artillery with flank and frontal attacks, the British took the fort in two hours, bagging irreplaceable regulars and scores of cannons. A chagrined Washington confessed there had been "warfare in my mind" about whether to evacuate the place. He had let Major General

Nathanael Greene, at this point one of the leading Bunker Hillists, talk him into leaving them there.

That bitter pill purged the last vestige of entrenchment tool illusions from Washington's mind. Two weeks later General Greene was across the Hudson River in Fort Washington's New Jersey twin, Fort Lee, when he learned from a local farmer that four or five thousand British troops had crossed the river at Dobbs Ferry, a few miles to the north, and were marching on the fort. Greene rushed a dispatch to Washington in Hackensack, asking for instructions. Should he stay and fight it out? Instead of a written answer, he got General Washington in person on a lathered horse. His instructions were one word: Retreat. Cannons, food, ammunition: everything was abandoned.

That was the day Washington began fighting a new kind of war in America. He was just in time, because in New Jersey the British too had some new ideas. Having demonstrated their ability to defeat the American army almost at will, they launched a campaign to win American hearts and minds. Along their line of march they distributed a proclamation offering rebels pardons and guaranties against "forfeitures, attainders and penalties." All they had to do was appear before a British official within sixty days and sign a statement promising to "remain in a peaceable Obedience to His Majesty." New Jersey, the British hoped, would become a model of how to defuse the Revolution. It had a large percentage of loyalists who would support a restoration of royal government and back the king's troops against "the disaffected."

At first Washington thought he had a good chance to defend New Jersey. He had brought twenty-five hundred regulars across the Hudson with him, leaving some seven thousand men under General Charles Lee in Westchester to bar the British from the Hudson Highlands and New England. New Jersey had seventeen thousand militiamen on its muster rolls. He asked Governor William Livingston to call them all out and ordered General Lee to cross the Hudson and join him for a stand on the Raritan River around New Brunswick.

These hopes rapidly unraveled. The British reinforced their New Jersey army until it was ten thousand men strong, under the command of one of their most aggressive generals, Charles, Lord Cornwallis. Charles

Lee, a headstrong compound of radical political opinions and careening military ambition, ignored Washington's request to join him. Meanwhile New Jersey's militia declined to turn out. Not a single regiment responded to the governor's call. Only about one thousand individuals showed up at mustering sites, almost as useless as none at all. It was grim evidence of the power of Britain's shrewd combination of carrot and bayonet.

Soon down to three thousand men, and with the British crunching toward the bridges over the Raritan, Washington told Congress, "We shall retreat to the west side of the Delaware." Although New Jersey and the rest of the country saw this decision as mere flight, Washington was still thinking strategically. He wrote Charles Lee that he hoped the British would pursue him and attempt to pacify New Jersey by stationing garrisons across the state. He planned to "lull them into security" and, when he saw an opportunity, "beat them up."

The Revolution in New Jersey slid toward collapse. The legislature disbanded. As many as three to four hundred people a day flocked to British army posts to renew their allegiance. Major General Israel Putnam, the architect of Bunker Hill, wandered through the state, telling everyone the war was lost. The current army was about to disband, he said, and even if Congress could raise another one, there was no hope of resisting the British "in the plain country to the southward." Without a hill to fight from, Putnam was devoid of ideas.

Other generals were equally ready to give up. Charles Lee whined that the mass of the people was "strangely contaminated" by disloyalty, and he was soon captured by British cavalrymen—some suspect by prearrangement. General William Heath, who was guarding the Hudson Highlands, denounced New Jerseyans as traitors and cowards. Washington took a different view. In a reply to Heath, he wrote that "the defection of the people has been as much owing to the want of an Army to look the Enemy in the face, as any other cause." In this offhand, intuitive way, Washington enunciated a crucial addition to the strategy that was to win the American Revolution. It meshed with protracting the war, never risking a general action, and waiting until the enemy exposed a part of its army to insult or destruction.

Washington swiftly demonstrated his ability to implement tactics to match his strategy. He ordered General Heath to invade northern New Jersey from the Hudson Highlands, seize arms, and intimidate the many loyalists the British had encouraged to come out of hiding there. He gave another general three continental regiments to support a fairly good turnout of militia in Morris County. Finally, he marshaled the twenty-five hundred shivering regulars under his command and led them across the ice-choked Delaware River on Christmas night 1776 to kill or capture two-thirds of the fifteen-hundred-man royal garrison at Trenton.

A few days later Washington again invaded New Jersey. Cornwallis came at him with nine thousand men. On January 2, 1777, Washington wheeled his smaller army around the British left flank by night and chewed up three regiments at Princeton, then headed for the enemy's main base at New Brunswick. The frantic British abandoned West Jersey and marched all night to get there first. They flung themselves into defensive positions around the town—only to discover that Washington had slipped away to winter quarters in Morristown. There he coolly issued a proclamation announcing that anyone who had switched sides could return to the cause by showing up at any American post and pledging fresh allegiance to the United States.

With an army to look the enemy in the face and British power reduced to a narrow enclave along the Raritan, New Jersey underwent a magical revival of its revolutionary ardor. British commissaries and foraging parties were ambushed on the roads. Loyalism beyond the army's enclave collapsed. Brilliantly combining military force and patriotic persuasion, Washington had rescued the state—and the country.

Recruiting for a new army revived in the rest of the nation, and General Howe glumly reported to London that he now saw no hope of ending the war "but by a general action." Here was irony indeed: Washington had maneuvered the British into adopting the flawed strategy with which the Americans had begun the war. Moreover, he had already decided that a climactic battle was precisely what Howe was never going to get. For the next five years he stuck to his strategy despite criticism from hotheads in Congress and in the army, who still envisioned a general action as the answer to everything. In early 1777 Congressman John

Adams, who fancied himself a military expert, was still drinking toasts to "a short and violent war."

When the British tried to advance across New Jersey that summer to assault Philadelphia, they found Washington's army on the high ground in the center of the state, waiting to pounce on them and declining to come down from the hills to give all-out battle. A disgusted Howe abandoned the stunned loyalists of East Jersey as he had deserted those in the west after Trenton and Princeton, marched his army to Perth Amboy, and sailed them down the coast, then up Chesapeake Bay to attack Philadelphia from a seemingly undefended flank.

Howe found Washington's hard-marching regular army waiting for him in line of battle on Brandywine Creek, apparently ready to offer him the general action he wanted. But Washington positioned his men to give them the whole state of Pennsylvania into which to retreat if—as it transpired—victory eluded them. He followed the same policy a few weeks later at Germantown. Retreat, a dirty word in the American vocabulary in 1776, was no longer considered disgraceful. When the frustrated Howe settled into winter quarters in Philadelphia, former Bunker Hillist Nathanael Greene exulted that British rule did not extend beyond "their out-sentinels."

Meanwhile, to make sure the British did not conquer America piecemeal, Washington was extending his central strategic concept of a regular army to look the enemy in the face. When a British army under General John Burgoyne descended from Canada in 1777, Washington sent some of his best troops, in particular a regiment of Virginia riflemen under Daniel Morgan, to help General Horatio Gates's northern army. These men played a crucial part in the victory at Saratoga, inspiring thousands of militiamen to turn out to support the regulars. Although the regulars did almost all the fighting, the militia blocked Burgoyne's line of retreat and destroyed his supply lines, giving him no alternative but surrender.

At Valley Forge, Washington revealed another unappreciated side of his leadership. Disgruntled congressmen and not a few army officers, led by wealthy Quartermaster General Thomas Mifflin, blamed Washington for losing Philadelphia. They persuaded the victor at Saratoga,

General Gates, a born intriguer, to join them. These cabalists knew they lacked the votes in Congress to dismiss Washington. Their plan called for humiliating and embarrassing him in various ways, hoping he would resign in angry disgust. They made Gates head of an entity called the Board of War that gave him far more decision-making power than Washington had. They lured the marquis de Lafayette into accepting command of an invasion of Canada, launched without even consulting Washington. A congressional committee was dispatched to the camp at Valley Forge with orders to, in the words of Sam Adams's devoted follower Congressman James Lovell, "rap a demigod over the knuckles."

Washington's response to this covert assault was masterful. He made sure Lafayette was on his side before he departed to invade Canada, When the troops Gates promised failed to materialize, the marquis blamed Gates in a series of ferocious letters to Congress. Washington used his aide John Laurens as a back channel to build an alliance with his father, Henry Laurens, the president of Congress. At precisely the right moment he confronted some of the brashest conspirators, such as the French volunteer General Thomas Conway and the gutless General Gates, forcing them to eat their words more or less in public. When the knuckle-rapping committee, led by Francis Dana, Congressman Lovell's Harvard roommate, arrived, Washington presented them with a twenty-thousand-word essay ghostwritten by Alexander Hamilton, analyzing what was wrong with the way Congress was interfering in the army's operations, causing the semi-starvation and disarray in the ranks at Valley Forge. It was nothing less than America's first state paper.

After giving the stunned solons a day to digest the conclusions of this virtually unarguable document, Washington invited committee chairman Dana to dinner. Toward the close of a long and trenchant conversation, Washington said, "Mr. Dana. Congress doesn't trust me. I cannot go on thus." The overwhelmed Dana replied, "General, Congress does trust you. And so do I." He and his fellow would-be knuckle rappers returned to Congress and became the advocates of Washington's reforms, which enabled the general, rather than Congress, to choose talented officers as commissary and quartermaster generals. For a coup de grace, President

Laurens persuaded Congress to indict Thomas Mifflin for massive malfeasance as quartermaster general. He spent the next two years frantically defending himself against these charges, while Washington went back to fighting the war.

When the British shifted their main military effort to the South in 1779, Washington remained firmly wedded to his strategy of a protracted war fought by a regular army. He detached one of his most dependable generals, Benjamin Lincoln, and some of his best regiments to meet the threat. The British trumped this hand by trapping Lincoln and his army in Charleston and forcing them to surrender, a victory that more than balanced Saratoga.

Grimly Washington detached more regulars he could not spare and assigned them to an army led by Horatio Gates, who was chosen by Congress for the job. The Saratoga victor was still the darling of many New England congressmen. The regulars inspired another good turnout of militiamen, but Gates made the mistake of putting the amateurs into the line of battle alongside the regulars at Camden. A bayonet charge routed them, exposing the regulars to another horrendous defeat.

This time Washington riposted with his best general, Nathanael Greene, who had learned a great deal about the art of war at Washington's side since sponsoring the disaster at Fort Washington in 1776. Although he began with barely eight hundred ragged regulars, Greene adapted Washington's strategy to the South, summing it up admirably in a letter to the guerrilla leader Thomas Sumter: "The salvation of this country don't depend upon little strokes nor should the great business of establishing a permanent army be neglected to pursue them. Partisan strokes in war are like the garnish of a table, they give splendor to the Army and reputation to the officers, but they afford no national security. . . . You may strike a hundred strokes and reap little benefit from them unless you have a good army to take advantage of your success. . . . It is not a war of posts but a contest for States."

Greene soon demonstrated what he meant. He dispatched 350 regulars to South Carolina under Daniel Morgan when the state was on the verge of total surrender. These regulars rallied enough militiamen to win a stunning victory at Cowpens and reverse the momentum of the war.

While Washington supported armies to the north and south, he never forgot New Jersey. The state remained the cockpit of the Revolution for him. In three out of five years he made it the site of his winter quarters. In the other two years, the ones he spent at Valley Forge and at Newburgh in Westchester, he was never more than a day's march away. The payoff came in June 1780, when swarms of New Jersey militiamen turned out to join thirty-five hundred continentals in stopping a seven-thousand-man invading army. After two bloody collisions at Connecticut Farms and Springfield, the British withdrew and never invaded the state again.

One thing should now be apparent: Washington's strategy was far more complex than guerrilla warfare. Instead, it posited a regular army as an essential force to sustain the war, aided when necessary by guerrilla elements. In spite of his criticism of militia, Washington used them throughout the war. He had no other choice. He soon resigned himself to never achieving the forty-thousand-man army Congress had voted him in the aftermath of Trenton and Princeton. For most of the war he was lucky to have a fourth of that number under his command.

He called out militia to flesh out his regular forces, but he never depended on them the way he and his fellow generals had in 1776. In 1780 he told the president of Congress that militia were useful "only as light troops to be scattered in the woods and plague rather than do serious injury to the enemy." This kind of fighting, which he called *petite guerre*—a first cousin of the Spanish word *guerrilla*—was, as his lieutenant Greene made clear, never decisive.

Washington got the most out of his thin line of regulars because he seldom used them in a European way and because he was generously endowed with a trait essential to a great general: audacity. It runs like a bright thread through his whole military career. Even in early 1776, during the stalemated siege of Boston, he startled his Bunker Hill–infatuated colleagues by proposing a dawn assault across the ice of the Back Bay on the entrenched British, a gamble that might have ended the war on the spot. A council of war voted him down.

Trenton and Princeton were of course masterpieces of audacity, but not enough credit has been given to Germantown. There, just four weeks after losing a major battle on the Brandywine, Washington hurled his entire army in four columns at the main British camp. Only the confusion generated by an early-morning fog prevented him from winning this daring gamble. In Europe it was Germantown as much as Saratoga that convinced France the Americans were capable of winning the war and were worth the risk of an alliance.

By this time Washington had stopped paying much attention to Congress's military thinking. He refused to split up his army to give various parts of the country an unfounded feeling of security. Not even the president of Congress could persuade him to station some units closer to the politicians' 1778 headquarters in York. "It would give me infinite pleasure to afford protection to every individual and to every spot of ground in the whole United States," Washington wrote. "Nothing is more my wish [but] I cannot divide the army. If this is done I cannot be answerable for the consequences."

Still, Washington never stopped looking for a chance to strike at an exposed British position. In July and August 1779, when the war in the North seemed stalemated, he struck two ferocious blows. First, bayonet-wielding light infantry under General Anthony Wayne killed or captured the entire garrison at Stony Point on the Hudson. A month later Washington's favorite cavalryman, Light-Horse Harry Lee, repeated the performance against the smaller British outpost at Paulus Hook in present-day Jersey City.

Surprize [*sic*] was one of the favorite words in Washington's military vocabulary, and he was constantly studying ways to improve his technique for achieving it. Because the enemy expected surprise attacks at dawn, he recommended midnight. "A dark night and even a rainy one[,] if you can find the way, will contribute to your success," he told Anthony Wayne, advice Wayne put to good use at Stony Point.

But Washington tempered his audacity with caution. When Benedict Arnold wanted to organize an assault on British-held Newport in 1777, Washington told him to forget it unless he had "a moral certainty" of succeeding. More and more, as the war dragged on, he sought to avoid giving the British even the appearance of a victory. He was constantly aware of the importance of maintaining popular support. This not only was important politically but was a vital part of his military strategy. Militia would not turn out for a loser. In this context, Brandywine, which seems at first glance to contradict Washington's determination to avoid a general action, fits his strategy of maintaining an army to look the enemy in the face. He recognized that in the struggle for hearts and minds up and down a two-thousand-mile-long continent, there were times when the Americans had to fight even if the odds were heavily against them. To have allowed the British to march into Philadelphia without a battle would have ruined the patriots' morale.

A similar blend of pugnacity and public relations motivated the last major battle under Washington's sole command, Monmouth in June 1778. The French had entered the war, and the panicky British abandoned Philadelphia to retreat to New York. Now more than ever Washington was disinclined to risk everything in a general action. But he sensed the need to strike a blow. After a day of ferocious fighting in nightmarish heat in the New Jersey Pine Barrens, satisfied that he had won the appearance of a victory, he let the redcoats continue their retreat.

To maintain civilian morale, Washington at one point suggested Congress provide the army with "a small traveling press" to supply "speedy and exact information of any military transactions that take place." When the bankrupt Congress refused, Washington did the next best thing. He furloughed an ex-newspaperman, Lieutenant Sheppard Kollock of the Continental artillery, and set him up as editor of the *New Jersey Journal*, which at least stabilized public opinion in the Cockpit State.

On another front Washington displayed an audacity, and an imagination, few generals have matched. Throughout most of the war he was his own intelligence director. He proved himself a master of the game, running as many as a half dozen spy rings in Philadelphia and New York. He constantly urged his fellow generals to follow suit. "Single men in the night will be more likely to ascertain facts than the best glasses in the day," he wrote to Anthony Wayne in 1779.

One of the keys to his victory at Trenton was his use of a double agent, John Honeyman, to give him a thorough briefing on the enemy's defenses and to lull the local commander with stories of the American army's collapse. At Valley Forge, Washington manufactured in his own handwriting documents full of returns from imaginary infantry and cavalry regiments. Double agents handed those documents over to the British in Philadelphia, convincing them that the main army had been reinforced with eight thousand men and was too strong to molest.

In July 1780 Sir Henry Clinton decided to launch a preemptive attack on a French army that had just landed at Newport. A brilliant idea, it might well have succeeded if one of Washington's best New York agents had not rushed him news of the plan. Clinton actually had his men aboard ships when he was distracted by the capture of some "secret" papers that showed Washington was planning an all-out attack on New York. The jittery British general abandoned his coup de main.

The Yorktown campaign was the ultimate proof of the genius of Washington's generalship. The idea of trapping Cornwallis in the little tobacco port came from the French commander, the comte de Rochambeau. At first Washington was skeptical of its chances for success. But the execution of the plan depended totally on Washington's tactics and strategy. First he befuddled the British commander, Sir Henry Clinton, with a veritable blizzard of false information about an attack on New York. Then he took the huge gamble of marching his men south in a long, exposed line through New Jersey. Benedict Arnold, by that time a British general, begged Clinton to attack, but Sir Henry declined another encounter with "the bold persevering militia of that populous province" and let Washington march to victory.

Perhaps the most appealing thing about Washington's strategy was its strong link to freedom. It eschewed the militaristic idea of hauling every man into the ranks at the point of a gun. It rested instead on faith in the courage of free men. It was a realistic faith: He did not expect men to commit suicide in defense of freedom, but he did believe men would take grave risks if they thought they had a reasonable chance of succeeding.

Looking back in his retirement years, Washington, an innately modest man, was often inclined to attribute victory to the "interposition of Providence." But those who study the evidence—and ignore the statistics—are inclined to think Providence wore the shape of a tall Virginian who had the brains to conceive a way to win a war when it was on the brink of being lost and the ability to provide the leadership that converted this strategy into a military victory won by free men.

CHARLES FINNEY
Prophet of Social Reform

Frances FitzGerald

—

IN JULY 1827 EIGHTEEN RANKING CONGREGATIONALIST AND PRESbyterian clergymen from New York and New England held a nine-day meeting at a house in New Lebanon, New York. When the ministers descended from their carriages on the first morning, there seemed to be two groups, for greetings between some were cordial and between others stiff. After they moved into the drawing room, an energetic fireplug of a man introduced eight of the ministers, then turned to a younger, tall, strikingly handsome figure to introduce the rest. The first was Lyman Beecher, the most powerful clergyman in New England; the second, Charles Grandison Finney, a minister who in the past two years had become the most famous evangelist in New York State.

The previous year Finney had conducted a series of revivals in Oneida County with spectacular results: four hundred converts in Rome, five hundred in Utica, or a tenth of the towns' populations, and three thousand in the county as a whole. In Rome he had spent a month at one church, giving sermons every evening and holding prayer meetings in the daytime. People had thronged to the church from all over town, and secular business had been largely suspended. His prayers and preaching had produced powerful emotional reactions, even among physicians, lawyers, and merchants who had attended church for years and sat unmoved through other revivals. People had groaned, sobbed, and laughed, and one man had fainted dead away. In Utica and the surrounding towns he preached at a number of churches, a cadre of ministers conducted services concurrently with his, and as news of the excitement spread, itinerant preachers and lay exhorters flocked to assist him. His success had brought him strong support from the Oneida Presbytery and praise from such respected preachers as Dr. Samuel Aiken of the First Church of Utica. It also brought him detractors, and rumors started that he and his friends were wild fanatics who invaded churches, terrorized congregations with talk of the devil, and denounced their pastors as "cold," "stupid," or "dead."

These rumors, and more, had reached the Reverend Asahel Nettleton, who for years had been the best-known revivalist in New England. An old-school Calvinist, Nettleton had preached quiet, dignified revivals with an emphasis on fine points of doctrine, but his message no longer seemed to be reaching congregations. The previous winter he had arranged to meet Finney with the intention of taking him to task for his "calamitous" revival measures, but a shy, nervous man, he found himself unable to confront the younger preacher. Instead, he wrote Samuel Aiken and twenty other New York pastors, charging Finney and his exhorters with a long list of offenses, among them speaking with familiarity of God and the devil, turning young converts into exhorters, encouraging women to pray in mixed company, and "crushing" those ministers who would not immediately agree to their new measures. These young men, he wrote, were "creating disorganization and disorder" in the churches and stirring up "a civil war in Zion." He wrote his friend Lyman Beecher in Boston a version of the same letter, pleading with him to do something about Finney and his band. "Somebody must speak," he wrote, "and who, WHO, I ask, shall do it, if not someone from New England?"

Nettleton's letters created a storm, and for the next five months angry missives flew back and forth between the New York and the New England clergy. In a letter to one of the New Yorkers, Beecher wrote that Finney's new measures were violations of "civilized decorum and Christian courtesy," and their general adoption "would be the greatest calamity that could befall this young empire." We are, he thundered, "on the confines of universal misrule and moral desolation, and no time is to be lost in forestalling and holding public sentiment correctly, before the mass shall be put in motion by fierce winds before which nothing can stand." Beecher particularly deplored the western revivalists' view that "all men, because sinners, are therefore to be treated alike by ministers of the gospel without regard to age or station in the society." This attitude, he wrote, was especially dangerous "in republican governments where public opinion is the only law," for there it would lead to a "leveling of distinctions in society," and that would be "the sure presage of anarchy and absolute destruction."

Beecher had a tendency to rhetorical excess, but the report of Finney's activities had certainly alarmed him. In the 1820s America was in the midst of a period of intense religious revivals known as the Second Great Awakening. The revivals had begun at the turn of the century with explosive camp meetings in Gasper River, Kentucky, and Cane Ridge, Tennessee; they had then swept the country, moving west with the frontier and back through the rural areas of the eastern states. Led by Methodists, Baptists, and breakaway Presbyterians, the revivals were churching the unchurched in the rapidly expanding country. They were at the same time challenging the old religious and social order. Drawn from the backwoods people they served, the frontier evangelists championed popular sovereignty and condemned distinctions based on learning and property. They inveighed against the wealth and pretensions of the settled clergy and took particular aim at the Calvinists for their assumption of cultural superiority, for their abstruse theology, and in particular for their doctrine that only a predestined elect could achieve salvation. These evangelical insurgents had made astonishing numbers of converts. In the South, they had overwhelmed the Anglican Church, and in rural areas of the North, they had far outstripped the Puritan churches. To Beecher, Finney's revival methods seemed much like those of the frontier sectarians, and fearing that Finney was bringing insurgency into the heart of the orthodox church, Beecher girded himself for yet another battle in his ongoing struggle to defend Christian civilization.

As a student at Yale in the early years of the century Beecher had heeded the warning of Yale president Timothy Dwight that the church was under attack: on one hand, from the backwoods sectarians and, on the other, from Enlightenment rationalism that was driving many educated people from Calvinism into the heresies of Unitarianism. Beecher had done his best to maintain the alliance of church and state, but after Connecticut revoked its support of the Congregationalist churches in

1818, he had found other ways to extend the influence of the church. His friend the Yale theologian Nathaniel Taylor had revisited the doctrines of election, predestination, and human depravity and reasoned that God in his benevolence would grant salvation to all who chose it and that man had the ability to do what God required. Beecher, who realized that free will doctrines would make Calvinism more acceptable to the populace, had adopted what became known as the New School theology but qualified his views carefully enough to claim he remained quite orthodox. He preached revivals of the sort that would not offend the oldline Calvinists or draw the mockery of the Unitarians. He also mounted a temperance crusade and formed a host of voluntary associations for mission work and moral reform, among them American Tract and American Bible societies. A formidable organizer and coalition builder, he believed that these associations could unite the Puritan churches, mobilize public opinion to guard public morals, and "perpetuate forever our civil and religious institutions." As for mission work, the Congregationalists and Presbyterians had in 1801 established a plan of union for the evangelization of the West, but only recently had the orthodox clergy begun to catch up with the Methodists and Baptists in the settled areas of northern New York. In Beecher's view, Finney with his boldness and ardor could prove useful to the cause, but he would have to give up his barbarous frontier revival measures.

By June the New Yorkers had figured out that Nettleton had gained his information from the Reverend William Weeks, a cantankerous local pastor who had never attended a Finney revival. While some urged a counterattack on the two of them, others, fearful that "civil war" was becoming a reality, proposed a high-level gathering of ministers to settle the dispute. Beecher agreed to the conference and persuaded eight of his colleagues, including Nettleton and Weeks, to meet with Finney and an equal number of his supporters in New Lebanon.

Years later Finney wrote that he had not been concerned about the meeting. The purpose was simply to "get at the facts of the revivals . . . compare views and see if we could not come to a better understanding than existed before." He had an abundance of self-confidence, but at the time he can hardly have been so sanguine. Ordained just three years before, he had little theological training and no experience of Presbyterian doctrinal or sectional disputes. Nettleton and Weeks were clearly out to destroy him. Many of their charges were calumnies, but the New Englanders did not like emotional preaching and clearly objected to some of the measures he had used, such as calling sinners by name and permitting women to pray out loud in the presence of men. If they denounced his revivals, he would lose denominational support, and a formal church trial might follow.

Beecher came ready to lay down the law to the provincial clergy, but as the published minutes of the meeting show, the difficulties for his side began as soon as the formalities were over. The westerners asked for documentation of the charges about Finney's revivals, but Beecher, unwilling to expose his ally Nettleton, refused to divulge his source. The New Englanders then had to discuss revival measures in principle alone. On certain measures, such as the naming of sinners, compromises were found, but when the New Englanders proposed that women should not be allowed to pray aloud in mixed company, the westerners put up a spirited biblical defense of the practice. When the easterners objected that the clergy should not be denounced as "cold" or "enemies to revivals," New Yorkers countered that they should not be called "enthusiasts" or "disorganizers" either. Resolutions condemning measures allegedly used by Finney were countered by resolutions condemning criticisms based on rumor and hearsay. And so it went. For fear of splitting the church, Beecher never brought up the underlying ecclesiastical and ideological issues he had made so clear in his letter, and after nine days of fencing over increasingly trivial issues, he failed to bring Finney to heel.

Beecher went away furious, but weeks later, when his anger had cooled, he realized that to preserve his own influence, he had to conciliate Finney, so at the Presbyterian General Assembly that year he signed what amounted to a peace treaty with the New Yorkers.

Finney went on to become the greatest evangelist of his day. From western New York he took his revivals to all the major cities of the East Coast, from Wilmington, Delaware, to Boston and later to England and Scotland, preaching everywhere to enormous crowds. His spectacular Rochester, New York, revival of 1830–31 set off a series of sympathetic revivals across the northeastern United States, swelling church membership by an estimated hundred thousand people. In the 1830s he inspired most of the major reform movements of the period: temperance, educational reform, women's rights, and, above all, abolition. No one was more influential than he, directly and indirectly, in converting northerners to the cause of emancipation.

The contrast between Finney's vision and Beecher's was as great as the New Englander supposed. Whereas Beecher aimed to rebuild the religious and social order of the eighteenth century, Finney was a nineteenth-century man in tune with the spirit of Jacksonian democracy: its expansive individualism, its faith in progress, and its egalitarianism. In his preaching, the emphasis was always on the ability of men—and women—to choose their own salvation, to work for the general welfare, and to build a new society. To a great extent because of him, northern evangelicals took a different path from those in the South, not just in the matter of slavery but in the very definition of the Christian life. In New York City, where he had a church in the early 1830s, he inspired large-scale philanthropy. At Oberlin College, where he taught off and on for forty years, he espoused ideas far ahead of their time, among them the rights of Native Americans and the right of civil disobedience. The Social Gospel of the late nineteenth century owed much to his preaching.

Finney is not well known today, possibly because he was too radical a reformer for the ascendant Christian right and too much an evangelical for secular historians. But in the 1960s Perry Miller wrote extensively on the influence of this "revolutionary" on the nineteenth-century American mind, and Richard Hofstadter, generally no admirer of evangelicals, wrote that "he must be reckoned among our great men."

Finney's iconoclasm, and his appeal for his audiences, had much to do with his upbringing in the West and his education outside the church. Born in 1792, he, like many Americans of the period, grew up in pioneer country, unmoored from tradition. His father, Sylvester, a modest landowner of old New England stock, had fought in the Revolutionary War; two years after Charles was born, he uprooted his family from his farm in Warren, Connecticut, and joined the tide of immigration from the hills of New England to the open country of western New York. The

Finneys settled first in Oneida County and, fourteen years later, moved on to the town of Henderson in the wilderness of the north country near Lake Ontario. The seventh of nine children, Charles grew up a country boy, doing farm work, hunting deer and turkeys, and learning his ABCs in backwoods schools. He became a considerable athlete, adept at wrestling, riding, swimming, and sailing, but his formal education was spotty. At fourteen he went to a respectable local academy, but he had to leave after two years because of the move to Henderson. Not until the age of twenty-two was he able to finish his secondary education at an academy in Warren, Connecticut, where he earned his keep by working on his uncle's farm. His ambition was to go to Yale, but he hadn't the money or the patience to spend four more years as a student. Instead, uncertain what to do with his life, equipped with a slight classical education, a trained singing voice, and proficiency on the bass viol, he went to New Jersey to teach school.

In 1818, Finney returned to Henderson because his mother had grown infirm. On the advice of friends, he joined a law office in the nearby town of Adams and apprenticed himself to one of the partners. He took a liking to the law, and three years later his future seemed secure. He was trying cases, making a good living, and expecting to be licensed to the Supreme Court of New York. He was also engaged to be married to Lydia Root Andrews, a pretty young woman from Oneida County, whom he had met at the local Presbyterian church.

Finney had attended many churches in his life—Methodist, Baptist, and Congregationalist—but none of the preachers had made any impression on him, and he was, he later wrote, "as ignorant of religion as heathen." Because of his love for music, he had joined the Adams church as choirmaster and for the first time found himself "under an educated ministry." He bought a Bible, read it along with his lawbooks, argued with his pastor, the Reverend George Gale, over the meaning of passages, and gradually came to believe that he required redemption. One day in October 1821 he quite unexpectedly felt "a mighty baptism of the Holy Ghost." He was twenty-nine, but the experience was life-changing. Neglecting his work, he spent his time at prayer meetings and that winter took up theological studies with Reverend Gale.

Licensed as a preacher in December 1823 and ordained six months later, he traveled the backwoods of the north country on horseback, making home visits and preaching revivals for the Female Missionary Society of New York. Once ordained, he married Lydia, and in the fall of 1825 they moved south to Oneida County, now settled, prosperous, and just then expecting the completion of the Erie Canal.

AS AN EVANGELIST Finney had entered a crowded field. In part because of the burgeoning population in its fertile valleys, upstate New York was far more engaged in revivals than any other part of the Northeast. Itinerant evangelists had crisscrossed the region for years, lighting fires of religious excitement so intense that the historian Whitney Cross called the region "the Burned-over District." Yet Finney created enthusiasms not seen before in the region. As the historian William G. McLoughlin tells us, awakenings are periods of cultural revitalization that extend over a generation or more, during which time a profound reorientation in beliefs and values takes place. The years 1825–37, when Finney preached across the state and took his revivals into the cities, proved the climax of the Second Great Awakening.

A portrait painted of Finney in 1834, when he was forty-two, shows a youthful-looking man with an aquiline nose, a high forehead, light hair, and arresting blue eyes. He was six feet two, and according to a minister who knew him, he had "a fine physical frame, exceptional grace of movement," and a voice "of rare clearness, compass and flexibility." In the pulpit he radiated energy and threw his whole being into his work. He never wrote out his sermons but preached extemporaneously or from a bare outline, looking people in the audience straight in the eye and addressing them as "you." His gaze was piercing, and his speech plain and colloquial. "When men are entirely earnest about a thing," he wrote, "their language is direct, simple, in point. Their sentences are short, cogent, powerful." Instead of using literary allusions, he illustrated his points with examples taken from "the common of affairs of men." What struck many people was that he sounded like a lawyer making a case to a jury.

He made structured arguments, anticipated objections, and seemed to address each person directly. "It did not sound like preaching," the journalist Henry B. Stanton wrote of a Rochester sermon. "The discourse was a chain of logic, brightened by the felicity of illustration and enforced by urgent appeals from a voice of great compass and melody." Stanton became a convert.

Like most Presbyterians in western New York, Finney preached Taylor's New School theology, but unfettered by theological training, he preached free will and salvation for all in much blunter fashion than did Taylor or Beecher. He hated what he called "the promiscuous jumble" that many Presbyterians made of "election, predestination, free agency, inability and duty," confounding sinners with "you can and you can't . . . you'll be damned if you do and damned if you don't." Original sin, he declared, was not some "constitutional depravity" but rather a deep-seated "selfishness" that people could overcome if they made themselves "a new heart." "Sin and holiness," he said, "are voluntary states of mind," and every sinner "under the influence of the Spirit of God, is just as free as a jury under the arguments of an advocate" to make up his or her own mind.

In the beginning Finney, like most frontier preachers, concentrated almost exclusively on the need for conversion, but in the 1830s he broadened his focus to the responsibilities of Christians. Converts, he preached, did not escape life. Rather, they had the duty to begin new lives dedicated to "disinterested benevolence" and to work for the attainment of God's kingdom on earth. In the excitement of the 1830s he preached that the millennium might come in just a few years if Christians exerted themselves. Finney was not talking about Armageddon but of a prophecy just as well known to the heirs of the Puritans: that increasing righteousness would usher in a thousand-year reign of true Christianity that would culminate with Christ's return to earth. Jonathan Edwards had preached this optimistic eschatology at the height of the First Great Awakening in the 1740s, but he had believed in a millennium of invisible spiritual grace, whereas Finney had a less pietistic, less supernaturalist vision. Christians might, with God's grace, bring in the millennium if they rid the world of its ills. Personal piety and personal morality were not enough; Christians had to prove "useful in the highest degree possible in advancing God's kingdom."

Finney published few sermons before 1835, and his revival methods changed over time, but the Rochester revival of 1830–31, which attracted the religious press and ministers from all over the region, was well enough documented to permit historians to reconstruct not just what he said and did but how he affected his audience. According to Paul E. Johnson and Mary P. Ryan, he changed not only the spiritual life but also the politics and the social structure of the region.

Built on the falls of the Genesee River, just south of Lake Ontario, Rochester had until 1823 been a small market town, really no more than a village. But with the arrival of the Erie Canal linking the region with New York City, the Genesee Valley became almost overnight one of the greatest grain-growing regions in the world, and Rochester the nation's first inland boomtown. Rochester milled and exported Genesee wheat, and as the farmers of the region grew prosperous, it became a center of manufacturing, producing everything from guns to furniture. Small businesses, where workers were treated as family, became commercial operations with a workforce of unattached young men living in boardinghouses. By 1830 the village had become a town of more than ten thousand people, three-quarters of them under the age of thirty.

In the 1820s Rochester experienced considerable social and political turmoil. The leading manufacturers of the town, most of them from established families with a background of Puritan Calvinism, assumed that they had patriarchal responsibilities for the moral development of their workers. With the division of work from family life, however, they retreated into their own homes, while the young workingmen, living in their own society, drank, caroused, and brawled as they pleased. Alarmed by the disorder among their men and figuring strong drink the cause of it, the manufacturers pressed for temperance legislation, but with the extension of the franchise to men without property, they no longer controlled the city government. At the same time, issues such as Masonry and whether or not Sabbath observance should extend to prohibiting the Sunday mail rent the churches, setting one minister against another and wealthy laymen against their own ministers. To many, it seemed that the town had become ungovernable.

Finney arrived in September 1830 to take the vacant pulpit of one of the three Presbyterian churches in town. He had almost refused the urgent calls for his services because of the disarray in all three churches, but at the last moment he decided that all the reasons why he shouldn't go were reasons why he must. For the next six months he preached in the Presbyterian churches almost every night and three times on Sunday. On weekdays he and other ministers prayed with individuals and held group prayer meetings in churches and homes. Meanwhile his wife, Lydia, and other evangelical women worked in the neighborhoods, counseling families and praying with women for the conversion of their husbands.

According to Johnson, the revival began among church members rededicating themselves to Christ and spread to family members and friends. People of all denominations came to hear Finney, and soon the church services were so crowded that people prayed out in the snow. By spring the churches had gathered in hundreds of converts—six hundred for the Presbyterian churches alone. A temperance crusade led by Finney's coworker Theodore Weld had merchants smashing their barrels of whiskey and letting thousands of gallons flow down the streets and into the Erie Canal. Sectarian divisions were forgotten, as were the old disputes. Lawyers, millers, manufacturers, master craftsmen, and their wives were welded into an evangelical community that subsequently converted most of the workingmen of the town. Then, as the historian Mary Ryan tells us, men and women formed voluntary associations to discourage vice, to care for the poor, and to help women bring up their children. Temperance was largely observed, and eighteenth-century patriarchal households turned into nineteenth-century middle-class homes.

The transformation owed much to Finney's "new measures," Johnson writes. The revival was quieter than those in Utica and Rome, but as always with Finney, it involved emotional group prayer. In the daytime meetings the leaders prayed out loud; others joined in, and some broke into tears, confessed their sins, and blessed the Lord. The church services were also occasions for public prayer, and instituting one new measure, Finney put those on the verge of conversion on an "anxious bench" at the front of the church, where the whole congregation could see them when they felt the spirit and stepped forward. Prayer and conversion thus became public, intensely social events, where people—men and women—exposed their deepest feelings before a crowd. After people had humbly asked for mercy and watched dozens, or hundreds, of others do the same, they found a new sense of trust in one another. Family ties were strengthened, enemies made up, and strangers found a sense of community.

It was Finney's message that showed the direction of change. In the context of a society in which traditional patriarchal rule was disintegrating, his insistence that every person had "the power and liberty of choice" was doubly liberating. It pointed to a spiritual democracy in which all people—employers and workers—were equally capable of controlling their own lives. It also pointed to a spiritual equality between the sexes. Women of the period had no legal rights in a marriage, but Finney gave them the same moral authority as men and even the right to disobey their husbands out of obedience to God. Then, too, his concept of original sin meant that children were not depraved beings who had to be tamed but innocents to be nurtured and educated. Further, Finney preached that everyone, not just the ministers and magistrates, bore responsibility for the society. Thus every Christian had to work for the building of God's kingdom.

By the time of the Rochester revival Finney had already begun to preach in the major cities of the East Coast. In the space of four years, 1828–32, he preached protracted revivals in Wilmington, Philadelphia, New York, Providence, and Boston, as well as in western New York towns. In all those cities his message of a democratic Christianity and the building of God's kingdom resonated with laymen and the less conservative clergy, but in New York he found partners, men with the power to effect social reform on a national level. His hosts in the city were not clergymen but rather a group of prominent businessmen who were prospering in the rapidly expanding economy. Transplanted New Englanders, ambivalent about their new wealth, these men contributed generously to the missionary and Bible societies Beecher had helped establish. Under the leadership of two highly reputable silk merchants,

Arthur and Lewis Tappan, they were in the process of building national associations and linking them into a veritable empire of benevolence. New School men, they found the New York clergy too conservative for them, so they turned to Finney and his colleagues from upstate. In 1830 they persuaded Finney to spend six months in the city, and when no important minister would give him a pulpit, they simply bought a vacant church building for him. Two years later, to lure him back again, they remodeled a huge theater on Chatham Street into a church that could seat twenty-five hundred people.

In New York, as in other cities, Finney urged the newly rich businessmen on to greater efforts in philanthropy. "The world is full of poverty, desolation and death; hundreds of millions are perishing, body and soul," he preached. "God calls you to exert yourself as his steward, for their salvation, to use all the property in your possession, so as to promote the greatest possible amount of happiness among your fellow creatures." Inspired, the Tappans and their friends formally engaged to give away all their profits, putting aside only what they needed to support their families. In the early 1830s they took up a series of new causes, among them the establishment of free city churches, where the poor could come without having to pay the customary rent on the pews, and the abolition of slavery.

Finney had spoken out on slavery since he first arrived in New York. Northern evangelicals commonly regarded slaveholding as a sin, but by 1830 the importance of the cotton trade to the northern port cities had made many established preachers reluctant to condemn it. In New York alone, some seven thousand southern merchants, most of them slave owners, had taken up residence and were generally welcomed by northern merchants and bankers, who had growing markets in the South. But Finney preached against slavery in vivid terms, calling for an end to "this great national sin" and refusing to give communion to slaveholders. The Tappans, for their part, took up the cause with a passion. In 1833, just after the British Parliament outlawed slavery in the West Indies, they founded the New York Society for the Abolition of Slavery at the Chatham Street church while mobs gathered outside and threatened to burn the church down. Two months later the American Anti-Slavery Society was formed with Arthur Tappan as its president and its headquarters in New York.

The national society included groups in other cities, notably William Lloyd Garrison's New England Anti-Slavery Society in Boston, but the New York society contributed most of the funds and, almost on its own, created a mass base for abolitionism. Garrison, a crusading young journalist, whom Arthur Tappan had earlier rescued from a libel suit and a Baltimore jail, published a newspaper, the *Liberator*, which stirred up the South with harsh denunciations of slaveholders and calls for immediate emancipation. But his influence in the North was limited. He never dealt with the problems that "immediate emancipation" would create for black or white southerners, and as time went on, he diluted his message—and infuriated the New England clergy—with an equally passionate advocacy of feminism, pacifism, and anarchism. The New Yorkers were more practical. They called for the immediate beginning of a gradual emancipation process, and they focused on swaying public opinion. They too distributed a newspaper, the *Emancipator*, and antislavery tracts, but they soon realized that working directly with church communities was far more effective, and through Finney, they found a cadre of field workers and a leader in Theodore Weld.

A convert of Finney's and a ministerial student at an Oneida County college, Weld had a keen intelligence and a gift for persuasive oratory. After his triumph in Rochester, the Tappans had enlisted him in some of their new projects, among them the promotion of manual labor in colleges across the country and the foundation of a theological seminary in the West. In 1832 the Tappans chose Lane, a fledgling manual labor college in Cincinnati, as the site for the seminary. They provided the funding, and the following year Weld brought in forty ministerial students, most of them Finney converts from western New York, among them Henry Stanton. During his travels in the slave states Weld had become a committed abolitionist, and he soon persuaded his fellow students to organize an antislavery society and to teach literacy to the impoverished freedmen of the city. To his surprise, the Lane trustees, most of them local businessmen, were scandalized. When they voted to ban all student societies and all discussions of "matters of public interest," Weld and most of his classmates quit the college, along with one professor and the Reverend Asa Mahan, a Finneyite from Rochester and the one abolitionist trustee.

The Tappans then transferred their support to Oberlin, another struggling young manual labor college, whose founder offered to enroll the Lane rebels and promised that they could designate the faculty and all the rules. Mahan was appointed president, and the following June most of the rebels turned up at the campus thirty-five miles south of Cleveland. But Weld had already found his calling and, along with Henry Stanton, signed on as traveling agent for the national antislavery society. That fall Weld lectured on abolitionism on the campus, and in the next several months thirty students, including a number of the Lane rebels, joined the cause and for two years made up the bulk of the field staff of the national society.

In the next two years Weld campaigned for abolition across Ohio, Vermont, western Pennsylvania, and western New York, while Stanton labored in Rhode Island and Connecticut. Regarding abolition as a moral issue, Weld used Finney's evangelical language and many of his revival measures. In the towns he visited, he stayed for weeks, lecturing for two to five hours each night and recruiting local people to visit their friends in the daytime. Often mobs greeted him with a barrage of eggs, snowballs, or stones, but generally, after a couple of days, the disturbances stopped and his audiences grew. At the last meeting he would ask all those who had made a decision for abolition to stand up, and often the entire audience stood. As in the case of Finney's revivals, the enthusiasm spread to neighboring towns. In 1837, Weld's voice gave out, but that year the national antislavery society in New York counted a thousand local societies in the North, most of them in the regions where Weld and Stanton had worked. Abolitionism had become a self-propagating mass movement, one that every year sent wagonloads of petitions to Congress.

Finney, for his part, looked askance upon the movement he had inspired. The Tappans, he thought, had lost perspective. During one of his absences from the city they had virtually replaced religious preaching with antislavery lectures at the Chatham Street church. Mobs had gutted Lewis Tappan's house, attacked black church members, and burned black churches around the city. Slavery, Finney believed, was the national evil that cried out the loudest for reform, yet the abolitionists, he thought, were making a serious mistake in focusing exclusively on antislavery agitation. Slaveholding was, after all, a sin, and like all sins, it had to be addressed in a religious context. In Finney's view, the churches were currently abetting slavery by their silence, but if Christians of all denominations came forward and "meekly but firmly" branded slavery as a sin, "a public sentiment would be formed that would carry all before it." Otherwise, he predicted, the nation would be caught up in ideological strife. In July 1836 he wrote Weld asking if he did not fear that "we on our present course are going fast into a civil war." Abolition, he argued, should be made "an appendage of a general revival of religion . . . just as we made temperance an appendage of the Rochester revival." He feared, he wrote, "that no other form of carrying this question will save our country or the liberty or soul of the slave." But he could not convince Weld or the Tappan brothers.

Finney was sorry to see Weld and his classmates quit their ministerial training, particularly because in 1835 he had accepted a professorship at Oberlin. The future, he believed, lay in training "a new race of ministers," and Oberlin needed his help. Just as important, he needed a less taxing schedule. He had contracted cholera in New York during the epidemic of 1832 and had still not recovered from the effects of the cure. The arrangement was that he would return to New York in the winter, when the colleges had their long vacations, and pastor a new church his patrons were building for him. But his health was not up to the task. In later years, after he had regained his strength, he spent long periods away from the college, preaching revivals in the East and in England and Scotland, but for the time being he settled into Oberlin as a theology professor and the pastor of its church.

Arriving at Oberlin for the first time, Finney found the campus "in the heart of a great forest and a mud hole," but Arthur Tappan raised huge sums for the college, and the building proceeded apace. Before long, Finney and Lydia and their four children were able to move into a comfortable brick house, the first real home they had ever had. Yet no sooner had they moved in than disaster struck. In 1836, Arthur Tappan, whom many slaveholders considered their main enemy, lost his lucrative trade with the South and his New York warehouse to arson. The following year a financial panic struck the nation; the New York banks closed, and the Tappans and all their friends were driven so deeply into debt they could not redeem their pledges to Oberlin. Faculty salaries weren't paid, and by late fall Finney, who had sold his traveling trunk to buy a cow, wondered how he would feed his family through the winter. Help from a New England friend arrived on Thanksgiving Day; money was later raised in Britain, and the finances of the school gradually recovered.

Thanks to Finney's celebrity and to the school's policy of accepting women as well as men, students poured into Oberlin: two hundred in 1835, five hundred in 1840, and many more after that. To ensure that the Lane disaster was not repeated, Finney had made two conditions for his employment: that the trustees should not interfere with the internal regulation of the school and that black students should be accepted on the same basis as whites. In practice few black students arrived—by 1840 they made up only 5 percent of the student body—but as a manual labor college, an abolitionist stronghold, and one of the first coeducational colleges in the country, Oberlin attracted idealistic students and teachers. In an 1839 statement of principles, the faculty declared that its commitments included "recognition of equal human rights as belonging to all . . . deep sympathy with the oppressed of every color," and "a consecration of life to the well-being of suffering humanity." In a period of "ultraist" enthusiasms in the late 1830s, the school flirted with Sylvester Graham's unappetizing diet and regimen of cold baths, but in general it avoided fads and maintained a balanced Christian mission.

At Oberlin, students debated all the public issues of the day, and in his classroom Finney encouraged discussion. Rather than lecture courses, he gave seminars in which each student wrote on a theme and presented his thesis to the class. Finney and the rest of the students then posed questions or made counterarguments until "by the Socratic method," a common view of the issue emerged. The purpose, Finney wrote, was to "awaken thought," and thus "the utmost liberty should be given for the expression of opinion." He himself found these exercises valuable. "I have availed myself to the utmost of the learning and sagacity and talent of every member of my classes," he wrote, "and not infrequently, I am happy to say, I get some useful instruction from them." Such an approach to teaching was remarkable for a theology professor of the day, but then in his view, theology was not a study of fixed ideas but rather a process of discovery.

In New York, Finney had published a collection of sermons and a book, *Lectures on the Revival of Religion*, that sold hundreds of thousands of copies in the United States and Europe. At Oberlin, he published more than a dozen volumes of lectures on theology and numerous articles for the *Oberlin Evangelist*. His books were widely read in colleges and seminaries, and each time he published, the Old School Calvinists, centered at the Princeton Theological Seminary, wrote lengthy critiques of his work, denouncing him as a fanatic and a heretic who ignored essential Reformation doctrines. What particularly incensed them, and many New School Presbyterians as well, was the perfectionist doctrine that he and other Oberlin faculty members developed in the mid-1830s. The doctrine derived from John Wesley's belief that after conversion Christians could achieve a higher level of sanctification and a "second blessing" of the Holy Ghost. Finney thought the Methodists were too much concerned with states of sensibility, or feelings, and not enough with moral responsibility. For him, sanctification meant "a higher and more stable form of the Christian life" in which Christians devoted themselves entirely to loving God and their neighbors as themselves. Finney's version of perfectionism had nothing to do with that of the antinomian John Humphrey Noyes, who claimed that he was without sin. In Finney's view, all Christians, even sanctified ones, were subject to temptation, to backsliding, and even to losing their salvation. All he was really proposing was that Christians could grow in their faith and act more as Christ would have them. But what he was doing, as the Princeton theologians noted, was taking yet another step away from Calvinism with its doctrines of human depravity and the permanent election of the few. He was at the same time moving even farther from the simple message of the frontier revivalists, and southern evangelicals generally, that conversion, or the "born-again" experience, was the one touchstone of the Christian life.

Finney never read the critical literature on the Bible developed in

Germany, and he remained innocent of the economic and social changes caused by industrialization. Still, looked at from the perspective of the fundamentalist-modernist split of the early twentieth century, Finney's theology could be seen as a precursor of modernism and the Social Gospel. As for his social and political ideas, many seem modern even today. Finney had no elaborate political theory, but he addressed what he saw as the absurdities of the radicals and the conservatives of his day. Unlike the anarchists, Garrison and Noyes, he maintained that human governments were a necessity and that while God had made no form of government universally obligatory, democratic government was the most desirable form. He also maintained that in democracies Christians had a duty to participate in politics. "In popular governments," he wrote, "no man can possibly be benevolent or religious without concerning himself to a greater or lesser extent in the affairs of human government." Christians were "bound to meddle in politics . . . for the same reason they are bound to seek the universal good of all men." Finney, however, believed in majority rule, and he believed that in ordinary circumstances, citizens should obey the law. On the other hand, unlike Lyman Beecher and many other distinguished clergymen, he did not believe that the American Republic was a "divine ordinance" or that submission to its laws was "a duty of God." In fact, long before Theodore Parker and other religious liberals of the day, Finney preached a higher law doctrine.

In the 1830s, Oberlin became a hub on the Underground Railway to Canada. Ferrying slaves to freedom was illegal under the federal Fugitive Slave Act and under the laws of Ohio. Finney, who had been elected vice president of the Ohio Anti-Slavery Society in 1835, knew that well. At a meeting of the society in 1839, he submitted nine resolutions in legal language, calling the Ohio laws "a palpable violation of the Constitution of this state, and of the United States, of the common law, and of the law of God." He also asserted that no man was constrained by any oath or law "to do that which is contrary to the law of God." Thus citizens had the right to civil disobedience.

For Finney, higher law had a general application. "We are bound in all cases to disobey when human legislation contravenes moral law or invades the rights of conscience," he wrote. Also "No legislation can have any authority that has not the highest good for the whole of its end." Finney was no pacifist. In his view, both war and revolution were justifiable if the goal and the method of prosecution accorded with moral law. But if a war contravened that law, it was simply murder, and not even national interest could justify it. In the case of war, he wrote, "our duty is not to calculate the evils merely in respect to ourselves or this nation . . . but to look abroad upon the world and the universe and to inquire what are the evils resulting." Unlike many of his contemporaries, Finney did not believe in American exceptionalism—or blind patriotism. "There can scarcely be conceived a more abominable and fiendish maxim," he wrote, "than 'our country right or wrong,'" a maxim that, he noted, had been adopted in the case of the 1846 war with Mexico. On a national day of fasting in 1841, he called for a "public confession of national sins," identifying those he found particularly egregious. One of them was "the outrageous injustice with which this nation has treated the aborigines in this country." (He was referring in particular to the expulsion of the Cherokees from Georgia in 1838–39.) Another was of course slavery. By 1846 he had confronted the argument that slavery was a lesser evil than the division of the Union. "A nation," he exclaimed, "who have drawn the sword and bathed in blood in defense of the principle that all men have an inalienable right to liberty, that they are born free and equal. Such a nation . . . standing with its proud foot on the neck of three millions of crushed and prostrate slaves! Oh horrible! This is less an evil to the world than emancipation, or even than the dismemberment of our hypocritical union! Oh, shame, where is thy blush?" Finney, needless to say, supported war with the South when it came.

Finney never advocated women's suffrage or any other legal rights for women, yet the feminist movement owed much to his insistence on the liberty and power of every individual. His revivals encouraged women to take an active role in their communities, and abolitionism led logically to the idea of equal rights for women. Most of the leading feminists, among them Elizabeth Cady Stanton, Susan B. Anthony, the Grimké sisters, Lucy Stone, and Antoinette Brown Blackwell, started out as antislavery organizers, and some of them had close connections to Finney and his converts. Elizabeth Cady married Henry Stanton; Angelina Grimké married Theodore Weld; Lucy Stone and Antoinette Brown graduated from Oberlin; and Brown went on to study theology with Finney. These women had their differences with the evangelist, but they found a mediator in his second wife, the head of a female academy, who shared their view that God had created women to be the equal of men.

Finney lived to the age of eighty-three. A former student recalled that he trained himself like an athlete for work, eating healthily, getting enough sleep, and walking for many miles in the forest on hunting expeditions. He outlived two wives, Lydia and the strong-minded Elizabeth Atkinson, who played an important role in his revivals in Britain. At age seventy-eight, he married a woman of forty-one, the assistant principal of the Oberlin female department. His marriages were happy ones, and all four of his six children who survived childhood had successful careers. At his memorial service in 1876, former students recalled how frightened they had been when he trained his penetrating gaze on them from the pulpit, but how approachable he otherwise had seemed to be. One described seeing him and Professor John Morgan, an old friend and one of the Lane rebels, sitting on a sidewalk, their legs hanging in a ditch like schoolboys and so intent on their conversation as to be oblivious of the spectacle they made. At Oberlin, Finney could get off the stage and relax. "Oh Lord," he prayed at one church service, "we ask that Thou wilt give Brother Morgan great simplicity of utterance; may he preach the truth so clearly that we shall not be obliged to stand on tip-toe to grasp the thoughts he is about to present."

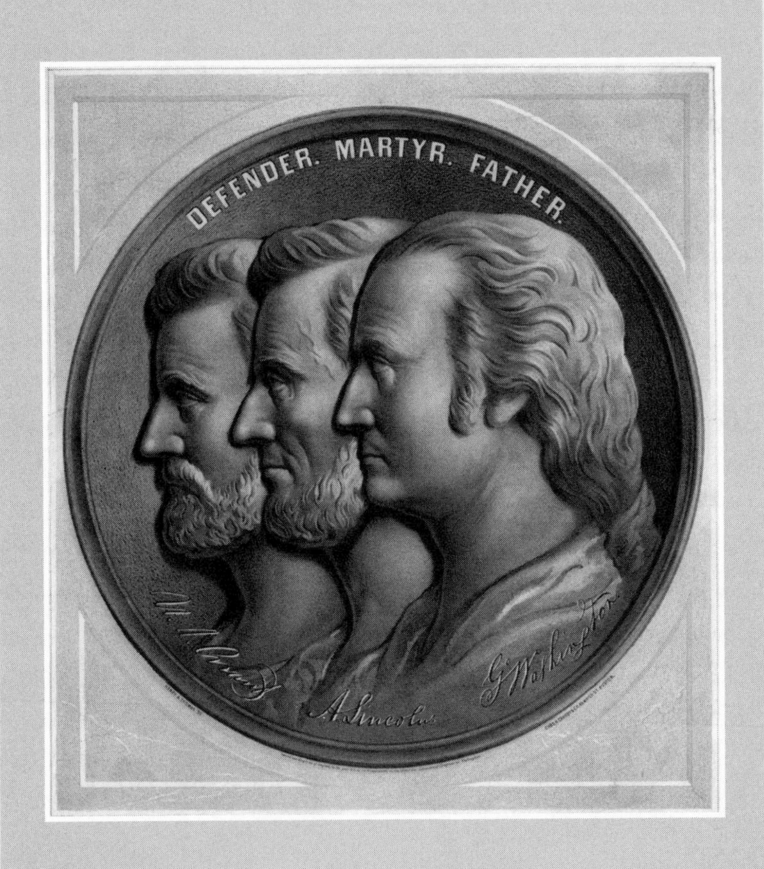
DEFENDER. MARTYR. FATHER.
A. Lincoln
G Washington

PRESIDENT ULYSSES S. GRANT AND THE BATTLE FOR EQUALITY

Sean Wilentz

—

During his triumphant postpresidential world tour in 1877, Ulysses S. Grant visited Chancellor Otto von Bismarck at the Radziwill Palace in Berlin. Bismarck was enthusiastic about meeting the American soldier-statesman, and their conversation lasted several hours, with Bismarck speaking in his slow but fluent English. The two leaders searched each other out on numerous topics, including the Franco-Prussian War and, above all, the American Civil War, which Bismarck described as "so terrible" and "so very hard."

"But it had to be done," the former president said, agreeably enough.

"Yes, you had to save the Union just as we had to save Germany."

This time Grant corrected his host. "Not only to save the Union, but destroy slavery."

Bismarck replied that he supposed, all the same, that pro-Unionism "was real sentiment, the dominant sentiment."

Yes, Grant allowed, it *was* early on. "But as soon as slavery fired upon the flag it was felt, we all felt, even those who did not object to slaves, that slavery must be destroyed. We felt that it was a stain to the Union that men should be bought and sold, like cattle."

Bismarck abruptly switched the conversation back to the strictly military aspects of the war, but Grant came around again to the imperative of emancipation, especially after 1862: "There had to be an end to slavery. Then we were fighting an enemy with whom we could not make a peace. We had to destroy him. No convention, no treaty, was possible—only destruction."

In correcting Bismarck, Grant overstated his case, possibly conflating his own opinions and reactions with those of northerners generally. From the attack on Sumter in 1861, when "slavery fired upon the flag," until at least the fall of 1862, most northerners accepted the aim of preserving the Union without interfering with slavery where it had already existed, in accord with what they believed were the plain limitations imposed by the U.S. Constitution. President Abraham Lincoln did of course begin efforts at compensated emancipation in the border states as early as the end of 1861, and by the early summer of 1862 he had quietly but firmly decided on issuing some sort of emancipation measure. Thereafter the Emancipation Proclamation caused Lincoln enormous political trouble with moderate Republicans, as well as with Democrats, in the North. Yet Grant's remarks are a needed reminder that antislavery opinion in various forms did run high in the North even before the war. If Lincoln and his victorious Republican Party did not support abolition, they were pledged to undertake the beginnings of slavery's ultimate extinction by barring the institution's expansion into the territories, a position that was sufficiently radical to cause southern states to secede as soon as Lincoln won the White House. To a greater extent than recent historians have recognized, this antislavery outlook was based, as Grant put it, on repugnance at men being "bought and sold, like cattle." Moreover, once the shooting started, it became apparent soon enough that, as Grant recognized at the time, slavery would not survive a Union victory.

In his conversation with Bismarck, Grant also showed that he believed that the war had settled, or at least should have settled, once and for all the issue of slavery and racial subjugation in the South, as well as the Union's preservation. Through his two terms as president Grant held firmly to that belief even when doing so caused him heavy political losses. Heroically, if not always successfully, he upheld Lincoln's twin principles of Unionism and emancipation, and above all, he wrote, Lincoln's "desire to see all the people of the United States enter again upon the full privileges of citizenship with equality among all." For this steadfastness over Reconstruction and more, Grant, long an object of derision, indeed obloquy, deserves to be honored as a major American leader, one of the best presidents of his day, if not in all American history.

Grant's reputation as a political leader has had a curious and telling history. That his presidency has ranked so low for so long says practically nothing about his public standing at the time. Grant won election in 1868 with just under 53 percent of the popular vote, a larger margin than expected, even though he narrowly lost New York and New Jersey. Four years later he crushed his opponent, Horace Greeley, in both the popular vote and the electoral college. Grant thereby became only the second president since Andrew Jackson to win reelection (Lincoln was the other), and he was the only president over the decades between Jackson and Woodrow Wilson to serve two full consecutive terms. Although his second administration was marred by allegations of scandal and by Democratic resurgence at the polls, Grant left office enormously popular, hailed as the most admired American on earth. During his world tour of 1877–79, the first time any former president had traveled so widely, crowds enthusiastically greeted him and his party on stops from London to Yokohama; large crowds also gathered to cheer his return to San Francisco and reappeared along his railroad route back east. "In stark contrast to what the literature might suggest," the historian Joan Waugh observes, "Grant retained much of his iconic status during his presidency and regained what had been lost in his postpresidential years." There were even serious efforts to nominate him for president on the Republican ticket once again in 1880.

During his presidency, to be sure, Grant could count on the Democratic press to condemn and mock him as at once feeble, corrupt, and imperious, attacks similar to those the Democrats had made on Lincoln. Even nastier were the rebukes of the so-called Liberal Republicans, members of Grant's own party, including Charles Sumner and Carl Schurz, who for a combination of reasons—displeasure with Grant's executive appointments, disgust at his friendliness with party organization pols, opposition to his resolute Reconstruction policy, all of it colored by a snobbish hauteur—came to despise the president and oppose his reelection. The most famous slurs emanated from Henry Adams, who thought that Grant was unfit to be president and who, many years later, observed acidly that "the progress of evolution from President Washington to President Grant, was alone enough to upset Darwin." The *bien-pensants* of the *Nation* called Grant "an ignorant soldier, coarse in his taste and blunt in his perceptions, fond of money and material enjoyment and of low company." When Grant died in 1885, the *New York Tribune* lauded his military career but charged that "the greatest mistake of his life was the acceptance of the presidency."

Yet Grant's admirers greatly outnumbered his detractors, and his death brought a wave of emotional eulogizing for the fallen leader. On the very next day after Grant was laid to rest in New York City, his adopted home, talk began of replacing his temporary vault overlooking the Hudson River with a grand memorial. A dozen years later the gigantic domed edifice that is familiarly known as Grant's Tomb was dedicated, and for the succeeding two decades, the memorial was New York's most popular tourist site, attracting more than five hundred thousand people annually, far more than the Statue of Liberty did. Observers as astute as the Scots-born James Bryce, in his formidable and influential *The American Commonwealth*, published in 1888, asserted that although American presidents had not usually been the greatest men available, four of them did "belong to a front rank": Washington, Jefferson, Lincoln, and Grant.

Grant's standing eroded drastically after 1920 because of several currents, cultural and intellectual, that emerged from diverse quarters. First, the rising racist, pro-southern, so-called revisionist, or Lost Cause, school of American historians (pioneered at the turn of the century by William Dunning of Columbia University) portrayed Grant as a butcher during the war and a tyrant during Reconstruction, a symbol of all that was hateful about Yankee domination and the financial corruption of the postwar decades. General Robert E. Lee, the man whom Grant had defeated on the battlefield, now became widely viewed, in and out of the academy, as the great military hero of the war, lionized in the South and respected in the North as the gentleman soldier who supposedly embodied the courage and gallantry of the outnumbered Confederacy. Abraham Lincoln became the true giant of the Union cause, now regarded even by some in the South as the forgiving man who, had he lived, would have spared the country the disgrace of Reconstruction. Grant, by contrast, seemed to have possessed not an ounce of decency or forgiveness. Demonized as an inept, even venal president, Grant emerged from these accounts as the lowlife who presided over the "blackout of honest government" (as Dunning put it, crudely) during the Reconstruction years, and who personally ushered in the excess and dishonesty associated with the Gilded Age of the 1870s and 1880s.

The disillusionment among the American intelligentsia about World War I—and about all professions that waging war advanced democracy—further damaged Grant's image during the 1920s. The leftist climate of the 1930s led to renewed attacks on his presidency as an emblem of Gilded Age corruption, in books such as Matthew Josephson's *The Robber Barons*, published in 1934, and *The Politicos*, which appeared four years later. In the South, and not just in the South, the success of the Pulitzer Prize–winning novel *Gone with the Wind* and then of its spectacular film version in 1939 marked the final triumph of the Lost Cause in mass commercial culture and the culmination of a distorted popular history of the Civil War era that had begun with D. W. Griffith's *The Birth of a Nation* a quarter century earlier. The rising historians of the 1940s and 1950s, even as they challenged both the Dunning school and the leftist simplicities of the Depression years, affirmed that Grant's political career was disastrous. Richard Hofstadter, among the most respected new historians, could write in 1948, without fear of contradiction, that "Grant's administrations are notorious for their corruption."

In 1962, in his major study of the literature of the Civil War, *Patriotic Gore*, the influential critic Edmund Wilson revived Grant's reputation by praising his performance in battle and (even more) lauding the taut, sinewy prose of Grant's *Personal Memoirs*, completed just before his death.* But Wilson had nothing good to say about Grant's two presidential administrations, under which, he wrote, "there flapped through the national capital a whole phantasmagoria of insolent fraud, while a swarm of predatory adventurers was let loose on the helpless South." The civil rights and Vietnam War era brought renewed attacks on Grant, most ably in William S. McFeely's

* Gertrude Stein had earlier praised Grant's prose in her *Four in America*, written in 1932–33 but not published until 1947 as part of the Yale edition of Stein's previously unpublished writings.

Pulitzer Prize–winning work *Grant: A Biography*, as a brutal Union commander and a halfhearted defender of the ex-slaves during Reconstruction, whose unenlightened views on race led him to vacillate and finally to retreat from resisting the forces of white supremacy. Curiously, in the 1960s and 1970s, even after a wave of new scholarship had finally overturned the racist, anti-Grant interpretations of the Dunning school, Grant himself remained an object of ridicule and contempt. "Sensitive intellectuals, then and since," the distinguished Civil War historian Charles Royster observed in 1992, "have looked at Grant's career and marveled that he could hold his head up without shame or remorse."

Only recently, amid the long conservative political era of Ronald Reagan, has Grant's reputation come in for reconsideration and upgrading, by authors including Richard N. Current, Brooks D. Simpson, Jean Edward Smith, and Josiah Bunting III. Yet this Grant revival has only begun to make a dent on historians' perceptions generally, let alone on popular impressions, and to undo the decades of vilification initiated by the Lost Cause scholars and crusaders. According to the most recent scholarly presidential rankings, Grant no longer languishes in the lowest depths, as he had since such ranking began in 1948, but he has risen no higher than the middle of the pack, on a par with Gerald Ford and Calvin Coolidge. He deserves much better.

HISTORIANS HAVE HAD difficulty pinning down Grant's politics before his presidency, especially before the Civil War, and how they may have shaped his thoughts and actions in the White House. As a West Point graduate Grant considered himself a military officer, even after he was cashiered out of the army in 1854, and as such he purposefully avoided any fixed party allegiance. Yet on the basis of some scattered facts, chiefly about his wife, Julia, and her father, the vociferously proslavery Missouri planter, Colonel Frederick Dent, some scholars have surmised that Grant's partisan political leanings were decidedly conservative, especially on issues connected to slavery. In fact, although he never became anything resembling an abolitionist before the war, Grant's early life was deeply rooted in antislavery politics.

Grant's father, Jesse, was a tanner who, in the 1820s, moved his business and his family from Kentucky to the river town of Point Pleasant, Ohio, because, he later wrote, he "would not live where there were slaves, and would not own them." Jesse wrote articles for the local antislavery newspaper, *The Castigator*, and was a close associate of its editor, David Ammen. (Ammen also published the antislavery letters of the Reverend John Rankin of nearby Ripley, Ohio, an abolitionist hotbed, and, when collected in book form, Rankin's writings went on to influence deeply William Lloyd Garrison's decision to become an abolitionist.) Ammen's son Daniel was Ulysses Grant's best friend; the two renewed their friendship during the Civil War, and as president Grant promoted Ammen (who attended the U.S. Naval Academy) to the rank of admiral.

Jesse Grant sent Ulysses to West Point in the hope that he would train to be an engineer, but apart from his accomplished performances as an equestrian—he was the best horseman of all the cadets—young Grant excelled in art and literature. (Contrary to the later slanders against him as a coarse brute, he was an excellent amateur painter and became president of the school's literary society.) Three years after graduation he served as a lieutenant under Generals Winfield Scott and Zachary Taylor in the war with Mexico, saw combat in several battles, and was twice brevetted for bravery. Yet even as he served his country beyond the call of duty, Grant bitterly opposed the war, and he later expressed his opposition in terms that closely resembled the arguments of the abolitionist Liberty Party. "The occupation, separation and annexation [of Mexico]," he wrote in his *Memoirs*, "were, from the inception of the movement to its final consummation, a conspiracy to acquire territory out of which slave states might be formed for the American Union." Looking back, he asserted that he believed the southern impulse for secession in 1860–61 originated in this conspiracy to plunder Mexico, another view popular among the abolitionists.

After the war Grant married the socialite Julia Dent and, after unsuccessfully trying to get an assignment to Washington, D.C., was posted to remote California. There, separated from his bride, he turned to hard drinking in what became a pattern of chronic (albeit infrequent) alcohol binges. Early in 1854, under threat of being charged with dereliction of duty because of his drinking, he abruptly resigned his army commission as captain. Over the next six years, reunited with Julia and now the father of a growing family, he sank to the lower social depths, as one business venture after another, fronted by his wealthy father-in-law, failed. At his most desperate point, running a down-and-out farm in Missouri that he had facetiously called Hardscrabble, Grant had to make ends meet by selling firewood on street corners and to friends in St. Louis. His income rarely exceeded fifty dollars a month. "Great God, Grant, what are you doing?" asked one of his former fellow army officers when they bumped into each other by chance.

"I am solving the problem of poverty," Grant said.

Although Colonel Dent had refused Grant a loan, he did provide three slaves to help work the farm in 1858. From this, and from Grant's later ownership of a slave, some historians have concluded that his views on slavery resembled those of his father-in-law. But Grant aroused the ire of his neighbors by working side by side with Dent's slaves in the field, as well as by paying the black day laborers who cut his firewood higher than the going rate; one of the slaves later recalled Grant as a kindly man who "always said that he wanted to give his wife's slaves their freedom as soon as he could."

At some point in 1858, under circumstances that remain murky, Grant came into possession of a thirty-five-year-old slave named William Jones, but in late March 1859, even though he was in penury and even though able-bodied male slaves were worth a thousand dollars and more on the auction block, Grant filed manumission papers to set Jones free. The courthouse where Grant formally freed Jones was the same building where the freedom suit case of the slave Dred Scott had been first argued in 1850; the Taney Court's notorious final decision in *Dred Scott v. Sanford* had come two years to the month before Grant acted. In May 1857, Henry Taylor Blow, of the well-known antislavery Blow family, whose parents had actually owned Scott years earlier and who had provided Scott with legal counsel and other support during the years his freedom suit dragged on, had finally arranged for Scott's formal emancipation, at the very same courthouse. It is hard to imagine that Grant missed the connections, for among his friends and steadiest firewood customers in St. Louis was the very same Henry Taylor Blow, whom Grant, as president, was to appoint ambassador to Brazil.

Five months after Grant freed Jones, John Brown led his fateful raid on Harpers Ferry, and Grant understood the personal connections immediately. Jesse Grant's family had crumbled when he was a boy in Ohio, and he had found himself apprenticed to a tanner in the town of Hudson named Owen Brown, who took him in as a member of the family. Brown's son, John, was six years younger than Jesse but made a lasting impression; the two also met up after Jesse had struck out on his own. "I have often heard my father speak of John Brown, particularly since the events at Harpers Ferry," Ulysses Grant wrote in his *Memoirs*; the elder Grant recalled Brown "as a man of great purity of character, of high moral and physical courage, but a fanatic in whatever he advocated," and it made sense to his son, who wrote that "[i]t was certainly the act of an insane man to attempt the invasion of the South, and the overthrow of slavery, with less than twenty men." Both Jesse and Ulysses Grant regarded Brown as a lunatic, yet neither man expressed disapproval of Brown's abolitionist ideals.

Grant, to be sure, was hardly a committed Republican in the late 1850s, let alone an abolitionist. Whatever he may have thought about the future of slavery, he was a staunch unionist who regarded the mounting sectional crisis with dismay, and in 1856 he voted for the Democrat James Buchanan because he believed that a victory for John C. Frémont and the Republicans would incite the disunionist southern fire-eaters and tear the country to pieces. (There are also hints in the record that Grant had encountered Frémont, already a celebrity as "the Pathfinder," in the army and distrusted him.) But when Buchanan dithered during the secession crisis, Grant turned bitterly against him and his cabinet and condemned the president as actively disloyal. Although torn, in the election of 1860, between Stephen A. Douglas and Abraham Lincoln—he remarked that he didn't quite like the position of either party—he was not eligible to vote, having recently relocated from Missouri to his family's town of Galena, Illinois. He later wrote, though, that finally he wanted "to see Mr. Lincoln elected."

Days after the bombardment of Fort Sumter, Grant announced that he would rejoin the military, and thence began his legendary rise through the ranks, from a recruiter and instructor in the Illinois militia in mid-1861 to lieutenant general and general in chief of all the Union armies in March 1864. From the very start of the war he understood the conflict in terms of slavery's future: If the southerners did not swiftly renounce secession but instead, as he expected, fought hard, Grant told associates, the existing protections granted to slavery by the North would evaporate. "In all this I can but see the doom of slavery," he wrote to his pro-Confederate, slaveholding father-in-law.

Throughout the war Grant presented himself simply as a military commander and not as one of the Union command's numerous political generals. "*I have nothing to do with opinions*," he told the citizens of Paducah, Kentucky, in early September 1861, when his soldiers pushed out Confederate forces and captured the town. "I shall deal only with armed rebellion and its aiders and abettors." Yet Grant could not evade politics or the larger goals and meaning of the war, quite apart from the military-political maneuvering required of any successful general. His record was not impeccable. At the end of 1862, Grant issued an order aimed at halting black-market activities in southern cotton that expelled all Jews from the military district composed of portions of Kentucky, Mississippi, and Tennessee. After a wave of protests from Jewish groups around the country hit the White House, Lincoln rescinded the order, Grant, who had Jewish friends and no history of anti-Semitism before or after the war, renounced the document and blamed its composition on a subordinate, yet the incident dogged him when he entered politics after 1865.

On the more important, overriding issues of slavery and race, Grant cooperated fully with Lincoln and the Congress over such matters as the implementation of emancipation and the recruitment of black troops for the Union army. Yet Grant's cooperation marked far more than his political intuition or a professional obeisance to his civilian commander in chief. Of particular significance was Grant's policy toward slaves who had escaped to his lines, the so-called contrabands. Well before Lincoln issued the Emancipation Proclamation, as Union armies began marching south, slaves ran to Union encampments by the thousands, leaving each commanding officer to invent his own policy on how to treat the fugitives. Grant, who had already been putting the contrabands to work for his army as paid teamsters, cooks, and hospital attendants, appointed a chaplain, John Eaton, to take charge of the matter in his district in November 1862. Eaton was reluctant to accept the job, but Grant, he recalled, was thoughtful as well as persuasive in his counterarguments. "Never before in those early and bewildering days," he wrote, "had I heard the problem of the future of the Negro attacked so vigorously and with such humanity combined with practical good sense."

Although open to abuse and not lacking in racial paternalism, Grant's policy, worked out by Eaton—for contraband camps to supply the fugitives with food, clothing, and other basic necessities, as well as wage-work and schooling—solved the immediate humanitarian problem while extending to the ex-slaves an important measure of respect and dignity. It was the sort of policy one could have expected from the man who, before the war, worked alongside black slaves and paid his free black workers well, and although thrown together out of necessity, it became one foundation for federal policy on behalf of the freedmen after emancipation and after the war. "It was at this point, probably," Grant later wrote about appointing Eaton, "where the first idea of a 'Freedmen's Bureau' took its origin." As president Grant tried to hasten sectional reconciliation while also defending the social and political rights of the former slaves, the chief purpose of the controversial Freedmen's Bureau, established during the war's final months. But to do so required cleaning up the mess left behind by the pro-southern obstructionist president Andrew Johnson.

HAVING NARROWLY ELUDED the conspiracy that murdered Abraham Lincoln, Grant, still commander of the U.S. Army, emerged as the greatest living Union hero of the Civil War, far greater than the relative unknown who succeeded Lincoln as president. Andrew Johnson understood the importance of Grant's popularity and did his best to secure his allegiance, to the point of naming him in 1866 to the supreme position, newly created by Congress, of general of the army of the United States, the equivalent of a four-star general, the first such in American history. But after an initial period of public friendliness Grant's and Johnson's relations soured. Their first important disagreement came early when ironically, Johnson sought to initiate proceedings against Robert E. Lee and other generals of the defeated Confederacy for treason, contradicting the terms of the unconditional surrender that Grant had dictated at Appomattox. Grant prevailed, and thereafter, when Johnson shifted his stance, hardened his defense of white supremacy, and obstructed congressional efforts to guarantee the civil and political rights of the ex-slaves, Grant became disgusted. Johnson, he later wrote, "seemed to regard the South not only as an oppressed people, but as the people best entitled to consideration of any of our citizens . . . The Southerners had the most power in the executive branch, Mr. Johnson having gone to their side; and with a compact South, and such sympathy and support as they could get from the North, they felt that they would be able to control the nation at once, and already many of them acted as if they thought they were entitled to do so."

The last straw was Johnson's accusation, in a cabinet meeting, that Grant had betrayed him by refusing to go along with Johnson's violation of the Radicals' Tenure of Office Act and take over as Edwin Stanton's permanent replacement as secretary of war, a fracas that helped soon bring about Johnson's impeachment in late February 1868 by the House of Representatives. On May 21, 1868, five days after Johnson had escaped removal from office by a single vote in the Senate, the Republican National Convention thunderously nominated Grant as its presidential candidate. Winning the election under the slogan "Let Us Have Peace," Grant entered the White House determined to change the nation's course by securing national reconciliation, but on the terms of the victorious Union instead of those favored by the "compact South." He would devote his best efforts, he said, to ensure "security of person, property, and free religious and political opinion in every part of our common country."

The first momentous reform would be the ratification of the Fifteenth Amendment, banning disenfranchisement on account of race, color, or previous condition of servitude, a measure that Grant specifically promoted in his inaugural address and thereafter supported vigorously. Congress had finished approving the amendment less than a week before Grant was sworn in, although some Radicals, including Charles Sumner, withheld their support because the amendment did not explicitly ban poll taxes and other subterfuges that might disqualify black voters. The more expansive version might have had trouble getting affirmed, but the amendment, as worded, was enough to enrage recalcitrant white southerners and turn sporadic brutal violence in the South into an eruption of terrorism that at times resembled a guerrilla insurgency. Even before the amendment was finally ratified by the states at the beginning of February 1870, masked raiders led by the Ku Klux Klan began a campaign of arson, murder, kidnapping, and intimidation, with the express purposes of scaring black voters from the polls, obliterating the Republican Party in the South, and, in time, reestablishing white supremacy as the cornerstone of southern life.

Southern Republicans, unable, except in a few isolated places, to compel local law enforcement officials to curb the Klan violence, turned to Congress and the White House for help. The degenerating situation forced a difficult choice upon national officials. On the one hand, most Americans assumed that reconciliation between North and South would mean not just a speedy return of the former Confederate states to their former status in the Union but a restoration of the constitutional order that sharply limited federal power to interfere with the police powers of the several states. President Grant, as a career military officer, was particularly sensitive about any display of executive power that might be interpreted as the actions of a would-be Caesar. To heed the pleas of the southern Republicans and use federal force against the Klan would mark a clear expansion of federal jurisdiction and inevitably raise charges from northerners as well as southerners that the government had turned its back on national accord. Yet if Washington did nothing, the Klansmen's atrocities would go unpunished, and the freedmen and their southern white Republican allies would be abandoned to their fate. For Grant, who hailed the ratification of the Fifteenth Amendment as the completion of "the greatest civil change . . . since the nation came into life," nothing less than the war's outcome hung in the balance, as the terrorists and their wellborn political leaders attempted to reverse the outcome at Appomattox.

Congress, seizing upon the enabling clauses of the Fourteenth and Fifteenth Amendments, passed the first two of three enforcement acts in mid-1870 and early 1871, making the denial of any citizen's civil or political rights a federal offense and providing federal oversight of voter registration and elections. Grant meanwhile appointed the committed egalitarian Amos T. Akerman, a citizen of Georgia who was born and raised in New England, to replace the ineffectual Ebenezer R. Hoar as attorney general. The Department of Justice, recently created by Congress, began vigorously pursuing and prosecuting the Klan. Yet despite these initial efforts, furious violence accompanied southern elections in the autumn of 1870, indicating the need for additional federal muscle, to smash what Governor William W. Holden of North Carolina called "[a]n organized conspiracy . . . in existence in every County in the State," whose "aim is to control the government."

Five days after Congress convened on March 4, 1871, Grant requested special new legislation, a third enforcement act, aimed directly at the Klan, calling it the premier issue of the day. With Grant then repeatedly prodding, congressional leaders devised a bill that would make it a federal crime to conspire to overthrow the U.S. government or to conspire to prevent citizens from holding office, voting, or otherwise enjoying equal protection under the law. The measure, known as the Ku Klux Klan Bill, also authorized the president to use the military to enforce its provisions as well as to suspend the writ of habeas corpus in areas he declared in a state of insurrection. Nothing like it had ever been approved in peacetime, making private acts of violence answerable in federal court and vastly expanding federal power generally and executive power specifically. Democrats, North and South, not surprisingly assailed the bill as the death knell of states' rights, but so too, in the beginnings of what was becoming the Liberal Republican schism, did many Republicans, who objected to the bill as injurious to individual liberty in the pursuit of a failing, coercive southern policy. By late spring the bill seemed doomed, as an unanticipated weakness in northern support emboldened a piebald coalition of white supremacists, strict constructionists, civil liberties advocates, disillusioned reformers, and an assortment of Grant's disgruntled Republican political rivals.

In mid-April the House pressed for an adjournment of Congress without taking action on the bill, but the Senate insisted on a showdown vote. Grant took the unusual step of personally appearing on Capitol Hill, accompanied by his cabinet, to meet with the bill's chief supporters from both houses, where, he had earlier intimated, he would issue a direct appeal for the bill's passage. On the way up Pennsylvania Avenue, the president informed Treasury Secretary George Boutwell (whom he had asked to accompany him to the Capitol) that he now doubted the wisdom of delivering a message, lest it appear that he was an ex-general directly requesting military power over the government. It was a subtle and shrewd assessment of the delicate political circumstances: Grant could ill afford to make a difficult situation worse by appearing heavy-handed, and his own fortunes would crumble if the bill failed after he had done his utmost until the bitter end. But at the Capitol the Senate Republican George F. Hoar of Massachusetts reminded Grant of the scope of the Klan's atrocities and argued that without strong executive action, the outrages would worsen. The president, Hoar suggested, faced a choice. If Grant asked Congress to grant him special powers instead of seizing them himself, it would be (as Hoar later recounted his remarks) "much less likely to be imputed to him that he was acting in the manner of a soldier and not of a statesman." Grant immediately dropped his misgivings and wrote a strong statement on the spot, calling for legislation powerful enough to meet the emergency conditions in the South and to ensure "life, liberty, and property, and the enforcement of law, in all parts of the United States." The bill passed the House, 93–74, and the Senate, 36–13, with the votes divided along party lines.

Less than two weeks later, after southern terrorists responded to the new law with a fresh wave of violence, Grant ordered troops stationed in the South to aid federal officials in breaking up "bands of disguised night marauders." In October the president suspended habeas corpus in nine backcountry South Carolina counties, and with Attorney General Akerman taking personal charge of field operations, federal marshals, aided by U.S. troops, arrested hundreds and restored a testy order to the afflicted areas. Throughout the South federal grand juries returned more than three thousand indictments in 1871, and after many escaped punishment by turning informers, about six hundred of those charged were convicted. By 1872 Grant's policies had effectively destroyed the Klan, and that year's presidential election proceeded smoothly in the South. The national campaign's chief issue became Grant's Reconstruction policies, as the Liberal Republican favorite Greeley, also nominated by the Democrats, ripped into what he called the president's imposition of "bayonet rule" and obliteration of states' rights and self-government. Grant won in a landslide, carrying, on the strength of black votes, all but three of the eleven former Confederate states, including victories by lopsided margins in South Carolina and Mississippi. With Grant at the head of their ticket, the Republicans also picked up sixty-three seats in the House, giving them a majority of over two-thirds to go along with their majority of nearly two-thirds in the Senate.

Grant understandably regarded the results as a personal as well as political triumph and, above all, as a vindication of his southern policies. Moreover, those policies secured what, by 1872, was beginning to look like a thoroughgoing social and political revolution, one that would have been inconceivable before the Civil War and only slightly less so before 1868. Throughout the South freedmen were joining political organizations and winning election to all levels of government, including a majority of seats in the legislatures of South Carolina and Louisiana. By the time Grant won reelection, biracial Republican state governments were introducing numerous improvements and fundamental reforms, including the building of new hospitals, asylums, and penitentiaries and the introduction of public school education (albeit segregated) for black and white children. Recent historians of Reconstruction have emphasized, correctly, that much of the credit for these innovations belongs to ordinary freedmen and women and their courageous white allies, long vilified as ignorant, vengeful blacks, treacherous scalawags, and greedy carpetbaggers.

But without Grant's determination to reverse the policies of the Johnson administration, pair national reconciliation with equal civil and political rights regardless of race, push for ratification of the Fifteenth Amendment, and then intervene to halt southern white resistance, none of the advances of the late 1860s and early 1870s would have been possible.

GRANT DID NOT CONFINE his reformism to the issues stemming from Reconstruction. Appalled at the corruption and inhumane abuses that plagued the federal Indian Bureau, he called in his first inaugural address for "the proper treatment of the original occupants of this land." He proceeded to shake up the bureau and pursue a new policy designed to gather the Indians on large reservations, where they would receive, with federal aid, food, clothing, and schooling as well as protection from violence. Although the reforms produced meager improvements and led to renewed military conflict with those tribes that refused to comply, Grant at least attempted to ensure that the Indians would be treated with respect. On another front, he responded to continuing conflicts between Protestants and Catholics over religious training in public schools with appeals to the strict separation of church and state and, in time, with a proposal for a constitutional amendment that would require every state to establish and maintain a public school system open to all children, without regard to sex, color, or religion and that would be strictly secular. Grant's larger goals, once again, proved elusive, but his efforts helped temper the sectarian debate while encouraging fresh departures in reforming public education.

Still, Reconstruction remained of paramount importance. Yet despite the administration's effective enforcement of the Ku Klux Klan Act and despite the mandate he received in 1872, Grant faced renewed troubles in the South that dominated, and made a misery of, his second term. Encouraged by the Liberal Republicans' call for a "New Departure" in policy that would end the federal military presence in the South, southern Democrats moderated their rhetoric and agreed to guarantee the ex-slaves' rights in exchange for home rule, while all along, they quietly conspired with new paramilitary organizations to intimidate and attack black voters and Republican politicians. In the North the financial Panic of 1873 and ensuing severe depression badly sapped what was left of voters' commitment to racial justice in the South. So did the exposure, on the eve of the 1872 election, of the Crédit Mobilier scandal involving bribes to Republican officeholders in the building of the Union Pacific Railroad, events that, even though they occurred before Grant even took office, began creating in the public mind the image, eagerly promoted by a hostile, scandalmongering press, of a White House engorged by spectacularly sordid corruption. In 1874 the Democrats enjoyed an enormous political comeback and, in the midterm elections, picked up an astonishing ninety-three seats in the House of Representatives, enough to plunge the Republicans into the minority and all but doom any future efforts at crushing southern white resistance.

Grant, beleaguered, was not always his own best champion. By nature taciturn and measured, he reacted angrily in private to personal attacks but refused even to acknowledge publicly the calumnies about him spread in the press, only deepening the newspapers' hostility. When the White House finally did become directly implicated in scandal, most grievously in the so-called Whiskey Ring corruption, in which his personal secretary, Orville Babcock, was allegedly involved, the president could do no more than unstintingly defend Babcock, thereby giving the appearance of either complicity or astonishing credulity. Even though Grant's own treasury secretary, the former solicitor general Benjamin Bristow (appointed to the Treasury Department in 1874) was responsible for cracking open the ring and prosecuting its participants, with Grant's support, and even though Babcock was eventually tried on flimsy evidence and acquitted on all charges, and even though unfriendly newspapers such as the *New York Tribune* conceded that the scandal "had been met at the entrance of the White House and turned back," the administration's most acidulous critics refused to be placated. To this day Grant is widely believed to have connived in, at the very least, getting a guilty Babcock off the hook.*

* Far more serious was the scandal involving Grant's old friend Secretary of War William Belknap in a kickback scheme involving private contracts to run military trading

Beneath the sensationalism and corruption charges, Grant's determination to do what he could to stem the white southern reaction caused him the greatest political grief. Here as well, he incurred some deep self-inflicted wounds. The Supreme Court proved especially disastrous. Grant ended up filling four vacancies on the Court, an exceptional opportunity for any president to buttress his policies and ensure his legacy. But because of a combination of bad luck and fierce opposition in the Senate, he failed to get his first choices and wound up appointing three justices who turned against his Reconstruction policies and, in the end, helped eviscerate both the Fourteenth and Fifteenth Amendments. Particularly unfortunate was his nomination, on the advice of his cabinet, of an obscure, mediocre Ohio lawyer, Morrison R. Waite, as chief justice in 1874, for two years later Waite wrote the majority opinion in the momentous case of *United States v. Cruikshank*, which killed enforcement of the Ku Klux Klan Act by declaring that the protections of the Fourteenth and Fifteenth Amendments applied to actions only by individuals and not by the states.

It was all the more galling for Grant that the *Cruikshank* case arose from the administration's efforts to punish perpetrators of the bloodiest racial outrage of the entire Reconstruction era, the notorious massacre in Colfax, Louisiana, in 1873, part of a chain of events that led to Grant's last effort to quell the white southern uprising. The affair began when Louisiana's fractious statewide elections in 1872 brought uncertain results, with both Republicans and Democrats claiming they had won the governor's race. A federal judge ruled in the Republicans' favor, and Grant dispatched federal troops to enforce the decision. The state's unyielding white population responded by forming new paramilitary groups.

Very quickly white supremacists gained control of several rural par-

---

posts. But Grant accepted Belknap's resignation as soon as the secretary tendered it and instructed his attorney general, Edwards Pierrepont, to investigate whether charges ought to be brought against Belknap. Pierrepont concluded that there was insufficient evidence to proceed, and there the scandal basically ended, with no further implication of the president.

ishes, and elsewhere they mounted ferocious, coordinated attacks on blacks and Republicans. In the county seat town of Colfax, at the center of the state near the Red River, friends of the black-controlled government of surrounding Grant Parish, backed by state militiamen, dug trenches and took up arms to protect the county courthouse.* On Easter Sunday 1873 a force of some three hundred whites, led by a local white supremacist named Christopher Columbus Nash, attacked with rifles and a small cannon, and by day's end more than one hundred blacks had been killed and the courthouse, set afire, had been destroyed. The Republican governor immediately sent in fresh forces, and several days later two companies of federal troops arrived to restore order. A total of ninety-seven men were indicted in connection with the massacre; six were tried; and three convicted. But the court appeals of those convictions led to the disabling *Cruikshank* ruling in 1875. The Colfax events emboldened white supremacists, including Nash, who in May 1874 formed the first chapter of a new paramilitary organization, the White League. There was much more violence to come.

The election campaign of 1874 brought renewed unrest, and in mid-September some thirty-five hundred White Leaguers in New Orleans overpowered state militiamen commanded by the former Confederate general James Longstreet, took over state offices, and installed a new Democratic government. Grant responded swiftly by issuing a proclamation demanding that the rebels disperse within five days or face federal military intervention and by ordering five thousand troops and three gunboats to New Orleans. The insurgents immediately backed down, and within three days the uprising—what the historian Jean Edward Smith calls a coup d'état—was over. But the struggle for power in Louisiana did not end there. Even after the Democrats enjoyed their national resurgence in the 1874 elections, Grant sent General Philip Sheridan to the Deep South; Sheridan, after submitting a hair-raising report to the president on conditions in Louisiana and Mississippi, obtained authority to

* Grant Parish had been created by the Republican-dominated legislature in 1869 in an effort to build Republican support in the state and was named in honor of the president; the town of Colfax took its name from Grant's first vice president, Schuyler Colfax.

take command of the situation and helped set in motion the forced ejection of five Louisiana Democratic legislators installed under threat of violence to occupy seats that were still contested. A congressional committee vindicated Sheridan's actions, and at least for the moment Louisiana was quiet. Moreover, in the waning days of the Forty-third Congress the lame-duck Republican House and the Senate passed, and President Grant signed, the Civil Rights Bill of 1875, banning discrimination according to race in all public accommodations. (The last gasp of Grant's Reconstruction policies, the act was to be declared unconstitutional by the Supreme Court's rulings in the so-called Civil Rights Cases in 1883.)

By the time he signed the civil rights legislation, Grant had sustained heavy political losses as a direct result of his determination in Louisiana. Democratic cartoonists and editorialists berated his willingness to sacrifice the prostrate state of Louisiana on the altar of radical nostrums about equality. Apart from some stalwart Radical Republicans, much of the North as well as the South had grown thoroughly tired of any commitment to civil rights for blacks. And Liberal Republicans—as ever, the president's most spiteful, high-toned critics—especially abhorred Grant's actions in Louisiana. Grant's receptiveness, for example, regarding his emissary Philip Sheridan's attempt to crack down on the White League's leaders by having them tried by courts-martial struck Carl Schurz as "so appalling that every American citizens who loves liberty ought to stand aghast."

For the last two years of his presidency, surrounded by an indifferent cabinet, a hostile Congress, and an avenging Supreme Court, Grant was virtually the only leading figure inside the federal government who was still concerned about protecting equal rights in the South. Where Grant could work out a modus vivendi with politically astute southern Republicans, as with South Carolina's governor Daniel Chamberlain, he was able to stave off for a time the violent white supremacist insurgency. But in states where idealism outstripped realism and where compromising internecine politics came into play, as in Mississippi, with its ineffectual governor, Adelbert Ames, the son-in-law of Grant's nemesis Benjamin Butler of Massachusetts, local equivalents of the White Leaguers, working hand in glove with Democratic politicians, gave no quarter. By the end of Grant's second term all but three southern states had been (in the term favored by the white supremacists) "redeemed" from so-called Black Republican rule. Grant's successor, Rutherford B. Hayes, in accord with the deals that settled the disputed presidential election of 1876, turned the South over to the Democrats and white insurgents, ending Reconstruction and commencing the long regression of race relations that was to culminate in black disenfranchisement at century's end.

Grant, embittered by his failures in the South, remarked upon them during his postpresidential world tour and said that only an extension of military rule could have "enabled the Southern people to pull themselves together and repair material losses." It would have been better, he explained, to have postponed black suffrage, readmission of the Confederate states, and the rest of Reconstruction for ten years and held the South in a territorial condition, in order to prepare the way for momentous reforms and thereby to permit the citizens of the South to put aside what Grant called "the madness of their leaders" who had come to power in the 1870s. Still, Grant recognized that suffrage, once given, could not be revoked, "and all that remains now is to make good that gift by protecting those that received it." About the only merciful thing about Grant's excruciating death from throat cancer in 1885 was that it spared him from having to witness how badly the federal government failed the freedmen and their children in the 1880s and after and allowed the cornerstone of Grant's southern program, black suffrage, to be revoked for generations to come.

RECONSTRUCTION WAS NOT, to be sure, the only controversial aspect of Grant's presidency, yet his record in other areas, although mixed, is better than the generally bleak appraisals of his political leadership suggest. In foreign policy, Grant's stubborn efforts to annex Santo Domingo, an action in which that country's government had expressed interest, must count as a failure, but so, too, the settlement, by international arbitration of the so-called *Alabama* claims cases, arising from attacks by British-built warships on northern vessels during the Civil War, must be counted as a great success, for Grant as well as for his secretary of state, Hamilton

Fish. Although the Panic of 1873 and the severe economic depression that followed were not caused by Grant's actions, they inevitably tarnish his presidency's reputation, yet sufficient credit is rarely given to Grant for his swift actions, three years earlier, to upset the efforts by his sometime associates Jim Fisk and Jay Gould to corner the gold market.

Still, if Reconstruction was not the only issue facing the country during Grant's presidency, it was certainly the gravest, and his standing as a president depends chiefly on evaluations of how he handled it. In a perverse way, it is possible to judge Grant's Reconstruction as both a dismal defeat and a stunning victory, for even though while in office, Grant polarized Republicans against Democrats, northerners against southerners, and whites against blacks, he left the presidency with political, social, and economic relations between North and South restored as at no time since 1861. The price for that success, however, was the subjugation of the freedman and the reversal of Grant's egalitarian hopes.

There is an argument to be made in Grant's defense that between 1868 and 1876 blacks and their political allies laid some of the foundations for later advances, not least with the signing of the Civil Rights Act of 1875. Yet once the reaction against Reconstruction took hold, everywhere from the violently "redeemed" towns and countries of Dixie to the genteel chambers of the U.S. Supreme Court, a full century was to pass before the nation returned to where Grant had helped lead it. For the entire history of American democracy, but especially for the intervening generations of black Americans, it was a cruel sort of success.

How much blame must Grant bear? Certainly, he could not prevent the resurgence of white supremacy in the South and the obliteration of the postwar experiment in biracial southern democracy, any more than he could keep public opinion in the North (never solid on the matter of freedmen's rights) dedicated to the cause. But given all that he was up against, not simply from southern white terrorists but from high-minded factional opponents and schismatics from his own political party, it is all the more remarkable that Grant sustained his commitment to the freedmen for as long and as hard as he did. Given the limitations imposed on executive power by the U.S. Constitution, it is more remarkable still that he acted as boldly as he did.

In retrospect, it may appear as if any attempt, only a few years after Appomattox, to foster amity between North and South while at the same time upholding the civil and political rights of the ex-slaves was doomed from the start. But this was not Grant's failure; it was the failure of most of the citizenry of an entire nation, a failure that he did his utmost to avert. Finally, Grant left behind the most admirable and politically courageous record on race relations of any president from Abraham Lincoln to Lyndon B. Johnson. For that leadership, he sustained broad approval among the American people—but he earned the enmity of southern racists and northern "liberal" reformers of his own time and then earned, from generations of later historians, a lasting reputation for incompetence and worse. It is long past time that the reconstruction of our understanding of Reconstruction came to include President Ulysses S. Grant.

J. PIERPONT MORGAN

He Knew He Was Right

Jean Strouse

TO MALAPPROPRIATE A FAMOUS LINE FROM *TWELFTH NIGHT*, SOME are born leaders, some attain positions of leadership, and some have leadership thrust upon them.* In the life of J. Pierpont Morgan, all three propositions turn out, improbably, to have been true. Not many people in the second or third generations of wealthy American families have taken up significant positions of authority and power on their own, and few individuals find themselves uniquely qualified to step into a leadership vacuum when historical circumstances require it.

For almost the exact span of Morgan's life, the United States had no central bank to regulate the nation's supply of money and credit, no official lender of last resort, no federal recourse in times of financial crisis or panic. Andrew Jackson effectively destroyed the Second Bank of the United States in 1836, a year before Morgan was born, and Woodrow Wilson signed the Federal Reserve System into law at the end of 1913, nine months after Morgan died. Over a period of about thirty years Morgan served as the country's unofficial central banker, amassing private reserves when he sensed a crisis coming, supplying gold to the Treasury when the federal government ran out of that commodity, working to keep the United States on the international gold standard, leading teams of bankers to stop major panics.

* Shakespeare's line "Some are born great, some achieve greatness, and some have greatness thrust upon 'em," is actually a cruel joke, part of a letter that tricks Malvolio, steward to the countess Olivia, into thinking she is in love with him.

He also organized giant railroad systems and industrial trusts, including General Electric, U.S. Steel, International Harvester, and the modern form of AT&T. With almost no government regulation of the financial or corporate marketplace, Morgan assumed de facto command. He effectively presided over a massive transfer of wealth from Europe to the United States and helped transform a largely agrarian society into a modern industrial state.

Financial leadership in this democratic country has always been politically contested, and Morgan's actions entered him into a struggle over the nature of America's identity that dates back to Jefferson and Hamilton.

His admirers regarded him as the Napoleon of Wall Street, the financial Moses of the New World, and a modern Medici prince. His critics saw him as the boss croupier of Wall Street, a great financial Gorgon, and "a bull-necked irascible man" . . . "with fierce intolerant eyes set just close enough to suggest the psychopathology of his will." The first part of that quote comes from John Dos Passos's *1919*, published in 1932; the second, from E. L. Doctorow's *Ragtime*, in 1974.

Morgan was importing cultural as well as financial capital for the young United States. The critic Robert Hughes has described the country in the mid-nineteenth century as breathing "thin aesthetic air," with no tradition of royal collecting, no church treasure, no great public repositories such as the Louvre, the British Museum, and the Vatican. Morgan was a founder or early patron of the American Museum, of Natural History, the Metropolitan Museum of Art, the New York Botanical Garden, the Metropolitan Opera, and the American Academy in Rome. He spent about half his fortune on art between 1890 and 1913 and said in his will that he wanted his collections made "permanently available for the instruction and pleasure of the American people."

His second career in the art world, like his work as a financier, gave rise to conflicting assessments. Bernard Berenson, who toured Morgan's art-filled London house in 1906, described it to his own patroness, Isabella Stewart Gardner, as looking like "a pawnbrokers' shop for Croesuses." Roger Fry, who worked as an assistant curator of paintings at the Metropolitan Museum of Art while Morgan was president there, said years later that "a crude historical imagination was the only flaw in [Morgan's] otherwise perfect insensibility [to art]." On the positive side, Wilhelm von Bode, the director of the Kaiser Friedrich Museum in Berlin, who occasionally advised Morgan about purchases, called him "the greatest collector of our time."

That people could have such contradictory appraisals of Morgan derives in part from his monumentally reticent nature. Neither introspective nor articulate, he was, as Henry Adams said of Theodore Roosevelt, "pure act." He never said anything about why he did most of the things he did, and he posted NO TRESPASSING signs all over the place.

He burned thousands of letters he had written to his father twice a week, every week, for thirty years. He kept a white enamel plaque over the mantel in his study that said, in blue Provençal script: "*Pense moult, parle peu, écris rien.*" His silence itself became famous. After he attended a dinner in his honor in Chicago in 1908, the *Tribune* ran the headline: MONEY TALKS, BUT MORGAN DOESN'T.

There were many reasons for his silence, among them the confidentiality that has always governed the high-stakes, high-risk world of investment banking. As the most powerful private banker in the world, Morgan could not cross the street, much less the Atlantic, without arousing speculation in the stock market and the press. He had more personal reasons as well, including his unorthodox private life. His first wife, Amelia Sturges, died of tuberculosis in 1862, just four months after their wedding. He was twenty-four. In some ways he never got over that loss. He married again in 1865 and had four children with Frances Louisa Tracy. The couple's tastes and inclinations differed significantly, however, and after about fifteen years they lived essentially separate lives. Morgan would travel with his mistress, much the way European aristocrats did, while Fanny stayed in New York; when he returned, he would send his wife to Europe with a daughter, a driver, and a paid companion.

Though he played a domineering role in the art world, in the capital markets, and with his family and friends, he was extremely shy in public, partly because of a skin condition called rhinophyma that turned his nose, in his fifties, into a hideous purple bulb. This condition is often preceded, as it was in Morgan's case, by severe adolescent acne rosacea, which ran in his mother's family. Appearing long after Morgan's sense of himself had been formed, the terrible nose did not dramatically change his life. It did make him avoid the general public. He met new acquaintances with a look of challenge, as if daring them to look him full in the face and not flinch at the sight.

Edward Steichen's iconic 1904 photograph of Morgan, in which the banker glares at the camera with what looks like a dagger in his hand (it is the arm of a metal chair), helped create the image of satanic majesty that dominated the popular imagination for most of the twentieth century.

MORGAN WAS BORN in 1837, into the upper echelons of American society. Both sides of his family had come to North America before the Revolution. One of his maternal ancestors, James Pierpont, was a founder of Yale, whose daughter Sarah married Jonathan Edwards. The Edwardses' grandchildren included Timothy Dwight (author, Congregational clergyman, president of Yale), Theodore Dwight (lawyer, prominent Federalist), and Aaron Burr.

Further down this line, Pierpont Morgan's grandfather John Pierpont graduated from Yale, was briefly regarded as America's leading poet, then went to Harvard's new Divinity School and embarked on a career in the Unitarian Church. The Reverend Pierpont was a radical abolitionist and temperance advocate who spoke out so stridently against slavery and "demon rum" from his pulpit at Boston's Hollis Street Church (he also delivered sermons on phrenology, Masonry, imprisonment for debt, disbanding of state militia, and prison reform) that the church elders censured and ultimately fired him. That John Pierpont managed to get kicked out of a Unitarian church offers a measure of his fanaticism.*

Emotional instability, a vulnerability to depression and manic excess, alcoholism, and countless physical and "nervous" ailments characterize this branch of the Pierpont family tree.

* Emerson, writing in private to Theodore Parker about Mr. Pierpont's protracted fight with the church, said, "I think the people almost always right in their quarrels with their ministers, although they seldom know how to give the true reason of their discontent."

The Reverend Pierpont's daughter Juliet brought a hardy strain into the family gene pool when she married Junius Spencer Morgan in 1836. A journalist visiting Junius Morgan's estate outside London decades later described his handsome white-haired host as "the most beautiful thing in the house . . . a man used to giving orders and having them obeyed; taking decisions quickly and taking the right ones."

About the only thing the intellectual, ecclesiastical Pierponts had in common with the practical, entrepreneurial Morgans was two hundred years of New England American heritage. In 1817 Junius's father, Joseph, descended from a Welshman who had sailed to Boston in 1636, moved down the Connecticut River from Springfield, Massachusetts, to Hartford, Connecticut. There he involved himself in every significant new opportunity offered by the young republic's market revolution, operating stagecoaches, taverns, and hotels; helping organize banks to finance Hartford's economic boom; investing in steamships, railroads, bridges, and canals; helping found the Aetna Insurance Company. When Joseph died in 1847, he left an estate worth about one million dollars, roughly fifteen million in early-twenty-first-century dollars.

Junius Morgan was the single most important person in the life of his first child, born in Hartford in 1837 and named after his radical grandfather—John Pierpont Morgan. A successful merchant in Hartford and Boston, then a merchant banker in London, Junius focused fierce attention on every detail of this son's moral and practical education. He personally taught Pierpont about history, great men, commerce, and foreign travel; took him to his office and gave him tasks; lectured him about the Yankee virtues of industry, prudence, restraint, veracity, thrift; brought him along on stockholders' excursions; spent hours with him one night going over an arithmetic problem until they proved that Pierpont's answer, which did not agree with the text, was correct.

When Pierpont at thirteen went to a new boarding school, Junius warned him to be "very careful with what boys you associate not to get intimate with any but such as are of the right stamp & whose influence over you will be good. You must bear in mind that *now* is the time for you to form your character & as it is formed so it will be likely to remain. You cannot have this too strongly impressed upon you."

Juliet Pierpont Morgan also directed a stream of moral platitudes at her eldest son, along with a litany of complaints about her own health and moods. By the time Pierpont was ten she had lapsed into the "nervous" invalidism, depression, and cranky self-absorption that was to dominate the rest of her life.

Illness punctuated Pierpont Morgan's own life with the unpredictable regularity of bad weather. He nearly died of febrile seizures as an infant. Later a series of vague, unnamed maladies frequently kept him out of school. The adolescent acne rosacea marked his face and ears with painful "boils." He came down with rheumatic fever at age fifteen and was sent off by his parents to the Azores—alone—for a long rest cure in the sun.

After he had recovered, he finished high school in Boston, giving a graduation speech on Napoleon, then moved with his family to London in 1854, when Junius joined the Anglo-American merchant banking firm of George Peabody & Co. Pierpont was longing to start a business career of his own—he had his eye on the East India shipping trade—but his father sent him to school in Europe first, to learn French and German. Junius himself spoke no foreign language and did not intend his eldest son to have the same deficit. Pierpont went to a Swiss boarding school for two years, then on to the university at Göttingen, Germany. He did so well in mathematics that one of his professors asked him to stay and make a career in the field, but the young man had other plans for his facility with numbers.

At last, in the summer of 1857, Junius sent him to New York to work as an unsalaried clerk at an investment firm. The American Polonius dispatched an anxious last-minute note to his departing son on board ship: "I want you to realize the importance of the step you are now taking & the influence it is to have on your future life. *Be true to yourself* & all is well."

—

BY THE TIME PIERPONT began his banking career in New York at age twenty he was fluent in French and German and familiar with more cultures than most Americans would ever see. He served his time as an apprentice, did well as a fledgling banker, and in 1862 formed a partnership with his cousin James Junius Goodwin. Ten years earlier the cousins had traded goods between Hartford and Boston as the fictional Goodwin, Morgan & Co. The real partnership in 1862, accurately reflecting their relative professional stature, was called J. Pierpont Morgan & Co. Jim said later, "I was the Co."

Junius hovered anxiously across the Atlantic. When Pierpont and a friend briefly cornered the gold market in 1863, netting sixty-six thousand dollars each, Junius had a fit, objecting to the maneuver not because it took advantage of the Union's monetary troubles for private gain, as other critics charged, but because it testified to character flaws: willful disobedience, recklessness, and greed. He threatened to sever his professional connection with his son, fuming to Jim Goodwin that "P." had ignored "my repeated admonitions. His head seems to have been turned by the position he has been able to attain & he thus goes on disregarding any opinion but his own." Pierpont's share of his New York firm's net profits in 1863 was fifty-eight thousand dollars. The gold speculation (which Wall Street regarded as a clever coup, hurting only other speculators) more than doubled his earnings. To Junius, anyone who took such speculative risks could not be trusted with other people's money, and their business depended entirely on trust. Junius did not in the end withdraw the London accounts from New York. He did, however, make sure for the next two decades to have a senior partner in New York to keep a firm hand and eye on his headstrong son.

After the death of his first wife, Pierpont began to suffer mysterious "nervous" breakdowns, periodically collapsing with headaches, general weakness, and depression. He rarely said anything about these "black" spells, but blamed what we would now call his "workaholic" nature. "When I have responsibility laid upon me," he wrote at age twenty-five to his father, "I cannot throw it upon anyone else however competent the party may be. I am never satisfied until I either do everything myself or personally supervise everything done even to an entry in the books. This I cannot help—my habit since I have been in business has been so & I cannot learn to do otherwise."

His attention to minute detail and inability to delegate had to do with his perfectionism and instinctive assumption of command as well as with his father's exacting surveillance. Later observers disagreed over whether Morgan was a "detail" or a "big picture" man. He was both. In these early years he made himself master of every entry on the books and every aspect of every deal he made. Eventually circumstances forced him to delegate, but he claimed even late in the game that he could sit down at any desk at his firm and take up wherever the clerk had left off.

Most likely he was bipolar. His dark moods alternated with periods of extraordinary energy (he put together the gargantuan U.S. Steel Corporation in twelve weeks) and art-buying sprees (which, as it happened, he could afford). His self-prescribed treatments included bombarding himself with friends, "taking the waters" at American and European spas, keeping a doctor always at hand, and traveling abroad.

Not at all certain in his thirties that he wanted the responsibilities "laid upon" him (primarily by Junius), he told his father in 1871 that he might withdraw from their business altogether. Instead, Junius persuaded him to take a year off, which Pierpont spent with his young family in Europe and Egypt. He later said he could do a year's work in nine months but not in twelve, and he spent at least three months each year abroad. Travel seemed, for a time at least, to help ward off his depressions, but none of the remedies ever fully worked. Yet for all of Morgan's anxious sense of frailty, he was physically robust: He outlived and outworked several younger partners.

He continued, as his father had complained after the 1863 gold speculation, to disregard most opinions except his own, but in the 1870s he came around on his own to share his father's ethic and large sense of public responsibility.

For nearly thirty years Pierpont and Junius worked together, the former in New York, the latter in London, raising capital in Europe for the burgeoning U.S. economy. Railroads were the main force driving that economy from the 1860s to the 1890s, and they brought about productivity changes that were as revolutionary—and as lucrative—as those derived from information and communications technologies one hundred years later. The railroads changed the way the world worked, stitching together the vast North American continent, making it possible to ship crops from the country's farm belts to the East and West Coasts and then on around the world, and bringing manufactured goods from the coasts to the heartland. A new communications system, telegraphy, grew up alongside the railroads. In the 1860s, the Morgans helped underwrite the laying of the first successful transatlantic cable, which forever changed communication between the United States and Europe.

In the Gilded Age, as in every era of explosive economic growth, the prospect of earning immense wealth led to the building of excess capacity, fierce competition, widespread corruption, and periodic economic collapse. Nineteenth-century America saw a new economic crisis every ten to twenty years: in 1819, 1837, 1857, 1873, 1884, and 1893. John Kenneth Galbraith wrote that the intervals between panics corresponded "roughly with the time it took people to forget the last disaster."

There was not enough capital in the United States at mid-century to build enormously expensive railroads. The money had to be raised abroad. But Europeans who had been burned by speculators or had watched the value of their investments plummet in economic crises were not about to send more money three thousand miles across the Atlantic without some guarantee that it would be safe.

Over time the Morgans came to provide that guarantee. They obtained information in New York, through Pierpont and their American associates, about which railroad companies seemed likely to yield steady, long-term profits and which were primarily speculative ventures. Once the bankers had issued securities for a road, they took what they called "moral responsibility" for their clients' investments. If a Morgan-financed road went bankrupt, or if its managers were taking dangerous risks with investors' funds, Pierpont stepped in. In what came to be called Morganization, he and his partners fired the managers, handpicked new ones, restructured the company's finances, reorganized its operations, and appointed a voting trust to watch over the company until it was restored to financial health.

European investors in the nineteenth century might not know anything about the Illinois Central Railroad or the Philadelphia & Reading, but between the 1860s and 1890s, they learned that the Morgan name on an issue of securities promised a measure of safety.

ALTHOUGH THE MORGAN BANK developed a reputation as a white-shoe, blue-blood preserve, Pierpont Morgan himself was surprisingly meritocratic. Constantly on the lookout for the best person to run a railroad or design a yacht, he was drawn more to ability, energy, and new ideas than to credit line or pedigree. Junius kept assigning him partners who were members of their extended family or similarly certified; Pierpont, for the most part, shed the men Junius chose in favor of others he found better qualified—including, over his father's strenuous objections, an Italian Catholic, Egisto P. Fabbri, who proved to be an excellent banker and partner.

Another figure Pierpont backed over his father's objections was a brilliant young American inventor. From New York in the fall of 1878 he wrote to one of his London partners that he had been "very much engaged for several days past on a matter which is likely to prove most important . . . to the world at large [and] to us in particular in a pecuniary point of view. Secrecy at the moment is so essential that I do not dare to put it on paper. Subject is Edison's electric light." He had put it on paper.

Thomas Edison had just produced a brief incandescence by passing an electric current through a platinum wire filament in a partially evacuated bulb. England's Lord Kelvin, asked later why no one else had figured out how to do it, said, "The only answer I can think of is that no one else is Edison."

Edison promised to illuminate downtown Manhattan with a single five-hundred-horsepower engine and to have a complete system ready in a few weeks. He also said he would make electricity cheaper than gas.

(Interiors at the time were lit by candles or gas; society aesthetes preferred candles, saying that gas made diamonds look dull.)

News of the lightbulb brought inquiries from financiers all over the world, but Junius Morgan was evidently unimpressed. His skeptical response has not survived. Pierpont tried to answer his father's objections by mail, writing and tearing up several letters about "the Edison business," then gave up in frustration and decided to make his case in person when he went to London in the spring. "I feel sure," he wrote to Junius at the end of 1878, that "if you understood what was proposed [about the Edison matter] you would look at it with a different light." He did not appear to notice his apt double entendre.

Pierpont proceeded to finance Edison's work without his father's backing, though Junius eventually came around, and he put the lightbulb on prominent, first-class display. It took Edison four years, rather than a few weeks, to build a power system in downtown Manhattan. On September 4, 1882, the inventor walked from the just completed central power station on Pearl Street to the firm of his bankers, Drexel, Morgan & Co., at 23 Wall Street. Edison's electricians had wired the bank itself and many other buildings in lower Manhattan, including the *New York Times* building, then located at 41 Park Row. A few minutes before 3:00 P.M. an engineer at Pearl Street turned on the current in a generator called Jumbo, after P. T. Barnum's famous elephant. At 5:00, Edison flipped a switch at 23 Wall Street. That it was still daylight when the bulbs came on spoiled the dramatic effect, but by 7:00, reported the *Times* the next day, as the city grew dark, the electric light "showed how bright and steady it is . . . soft, mellow, and grateful to the eye." The *Herald* added: "From the outer darkness these points of light looked like drops of flame suspended from jets." Edison told the *Sun*, "I have accomplished all I promised."

Not entirely. The Pearl Street station had cost nearly three times the early estimates, making investors in other cities reluctant to pay for central power plants.

Morgan promoted electric lighting to influential friends on both sides of the Atlantic and continued to supply Edison with funds. His house at the corner of Madison Avenue and Thirty-sixth Street was the first private residence to be entirely illuminated by electricity. A reception Morgan held there in 1883 introduced four hundred of his friends to Mr. Edison's light. His daughter Louisa attended a costume party in the early eighties as "the spirit, it could hardly be called the ghost, of electricity," reported the *New York Herald*: "She was gowned in electric green satin, covered with a net work of embroidery done in electric wire." There were electric ornaments in her hair, and at the touch of a button concealed in the folds of her dress, all the tiny bulbs lit up.

Morgan continued to back Edison for another ten years. Then, in 1892, as the Edison companies lost ground to their competitors, he worked with the Boston bankers Lee, Higginson, & Co. to combine Edison General Electric with one of its chief rivals, the well-run Thomson-Houston Electric Company, into a single corporate unit called General Electric.

Fourteen years after Edison invented the lightbulb he had moved on to new projects, and it seemed clear to the bankers he relied on for capital that he was not the man to lead the electrical industry into the twentieth century. Charles Coffin, the head of Thomson-Houston, was. As the new president of General Electric, Coffin proceeded to rationalize the constituent companies into a model of integrated modern corporate enterprise. General Electric is the only company listed in the first Dow Jones Industrial Average, published in the *Wall Street Journal* in 1896, that remains in the average 114 years later.

JUNIUS MORGAN RETIRED in the early 1880s and died in 1890, by which time the center of world finance had shifted from London to New York, as had all the authority in the House of Morgan.

By the late eighties the United States had a massive but wildly chaotic and competitive national transportation system, and consumers as well as the managers of the roads thought it needed some kind of external control. In 1888 Morgan summoned the officers of a dozen major lines to a meeting at his house to try to impose order. The financial analyst John Moody wrote that every stockholder in Europe and America ought to give his proxies to this group, since only by concentration in a few "strong hands" could investment capital be protected against the "gigantic waste and fraud and duplication" endemic to the American railroad system. Charles Francis Adams, Jr., the president of the Union Pacific, agreed. He attended the meeting at Morgan's house and wrote in his private journal that ending the current anarchy would require "a railroad Bismarck." Would Morgan, Adams asked himself, become that figure?

Over the course of the following decade the answer made itself clear. America's "railroad Bismarck" ended the anarchy by organizing many of the country's railroad lines into centralized regional systems. And once the country's railroad infrastructure was essentially in place, Morgan turned to consolidating industrial companies.

In 1901 he bought out Andrew Carnegie and organized U.S. Steel, the largest corporation in the world, capitalized at $1.4 billion. The new corporate giant combined steel mills, blast furnaces, coke ovens, ore mines, barges, steamships, thousands of acres of coke and coal land, and several railroads, and it dominated world steel markets for half a century.

By 1900 many Americans were horrified at the power of big business and giant monopolies, or "trusts." Yale's president, Arthur T. Hadley, predicted in 1901 that unless the government checked the advancing power of the trusts, the United States would see "an emperor in Washington within twenty-five years." The inimitable Henry Adams told a friend, "Pierpont Morgan is apparently trying to swallow the sun."

A year later, in April 1902, Theodore Roosevelt occupied the White House. Morgan had, at Roosevelt's request, brokered an end to an anthracite coal miners' strike; he had also halted a panic on both sides of the Atlantic, organized a new consolidation of railroads in the Northwest, and been slapped by the new president with an antitrust suit; and he was beginning to set up a gigantic international shipping trust. Henry Adams again: "Pierpont Morgan . . . is carrying loads that stagger the strongest nerves. Everyone asks what would happen if some morning he woke up dead."

Morgan had just turned sixty-five, and though he had no intention of waking up dead (he made no clear provision for his successors at the bank or for the disposition of his art collections), he was easing out from under the nerve-staggering loads, spending increasing amounts of time traveling in Europe and collecting art. One of his British partners wrote to an American counterpart about Morgan in the summer of 1902: "We never see him and it is difficult to get hold of him. He spends his time lunching with Kings or Kaisers or buying Raphaels."

The "Old Man," as some of his banking colleagues called him in private, was by no means finished. Adams's witty question became more urgent in 1907, when an attempt by speculators to corner the stock of a copper company failed and set off a panic on Wall Street.

Morgan had come of age watching the Bank of England try to keep the British economy on track and observing what happened in the United States with no central bank. With his eye fixed on his firm's European investors, he had done what he could to keep the U.S. economy growing steadily—which meant, among other things, trying to even out the excesses of the business cycle, keep the country on the gold standard (since its major lenders and trading partners pegged their currencies to gold), and amass reserves when he sensed a panic coming on. He and his colleagues knew that the antiquated, decentralized U.S. banking system could not meet the economic needs of a dynamic industrial state. At the beginning of 1906, Jacob Schiff of Kuhn, Loeb warned a group of financiers that "if the currency conditions of this country are not changed materially . . . you will have such a panic . . . as will make all previous panics look like child's play."

Over the next eighteen months a worldwide credit shortage kept global markets in turmoil. The nine-year-old Dow Jones Industrial Average lost 25 percent of its value in the first three months of 1907, and the U.S. stock market crashed that March in spite of record corporate earnings. In the spring, banks failed in Japan, the Egyptian stock market collapsed, and the city of San Francisco could not float a loan. After the U.S. stock market crashed again in August, the *New York Times* estimated the losses at one billion dollars (roughly fifteen billion in 2010 dollars—pocket change compared with the bailouts of 2008–9, but enormous at the time).

Then, in October 1907, a run on New York trust companies set off a panic. Trust companies, the weakest link in the financial system, operated like commercial banks—accepting deposits, issuing loans, and financing speculative schemes—only with no regulatory supervision or mandated reserves. An attempt by speculators to corner the stock of a copper company failed that fall, and as word got out that the trust companies had made loans to the speculators, people with money on deposit at the trusts lined up to draw it out.

Morgan, now seventy years old, was attending an Episcopal Church convention in Richmond, Virginia, when the panic started. His partners kept him posted on the situation by messenger and wire, but insisted he not come back to New York early since a sudden change in his plans might exacerbate the panic. When he did return, arriving early Sunday morning, October 20, he went straight to his private library on East Thirty-sixth Street. There his partners brought him up-to-date. Reporters stationed themselves across the street. Bankers stopped by all day and into the night as Morgan gathered information and resources.

President Roosevelt was shooting game in the Louisiana canebrakes. He told a reporter that day: "We got three bears, six deer, one wild turkey, twelve squirrels, one duck, one opossum and one wildcat. We ate them all, except the wildcat."

Late Sunday night Treasury Secretary George Cortelyou sent word from Washington that the government would deposit six million dollars in New York's banks.

By the time the meetings at the library broke up after midnight, Morgan had appointed two groups of men to handle whatever came next: a high command consisting of himself, George Baker, and James Stillman—the presidents, respectively, of the First National Bank and National City Bank—and three young lieutenants who would supply the senior trio with information. (First National and National City eventually combined to form what is now Citigroup.) The bankers' immediate job was to determine which trust companies were essentially healthy and could be saved with fresh infusions of cash and which were hopelessly overextended and should be allowed to fail.

The Morgan lieutenants did not have enough time to ascertain whether the most besieged institution, the Knickerbocker Trust Company, had enough assets to secure a loan. On Tuesday afternoon Morgan let it fail. Banks around the country began withdrawing their reserves from New York. Stock prices plunged. The treasury secretary took an afternoon train to Manhattan. Morgan came down with a heavy cold.

The next domino to totter was the Trust Company of America. Two of the young men working for Morgan, Henry P. Davison and Benjamin Strong, stayed up all Tuesday night, studying its accounts. When they reported to the senior trio on Wednesday, Morgan mainly wanted to know whether the company was solvent. Strong said that its surplus was gone but its assets were essentially intact.

Morgan turned to Baker and Stillman and said, "This is the place to stop the trouble, then." That afternoon TCA employees filed into the Morgan offices with leather sacks and boxes full of securities certificates. Morgan, Strong, and the TCA president sat around a big table, adding up the value of the bonds and stocks. Stillman was on the phone to his bank. Morgan, sneezing and coughing, took notes, and as soon as he had sufficient collateral for a loan, he asked Stillman to send that amount over to the trust. By 3:00 P.M. the bankers had traded about three million dollars in cash for collateral, and the TCA stayed open. The treasury secretary announced that the government would deposit another twenty-five million dollars in New York to ease the crisis.

John D. Rockefeller provided ten million dollars to support the trust companies on Thursday, but the panic spread to the stock exchange. Financial institutions calling in loans were choking off the market's money supply. Stock prices plummeted again. At 1:30 P.M. the president of the exchange told Morgan that he was going to have to suspend operations before the 3:00 P.M. close. Out of the question, said Morgan; closing early would destroy public confidence. He promised to find money to lend the brokers. He summoned the presidents of New York's major commercial banks to his office, and in a few minutes they had pledged $23.5 million. Morgan sent word to the trading floor. "The rebound was instantaneous," reported the *Times*. The exchange stayed open till 3:00.

On Friday Morgan had to raise ten million dollars more to lend to the exchange. As he left his office late that afternoon, he told reporters that if people would leave their money in the banks, everything would be all right.

Saturday's newspapers reported that five million dollars in gold would be sent from London, that confidence had returned to the French Bourse "owing to the belief that the strong men in American finance would succeed in their efforts to check the spirit of the panic," and that "J. P. Morgan has a cold."

Roosevelt had been out of the picture all week while Morgan handled the crisis. On Sunday the newspapers published a letter from the president congratulating his treasury secretary and "those conservative and substantial business men who in this crisis have acted with such wisdom and public spirit." The fundamentals of the economy, wrote the president, were sound.

Still, the bankers had to bail out a near-bankrupt New York City, and the trust companies, source of the original trouble, were not in the clear. On Sunday night, November 3, Morgan gathered fifty trust company presidents at his library, told them to come up with twenty-five million dollars on their own, and left them in a room filled with Renaissance bronzes, paintings of the Madonna and Child, Gutenberg Bibles, and rare books. He withdrew to his librarian's office.

At 3:00 A.M. he called in Ben Strong for a review of one trust company's books. Strong gave his report, then headed to the library's front doors and found them locked. Morgan had the key in his pocket.

No one was to leave until the trusts anted up. The presidents continued to talk. At 4:15, Morgan walked in with a statement requiring each trust company to share in a new twenty-five-million-dollar loan. One of his lawyers read it aloud, then set it on a table. "There you are, gentlemen," said Morgan. No one moved. Morgan took the arm of Edward King, the head of the Union Trust Company, and drew him to the table.

"There's the place, King," he said, "and here's the pen." King signed. The other presidents signed. They set up a committee to handle the loan and supervise the final-stage bailouts of endangered trusts. At 4:45 A.M. the library's heavy brass doors swung open and let the bankers out.

As the stock market rallied and gold began to arrive from Europe, the two long weeks of crisis came to an end. For a moment Morgan was a national hero. Crowds cheered as he walked down Wall Street, and world leaders saluted his achievement with awe. The next moment, however, the exercise of that much power by one private citizen terrified a nation of democrats and revived America's long-standing distrust of plutocrats and concentrated wealth. The 1907 Panic convinced the country that its financial welfare could no longer be left in private hands. It led to the appointment of a National Monetary Commission and, ultimately, to the founding of the Federal Reserve.

Critics who claimed Morgan had engineered the 1907 Panic for his own profit might have been surprised to learn that his U.S. firms lost twenty-one million dollars that year. The crisis itself was relatively brief, but it brought on a severe nationwide contraction that destroyed not only speculative ventures but healthy banks and businesses as well, and threw people all over the country out of work.

Morgan helped the members of the National Monetary Commission who were developing plans for a central banking system. Two of them had served as his "lieutenants" during the 1907 Panic: Benjamin Strong, a vice president at Bankers Trust, and Henry P. Davison, a Morgan partner.

Convinced, however, that the country could not wait for government action on monetary policy (and that in any case the government would not regulate vast flows of capital as well as they themselves could), Morgan, Baker, and Stillman—the senior trio that had formed during the Panic of 1907—constructed a regulatory system of their own. In private notes and cables they called themselves the Trio. Their concerted actions as the nation's self-appointed central bankers brought on charges that they were running a "money trust." The United States needed monetary control so urgently, said the *Wall Street Journal* in 1911, that if a money trust did not exist, somebody ought to invent one.

Testifying in Washington in 1912 before the congressional Pujo Committee, which was investigating the "money trust," Morgan had the following droll exchange with Samuel Untermyer, the lawyer conducting the investigation.

Asked why he had bought a large amount of stock in the Equitable Life Insurance Company in 1910, Morgan said simply, "I thought it was the thing to do."

Untermyer: "But that does not explain anything."

Morgan: "That is the only reason I can give."

Untermyer: "It was the thing to do for whom?"

Morgan: "That is the only reason I can give. That is the only reason I have, in other words. I am not trying to keep anything back, you understand."

Untermyer: "I understand. In other words you have no reason at all."

Morgan: "That is the way you look at it. I think it is a very good reason. . . . Some of these days you will agree with me."

Untermyer: "You can never tell what may happen. Some of these days you may agree with me, Mr. Morgan."

Morgan: "Very well. That may be. If I do, I shall wait for a good reason."

A few weeks later Henry P. Davison proved to be better than his senior partner at explaining Morgan's "reasons." He told the Pujo Committee that a few prominent bankers had taken it upon themselves to monitor the capital supplies of the country's expanding industrial economy because of America's obsolete banking system. The picture the committee had drawn, of these financiers controlling the boards of companies with resources of twenty-five billion dollars, was misleading, Davison pointed out. Much of that money was invested in factories, land, and equipment; it was not available in cash "subject to the selfish use or abuse of individuals." The presence of bankers on corporate boards had to do not with a desire to manage daily operations or acquire securities at insider prices but with a sense of their "moral responsibility," as sponsors of the corporations' securities, to keep an eye on policy and protect investors' interests. "For a private banker to sit upon such a directorate," continued Davison, "is in most instances a duty, not a privilege."

To step out of the past for a moment, imagine how different things might have been in the tech and housing bubbles at the turn of the next century if someone like Morgan had been watching closely over the managers of companies such as WorldCom, Enron, AIG, General Motors, and all the major banks, investment firms, and mortgage brokerage houses that made foolish loans and sold incomprehensible securities derivatives. No single individual could wield the power in the twenty-first century's hugely complex and diverse global markets that Morgan had one hundred years ago. Still, what if corporate boards of directors, accountants, and government regulators had actually done the jobs they were supposed to do: paid attention to what managers were doing, intervened when they detected signs of trouble, and called a halt?

Morgan acted out of a strong sense of financial public duty, but he was not serving as proto-Fed out of altruism. The people he represented had billions of dollars invested in the emerging U.S. economy. He and his father had appointed themselves early on to watch over America's credit in international markets, to keep money flowing from wealthy "old" Europe to the "new" American economy, and the younger Morgan had expanded the job description: trying to stabilize economic growth, discipline reckless speculators, regulate competition, harness the markets' creative destruction.

Like his father, he believed that his work in the financial markets was a high calling as well as a profitable business. He acted at least in part out of a sense of noblesse oblige. He never doubted the wisdom of his actions and did not worry about passing through the eye of the needle. People suffered under the policies he promulgated: keeping the dollar strong and pegged to gold assured investors that their loans would retain value, but it was terrible for farmers and people running small businesses, perennially squeezed by falling prices and the rising cost of debt.

Certain that he was guiding the United States toward a spectacularly prosperous future, Morgan did not distinguish between his own and the national interest, though he was by no means an objective arbiter in the long struggle over the nature of America's identity; he was an active partisan.

After Morgan's death in 1913 and the probation of his estate, the newspapers reported his net worth as about eighty million dollars. Eighty million dollars was a lot of money in 1913—equivalent to more than one billion dollars in 2009—but it was not nearly as much as Morgan could have made if amassing wealth had been his primary goal. John D. Rockefeller, already worth one billion 1913 dollars, reportedly read the figure for Morgan's net worth in the newspaper, shook his head, and said, "And to think he wasn't even a rich man."

Morgan's power derived, as this anecdote suggests, not from the size of his personal fortune but from his financial leadership. After the United

States passed legislation establishing the Federal Reserve System in 1913, Benjamin Strong, who had worked for Morgan during the 1907 Panic, became the first governor of the Fed bank in New York. Milton Friedman and Anna Schwartz, in their book, *A Monetary History of the United States 1867–1960*, point out the "striking contrast" between Morgan's effective handling of the 1907 crisis and the failure of the Federal Reserve to contain the 1929 panic and limit the Depression of the thirties.

The authors also speculate about what might have happened had Strong not died in 1928: "Strong, more than any other individual, had the confidence and backing of other financial leaders inside and outside the [Federal Reserve] system, the personal force to make his own views prevail, and also the courage to act upon them. . . . If Strong had still been alive and head of the New York Bank in the fall of 1930, he would very likely have recognized the oncoming liquidity crisis for what it was, would have been prepared by experience and conviction to take strenuous and appropriate measures to head it off, and would have had the standing to carry the System with him."

Substitute Morgan for Strong: "More than any other individual, [he] had the confidence and backing of other financial leaders inside and outside the system, the personal force to make his own views prevail, and also the courage to act upon them."

CHIEF JOSEPH AND THE CHALLENGE OF INDIAN LEADERSHIP

Elliott West

HE WAS CALLED THE RED NAPOLEON, A MILITARY GENIUS WHO OUTwitted and outfought several army commands while being chased across nearly a quarter of the nation. He appeared too as an ideal of native nobility who, when finally run to ground, gave up the fight so his people would not suffer further. His dignity at that surrender and the eloquence of his hundred words, ending with "From where the sun now stands I will fight no more forever," secured his fame and his position as a worthy, even beloved opponent.

He was Joseph, a chief of the Nez Perce Indians of the Columbia Plateau. When the Nez Perces went to war with the United States in June 1877, Joseph was pictured, as so many before him, as a treacherous, irredeemably depraved savage. By the war's end he had emerged, improbably, as a hero, in particular as a model of leadership—cagey and dogged, courageous, brilliant in a fight yet humane toward innocents in harm's way, a great warrior who balanced determination with integrity. The image persists, with special resonance today among Indians asserting themselves in the nation that Joseph fought. A poster calling for political mobilization ("2.7 million Indians can make a difference") features a photo of Joseph taken within days of his surrender. "Chief Joseph used his power to lead," reads the caption. "Use your power."

He deserves his reputation. Of all Native American leaders during the torturous four centuries after Columbus, Joseph was among the most gifted. He was also among the most misunderstood. His gifts were not the ones the public praised so lavishly but were rather in the subtle game of reading the mood, values, and fantasies of his victorious enemies, then playing them to his people's advantage. In its wider context Joseph's life reveals another layer of the story of American leadership. He was one of many who were to learn that native understandings of society and authority—of who was in charge and what being in charge meant—were profoundly different from and opposed to those of the American nation. Like most other Indian leaders, he learned that lesson to his own grief. Unlike most, he took what he learned and applied it, turning it back on the government that had pressed its ideas of power on him and his people, challenging the Republic's leaders on their own terms. The shrewd intelligence of his performance was easy to miss, exactly because it needed to be, but once seen, it is all the more impressive and all the more instructive in the varieties of leadership that have shaped the American story.

THE NEZ PERCES met their first white people on September 20, 1805, when Meriwether Lewis, William Clark, and their Corps of Discovery stumbled into one of their camps after crossing the snow-choked Lolo Pass over the Bitterroot Mountains of the northern Rockies. They were starving and frostbitten, and after briefly considering killing them, the Nez Perces instead fed them salmon and berries, gave them shelter and rest, advice and canoes, and sent them on their way to the Pacific. On their return the corps lived with the Nez Perces for several weeks, during which time the two sides pledged their friendship. The Nez Perces would support the United States and fight with it in any conflict; Washington would bring the Nez Perces trade, especially firearms. According to Nez Perce tradition, Clark sealed the deal by siring a son, Halahtookit ("Daytime Smoke"), with the daughter of a prominent chief.

The several thousand Nez Perces were the most numerous and powerful people of the interior Pacific Northwest. They lived in what is today eastern Oregon and central Idaho, protected to the east, west, and south by mountains and to the north by allies. Their home country was enormously varied, ranging in altitude over eight thousand feet, and rich in resources, especially salmon and the nutritious bulbs of the camas lily. During the seventy or so years since they had acquired horses traded from the Southwest, they had bred large herds of splendid animals and developed superb equestrian skills. The Nez Perces had enemies, in particular the Shoshones to the south and the Blackfeet on the northern Great Plains, where they ventured to hunt bison, but at home they were unchallenged and confident. Understandably, then, they seem to have considered themselves at least equals to their new allies. Jefferson's emissaries did raise misgivings. Over the past couple of generations there had been prophecies of strangers from the east bringing catastrophe. But Lewis and Clark offered interesting advantages, in particular weapons to use against the well-armed Blackfeet, and to put it mildly, their arrival, hungry and lost, did not suggest that they spoke for a power that was much to worry about.

The Nez Perce response to that first meeting obviously was quite a miscalculation, one that wrenched their history in a disastrous direction. It took time, however, for them to realize how badly they had misread the situation and how awful were the consequences, a gradual education over nearly three-quarters of a century. Joseph, born thirty-five years after that first contact, lived into his leadership just when the accumulating lessons couldn't be missed or their disastrous implications avoided. His challenge would be to plot the best way through them.

The misunderstanding between the Nez Perces and the white newcomers arose from radically different notions of what a society was and how it was led. As had Europeans from their first arrival in the Americas, agents of the American Republic projected onto Indians a social and political structure like their own. Meeting a people who seemed to be related, they presumed they were a nation writ small. They gave them a common name—the Utes, Cheyennes, Shoshonis, or Nez Perces—and presumed that they saw themselves as part of a common order with established laws. They assumed too that an Indian "nation" like the Nez Perces had recognized leaders commanding an apparatus of power and making and enforcing decisions, much like a corporate flow chart, with authority by paths that everybody understood and generally went along with.

What they thought they saw, however, was not there. The Nez Perces (meaning "pierced nose"), who called themselves the Nimiipuu, or the "Real People," did speak a common language and recalled a common beginning. They had sprung to life from drops of bloody water flung about by the trickster hero Coyote after he had slain a terrible monster. But if one of the Nimiipuu were asked his or her identity, it would be with one of many distinct bands living in dozens of river villages. Pressed further, he or she would mention kinsmen and allies not only among the other bands but, much farther afield, among neighbors with whom the Real People had intermarried: the Cayuses, Wallawallas, Palouses, and others in the Columbia basin and the Flatheads across the Bitterroots. Bloodlines wove across an enormous region, from today's central Montana nearly to Portland, Oregon, and allegiance and amity followed the blood. Nez Perce identity, that is, was both more localized and more expansive than what whites expected. They were commonly bound as a people, yet fragmented among many groups rooted in particular places, but also linked into a tessellation of families and other tribes over a region many times larger than that of the Nimiipuu homeland. Anyone looking for the equivalent of a modern nation would have found it bizarre.

So too with Nez Perce leadership. It varied with place and circumstance. When bands came together in a joined effort, they chose as a leader someone with special gifts in the task at hand: a fine strategist and warrior to lead them on a raid, a coolheaded bargainer to negotiate with outsiders. His leadership was conditional and temporary. If he lost the confidence of those around him, he quickly lost his job, and in any case, whenever the work he led was finished, so was his leadership. Day-to-day leadership was by band headmen, sometimes called chiefs, men recognized for skills at dealing with other bands and for being modest, generous, fair, and always ready with kind words. A band headman usually held his position until death, so an outlander might assume he had considerable command over those around him.

But not so. Among the Nez Perces no person, from a headman down, could require any other person to do anything at all. They had plenty of rules, but instead of having someone to enforce them, they relied on a general understanding that everyone in the band relied on everyone else, and so any individual action threatening the mutual interest was self-defeating. Acting in the common good was just common sense. Acting against any other member of the band, even a chief punishing one of the lowliest, was a violation of a good order based on harmony and on trusting others to act rightly.

The majority of western Indian peoples, for all their dazzling diversity of cultures, in their basics lived similarly to the Nez Perces. Most were hunters and gatherers and fishers, an economy requiring them to live, like the Nez Perces in their bands, in groups no larger than about 150, often smaller. In that socially dense, face-to-face world—a scholar defines its upper limit as one where gossip involves everybody and, when hostile, can really hurt—the Nez Perce way of mutual enforcement of rules was common. Such a small-radius society was utterly alien from a modern nation measured in millions of square miles and millions of persons. When people from such a nation showed up, expecting a nation's formal structures of power, laws, and punishment, the result was at best confusion and often a hopeless snarl.

Confusion typically boiled down to the matter of leadership, since it was through leaders that the differences of the two worlds met, shaped evolving relations, dickered over disputes, and often argued toward war. The confusion ran both ways, of course. The Nez Perces and other indigenous peoples had no conception of a nation-state—how could they?—and not the slightest notion of how power, authority, and leadership worked within one. From that angle, the tortured history of federal-Indian relations hinges considerably on questions of leadership: how Indian and white leaders interacted, how they often misread each other, how they adjusted (or not), and how they sometimes managed to grasp the real contours of power well enough to plot a reasonable course through them. No instance offers a better view of the play of leadership than that of the Nez Perces, and no character in that story, and few in all native history, is as intriguing as Chief Joseph.

HE WAS BORN in 1840, with two names. His father, Tuekakas, was headman of the largest Nez Perce band that lived in a valley called the Wallowa, meaning "Land of the Winding Waters." The Wallowa, in today's far eastern Oregon, west of the Snake River, was isolated but spectacularly beautiful, with lakes, streams, and lush summer pastures. Tuekakas had been one of two band chiefs baptized in 1839 by the Presbyterian missionary Henry H. Spalding. The other chief took the Christian name Timothy. Tuekakas chose Joseph. He in turn christened his new son Ephraim but gave him as well a Nez Perce name, Heinmot Tooyalakekt, which roughly translated as "Thunder Rising to Loftier Mountain Heights." "Ephraim" never took hold, but whites later called the maturing son Young Joseph. After he assumed his father's role on Tuekakas's death, it was Chief Joseph.

The double naming was significant. Since meeting Lewis and Clark, the Nez Perces had purposefully straddled the line between their way of life and that of a distant America. They hoped to acquire something more than trade goods. To the Nez Perces and Indians generally, material power—in this case, rifles and ammunition, awls, knives, pots, coffee and coffee grinders, and much more—followed from the immaterial. Success and possessions in the here and now implied impressive connections among supernatural forces at work everywhere all the time, and it followed that if whites had so much in the seen world, they must have considerable clout in the unseen. Not only the Nez Perces but their neighbors and kinsmen the Cayuses, Wallawallas, and others wanted to share that influence.

Thus the double naming. Old Joseph's baptism came eight years after three Nez Perces and a Flathead had traveled to St. Louis to visit William Clark, now in charge of western Indian relations. They went there to promote better commercial connections and to look into the whites' spiritual teachings, including the "white man's book" they had heard about, but quickly the press ditched the first and inflated the second. The "Four Wise Men from the West" had come pleading to be saved from heathenism. "Who will go?" asked a prominent religious journal. "Who?" First to answer were the Methodists Jason and Daniel Lee in 1834, then the Presbyterians Marcus and Narcissa Whitman and Henry and Eliza Spalding in 1836. The Whitmans built a mission among the Cayuses, the Spaldings among the Nez Perces at a spot called Lapwai ("Place of the Butterflies") among the northern bands.

The Nez Perce response at first was exuberant. Sunday services and a new schoolroom were crowded, and with the first printing press in the Northwest Henry and Eliza produced a Gospel of Matthew in Nez Perce phonetic transliteration. Soon enough, however, the missionaries and the missionized realized that as in so much in Indian-white relations, each had utterly misread what the other was up to. The Spaldings and Whitmans expected their flocks to abandon both traditional beliefs and traditional lifeways. They were to take up farming and accept the full panoply of white culture, from dress and hairstyle to familial relations. The Nez Perces wanted to incorporate Christian spiritual power into their own rich spirituality so they might enhance, not replace, a life that had sustained them for centuries.

Old Joseph had taken the lead in exploring Christianity's promise, for a while moving close to Spalding's mission, but sometime in the early 1840s he reversed course, turning around and moving back to the Wallowa. Good leadership meant monitoring the results of chances taken, and it was increasingly clear that Nez Perce life was not getting better. It was getting worse. Most alarming, missionaries proved to be the advance guard, and Whitman an avid promoter, for white settlement in eastern Oregon. The numbers of immigrants passing through grew yearly. The twenty-five hundred in 1845 nearly matched the entire Nez Perce population.

The following year the balance tipped dramatically against the Indians. In June a treaty with Great Britain gave the United States all of modern Washington, Oregon, and Idaho, and in November the Cayuses, disenchanted with the Whitmans and blaming them for a devastating measles epidemic, killed them both and thirteen others. The massacre brought a crushing response from local militia and helped goad Congress into creating the Oregon Territory in 1848. More settlers poured in each summer, and in 1855 Isaac Stevens, governor of the new Washington Territory, pressed tribes of the Columbia basin to sign a series of treaties creating reservations that left the Nez Perce country mostly intact but drastically reduced the homelands of others. Resentment soon flared into a series of wars that by 1858 had broken the back of opposition among the Wallawallas, Yakimas, Coeur d'Alenes, and others across the Columbia Plateau. Before, the Nez Perces had been the most powerful people of the region. Now, in practical terms, they were the only people with any power at all.

Old Joseph meanwhile was feeling his way through the maze facing every Indian leader in dealing with whites. The Nez Perces' first assumption—that they and the United States were on a par—was clearly wrong, but exactly what they were up against, that was still a puzzle. Just as no one could have grasped the notion of a nation-state like the one stretching itself into their homeland, so none could know the numbers, the technological heft, and the raw power welling up in the East. In pulling back to the Wallowa, Old Joseph was stepping away to refigure the algebra of contact, trying for a sense of the weights on either side of the equation of two cultures coming together. That recalculation was to test Old Joseph in his last years. On his death his son discovered how great the imbalance was and how treacherous the challenge of living into it.

IN 1860, AS YOUNG JOSEPH was entering full manhood, the Nez Perces felt a shock of the sort that, more than any other, shattered the well-being of western Indians: a gold rush. News of strikes in the northern and central parts of the homeland brought thousands of gold seekers and with them the usual problems. Into the raw town of Lewiston came not only miners but what a visitor called "the last scrapings of the earth," thieves and cutpurses, sharpers, whores and whoremongers, who found prime targets in local Indians. Farmers grabbed land along the rivers, and ranchers pastured cattle on Nez Perce horse pastures and their vital camas fields. The treaty of 1855 had promised no white intrusion would be tolerated, but little was done to stop the rush, and by the time the strikes played out after a couple of years, whites were well entrenched in Lewiston and among the northern bands. Washington's response was not to enforce the old treaty but to demand a new one. The resulting council at Lapwai in June 1863 was a turning point in Nez Perce history and in the nature of their leadership.

Calvin Hale, who as the Washington Territory's Indian superintendent was the government's agent, insisted that one man, a "head chief," spoke for all Nez Perce bands, a claim that dated back more than twenty years. In 1842 the first federal agent to the region, Elijah White, had arrived with the usual projection of a nation onto Indians: The Nez Perces were one people and so must have one leader. Who was he? The baffled headmen finally tapped a young English-speaking subchief, although they clearly meant him to be only a liaison and interpreter. Ever since then the government had used that offhand act to claim that one man had authority over all the bands, and to a degree the bands went along, using the supposed "head chief" as their spokesman. In 1863 that man was Lawyer, a Christian friendly to assimilation and pliant to Washington's wishes.

At an all-night meeting during the council, however, whatever gauzy unity the bands had allowed since 1842 was ended. After hours of argument over the new treaty, those for and against it shook hands and, "with a warm and emotional manner," wrote an army officer who was there, "declared the Nez Perce nation *dissolved*." Now leaders of fully independent bands would speak for their people alone. A few hours later the bands opposed to a treaty left for home. That same day Lawyer and cooperating band chiefs signed what Washington was to claim was a treaty governing all Nez Perces. All the bands that signed the treaty would keep their lands. All that had refused and gone home would lose theirs. A pleased Calvin Hale wrote that for about eight cents an acre the government would gain just under seven million acres of valuable mining, farming, and grazing lands, 90 percent of what had been guaranteed the Nez Perces eight years earlier.

Many Nez Perces today still call this the steal treaty. Later Chief Joseph, who at twenty-three was almost certainly with his father at the council, explained in simple marketplace terms what had happened: "Suppose a white man should come to me and say, 'Joseph, I like your horses, and I want to buy them. I say to him, 'No, my horses suit me, I will not sell them.'" Then a neighbor tells the hopeful buyer: "'Pay me the money, and I will sell you Joseph's horses.'" The deal completed, the white man then demands "his" animals. "If we sold our lands to the government," Joseph explained, "this is the way they were bought."

For several years Washington nonetheless did not press its case, and some agents strongly considered simply letting the resisting bands be. The isolated Wallowa drew only slight attention from settlers. Old Joseph sensed what was coming, however, and as he was dying in 1871, his words were of vigilance. "You are the chief of these people. They look to you to guide them," his son recalled his saying. "Always remember that your father never sold his country. . . . A few years more and white men will be all around you. . . . This country holds your father's body. Never sell the bones of your father and mother." Young Joseph, now Chief Joseph, took the words to heart and never sold the Wallowa. Keeping it, however, was another matter.

A confrontation finally came, starting in June 1876, when a rancher in the Wallowa killed a Nez Perce man. Tensions tightened over the next weeks, and as it had so often before, Washington used the crisis to press its hardest case. When Joseph met that fall with a special presidential commission, present was a figure who would play prominently in the story ahead, Oliver Otis Howard, an ardent Christian abolitionist who had risen to general in the Civil War, along the way losing his right arm; headed the Freedmen's Bureau afterward; and fought Apaches in the Southwest before his appointment to head the Department of the Columbia in 1874. Howard and the commissioners backed off from all compromise. The treaty of 1863 was law, they said. Give up your lands, and come onto the reduced reservation. Crowd in with kinsmen now taking a different cultural path. You may keep up the hunt and the fishing and gathering if you can (an empty gesture under the circumstances); but if not, you must turn to farming, and in any case, you will send your children to white schools. In short, give up who you are.

It was Joseph's first significant test as a leader. Riding into the Lapwai agency at the head of sixty followers, he was physically impressive, well over six feet tall, with a powerful chest, broad shoulders, and a wide face with large dark eyes and a high forehead. As he sat down with the commissioners, his expression was unthreatening but unrevealing: a diplomat's face. He wore his hair in twin braids and in an upward sweep in front. This last was a sign of another resistance to the new order. Joseph followed a native religious movement that had arisen in the late 1850s. Like many others across the continent over the years, it promised the banishment of white invaders and the return of golden times if converts followed new rituals and certain commands, in this case to leave the earth inviolable, shunning farming and living by what the land and rivers gave naturally. Followers were called Dreamers, from the belief that God spoke to them especially in visions while asleep, and to show their allegiance, men wore their hair in a rearing pompadour like Joseph's.

The commissioners were struck by Joseph's "alertness and dexterity in intellectual fencing" and even more by his "serious and feeling manner" in expressing his people's fundamental beliefs. Calmly he explained that the Wallowa was "sacred to his affections." He was a child to it, and so to leave "would be to part with himself." Like his father, he asked for nothing except to be left alone. As for his people's turning to agriculture, the "Creative Power" had meant for people to live on the earth as they had found it and to feed themselves with what it freely gave. (How could I take up the plow, asked the founding prophet of the Dreamers, and "take a knife and tear my mother's bosom? Then when I die she will not take me to her bosom to rest.") Blunted again and again, the commissioners finally told Joseph that he faced a government now ruling from ocean to ocean. Surrender your homeland, they said, or face its full force. Joseph answered that he would not—could not—give up the Wallowa.

Over the next several months Joseph and his brother Ollokut ("Frog") tried to dance away from a showdown, but in mid-May 1877 they agreed to another council at Lapwai, this one for all bands rejecting the treaty. To speak for them, the band chiefs chose not Joseph but an older warrior and holy man among the Dreamers, Toohoolhoolzote ("Noise" or "Growler"), the leader of a band even more isolated than Joseph's. He was as confrontive and abrupt as Joseph was cool, and the more Howard pressed him, the harder he pushed back, sneering at the claim that his people were under Washington's authority ("The government . . . shall not think for us") and saying over and over that he "belonged to the land out of which he came" and could no more surrender his home than hand over who he was. Finally a frustrated Howard, saying, "I stand here for the President," drew a line. Would he, or would he not, comply with the treaty? "So long as the earth keeps me, I want to be left alone . . ." the old Dreamer answered. "I am NOT going on the reservation." With that Howard and another officer grabbed Toohoolhoolzote by the arms and walked him to the nearby guardhouse. Apparently cowed, the other leaders submitted. At a final meeting a week later Howard issued another, especially shocking order. The bands had one month to gather all belongings, round up their herds, and report to the reservation.

The Lapwai council was as stark a confrontation of native and national cultures as the nineteenth century offers. The steal treaty was almost incidental. The true clash was between different ways of addressing the world, two drastically different social orders, perceptions of identity, and relations with the divine. For seventy-two years after pledging their alliance as equals to the United States, Nez Perce leaders had kept their promise while maneuvering within the reality of an expanding nation. Now, as the resisting bands dismantled their lives and prepared to uproot, it appeared they would be one more people, like dozens across the West, giving in to the power they had so misjudged. In fact they were about to take a course unique among Indian peoples. It made them famous, even as it led them into their darkest time, and as it played out, Joseph found himself pressed into roles that none before him had faced and leading his people in ways he could not have imagined.

LEAVING BEHIND HUNDREDS of cattle, the resisting bands, led by Joseph, Toolhoolhoolzote, and White Bird, leader of another resisting band, packed up all they could and by June 14 had assembled at a traditional camping spot just south of the reservation. The next day they were to cross into new, constricted lives. Early that morning, however, three young men rode down to the Salmon River and shot and killed four white settlers and wounded another, and when they returned to boast in the camp, more warriors set off for killing of their own. Over the next two days fourteen more settlers were killed. Meanwhile a stunned Howard wired for several hundred reinforcements and sent what troops he had, a hundred green cavalrymen under Captain David Perry, to protect settlers crowding into the towns of Grangeville and Mount Idaho. When Perry learned the bands were camped at nearby White Bird Creek, he chose instead to ride against them. His attack at dawn on June 17 quickly reversed into a rout. In less than an hour the Nez Perces killed thirty-four soldiers while suffering only two wounded.

So began the Nez Perce War. It lasted fifteen weeks. The bands in the fight—the majority of Nez Perces by then were on the reservation and remained at peace—first led the army on a chase around their home country's rugged mountains and wide prairies. In several clashes they at least held their own, but they could maneuver for only so long. A month into the war they made a choice no other western Indians ever had. They would run for it. In mid-July they crossed the Bitterroot Mountains eastward to Montana over Lolo Pass, the trail Lewis and Clark had taken in the other direction to meet the Nez Perces nearly three-quarters of a century earlier. Their hope was to find temporary refuge among their Crow allies on the Montana plains and to return after passions had cooled, a hope based on the belief that by passing over the mountains, away from their immediate enemy, they would be out of harm's way.

They soon learned differently. A command under Colonel John Gibbon was dispatched in pursuit, and at dawn on August 9 at Big Hole, a traditional camping spot in western Montana, Gibbon struck. As with Captain Perry at White Bird Canyon, it was a surprise attack at dawn, but although they took heavy casualties, the Nez Perces once again turned back their attackers and nearly annihilated them. From August 26 to September 5 the Indians passed through the newly created Yellowstone National Park, killing a few tourists before breaking free of what had seemed an inescapable trap as they left. After their friends the Crows turned them away, they fought and bested their pursuers one more time and broke northward across the Montana plains. The bands' goal now was to reach Canada and live among the several hundred Sioux under Sitting Bull, who had fled there the year before. They nearly made it. Just forty miles shy of the international border, at the base of the Bear's Paw Mountains on the last day of September, a command under Colonel Nelson Miles caught them, drove off their horses, and laid siege to their camp. Joseph's famous surrender came a week later.

For sheer drama few western episodes can match the Nez Perce War.

There was its timing, coming a month after the end of the fighting with the Sioux. Excepting minor flare-ups and the police action against the Apaches in the Southwest, it was the nation's last Indian war and the culmination of four centuries of hostilities between North American native peoples and their invaders. There was the social dimension. The war was not a case of soldierly confrontation. The bands included about 800 persons, most of them noncombatant women, children, and elderly, and as they fled, they bore with them the essentials of starting a new life elsewhere, including more than two thousand horses. By the time this great moving community was caught it had traveled about fifteen hundred miles, the equivalent of from Washington, D.C., to Denver, Colorado. The brilliant maneuvers and cool ferocity of their warriors, who never numbered more than 250, won them admiration even from those they defeated. When officers were asked why the campaign had been so long and costly, one wrote simply: "Superiority of enemy." Over it all was the story's dramatic arc: the prelude of friendship and betrayal, the war's ugly beginning, the stunning break for freedom, the underdogs winning one improbable victory after another, then the heartbreaking end and capture within a breath of sanctuary.

That last moment is indelibly set in the public mind with Joseph and his words of surrender on the snowy afternoon of October 5:

> Tell General Howard I know his heart. What he told me before, I have in my heart. I am tired of fighting. Our chiefs are killed. Looking Glass is dead. Toohoolhoolzote is dead. The old men are all dead. It is the young men who say yes and no. He who led on the young men is dead. It is cold and we have no blankets. The little children are freezing to death. My people, some of them, have run away to the hills and have no blankets, no food; no one knows where they are—perhaps freezing to death. I want to have time to look for my children and see how many I can find. Maybe I shall find them among the dead. Hear me, my chiefs. I am tired; my heart is sick and sad. From where the sun now stands I will fight no more forever.

In the speech, as told, Joseph turned over his command, brilliantly executed, that had taken his people to the lip of freedom. The press first had predicted his quick defeat, but as the story unfolded, the praise for Joseph's generalship began to swell. In an early clash he was described riding up and down his battle line, barking orders and waving a red blanket to direct those more distant. After the Big Hole he was saluted as the leader of men with skills "as if they had been acquired at West Point," and the *New York Tribune* ranked him and his warriors above the "cavalry men of the Don and Volga." His compassion was said to match his generalship. Under his orders, readers learned, the Nez Perces had forgone scalping, spared women, children, and the wounded, and treated captives kindly. This is the Joseph who has survived in the popular perception, the master strategist formidable in a fight and, once a victor, as a western editor concluded, "almost too humane for belief."

Joseph's near veneration is another of the war's revelations, but not because its picture is true. Its lessons are in what the public needed to see and believe and in how a gifted leader learned those lessons and used them to find a way out of his people's dark time.

Joseph was never a war leader. Although always brave in the fight, he never devised strategy or led anyone in battle. If he had a role in the fray, it apparently was to watch over the camp and horse herd, and his greatest contribution was to save the animals at the start of the Big Hole fight. War was one of those unusual occurrences when men with skills for the moment—in this case their strategic gifts and special valor—were pulled into temporary service. In 1877 those leaders were Looking Glass, Toohoolhoolzote, Joseph's brother Ollokut, Rainbow, and others. Joseph's gifts were elsewhere, in diplomacy, and even so, he was one among several in that role. The band chiefs chose not him but Toohoolhoolzote to face Howard at the final showdown at Lapwai. Joseph's formidable presence in meeting white leaders, however, plus his being chief of the largest band, made him, in the government's eyes, the leader of all the resisters. It was one more projection of a national flowchart onto native society, and it followed that when talk gave way to war, he would command it. At the siege at the Bear's Paw, that impression seemed confirmed when he took the lead in negotiations. He was only stepping up, however, out of the background and into a moment that once again called for his gifts. The war was over. Time now for a bargainer. Besides, as he said in his supposed surrender speech, just about everybody else in authority was dead.

That speech solidified the public perception of Joseph the commander. But the speech was not his, at least not literally. He spoke virtually no English, and whatever he said was conveyed indirectly, through two couriers and a translator. The famous words were written down by Howard's aide-de-camp, Charles Erskine Scott Wood, and no one else present reported anything much like them. Wood was already an accomplished writer, sending from the campaign dispatches to periodicals, and his journal shows him increasingly drawn to those he was pursuing. In the decades ahead he became a prolific poet, a successful attorney and defender of radical causes, and a bitter critic of the government, especially of its treatment of Indians. After the surrender he and Joseph quickly took to each other, and years later Wood sent his son to spend two summers with the Nez Perce chief. Whether the writerly Wood composed or shaped the speech to cultivate sympathy for a man and a people he admired cannot be known, but it's a valid question.

Joseph was no historical fraud, however. To the contrary, behind the misperceptions is another story of heroism and masterful leadership. It does not end with the surrender but begins with it.

AT THE BEAR'S PAW, both Oliver Howard and Nelson Miles promised Joseph that his people would be sent back to Idaho, but in fact they were first marched to Bismarck, Dakota Territory, then taken by train to Fort Leavenworth, Kansas, where after a miserable winter and sweltering summer they were exiled to the Indian Territory (today's Oklahoma). They spent nearly seven years in what they called Eeikish Pah (the Hot Place, or the Heat). Nearly half of them died there, including most young children and many elderly, among them William Clark's son Halahtookit ("Daytime Smoke"). It was arguably the low point in all Nimiipuu history, which made the challenge at hand—to restore the people from the Heat to their homeland—as great as any their leaders had ever faced.

It began with grasping what they were up against. That education had been proceeding for more than seventy years, but on the eve of the war the Nez Perces still looked on whites and their world with a mix of canny understanding and profound ignorance. The resisting bands had prospered by getting to know and by trading shrewdly with whites close by, yet none of them had ever been to a town larger than Lewiston. They knew local authority well enough to stay free of it for generations, yet so poorly did they grasp the meaning of a nation that they believed that once in Montana they would be left alone. They were plenty acquainted with clapboard buildings and steamboats, but it is doubtful that any among the resisting bands had ever seen a telegram, and the first locomotive they saw was the one that carried them into captivity after their surrender. The war itself was a crash course in the scope and muscle of the nation and its power. Traveling over a mountain did not make them free; troops, ferried by rail from as far as Georgia and maneuvered within the telegraphic net, seemed to appear from nowhere. Once the Nez Perces were caught, traveling through cities like St. Paul, Minnesota, gawked at by crowds in the many hundreds, none could have missed the sheer weight of numbers against them. The implications must have been obvious.

The lessons made the challenge of leadership, which fell mainly to Joseph, in one sense utterly new: how to protect the Nez Perces inside this alien reality. But in another sense Joseph acted within an enduring tradition. As had the chiefs who met Lewis and Clark, in another world so long before, he gauged what advantage these whites offered, and he leveraged it as best he could. The advantage, one he could hardly have guessed, he apparently learned early in captivity, perhaps from Wood and more likely from his first postwar glimpse of white society in Bismarck. As he led the bands into town, protected by troopers, locals broke through the lines in a frenzy of admiring generosity, thrusting pies, boiled hams, and other eatables on people that, the last Joseph knew, had been condemned as rabid, degenerate savages. As for Joseph himself, a reporter who interviewed him wrote that this "ideal Indian," a "prince of misfortune," was "just the character to live in romance and poetry . . . A more noble captive has never graced our land." Later, as up to five thousand locals in a day came to see the Nez Perces camped in a malarial bottom at Fort Leavenworth, Joseph sat stoically in public view and granted interviews to fawning journalists. Although there is no way to know when and how well he grasped how he appeared to the nation or, what must have been more bewildering, how that image was being created and broadcast, there is one hint. Two days after he arrived in Bismarck, town fathers honored him for his "bravery and humanity." Joseph spoke briefly of his good sentiments, then ended: "I expect what I speak will be said throughout the land, and I only want to speak good."

During the next months and years he especially directed that good speech, always through a translator, at those with power to help. In January 1879 he was permitted to travel to the national capital and meet with high officials, including President Rutherford Hayes. While there he spoke for an hour at Lincoln Hall to members of Congress, cabinet members, and diplomats, and his dictated account of the war was published the following April in the *North American Review.* He waded into the social swirl. At a White House reception, a "model of courtly grace" in blankets and shell earrings, he bowed to the first lady and chatted with William Sherman as the social elite "pressed up to shake the savage hand." Reporters found him a living exhibit of the *beau sauvage*, dignified and regal, wearing "that melancholy air that makes him so interesting to the people who have abused him so." When he spoke publicly, it was of that abuse, but his message was subtler than that. He elevated the values enshrined in postwar America and deftly used them to his purpose.

He now knew his people must change and be part of this nation, he said, but the nation's leaders ought to change too. They should act as they professed. If all were to live under one law, as the Nez Perces had been told for so long, then all should be treated alike: "Let me be a free man—free to travel, free to stop, free to work, free to trade . . . free to follow the religion of my fathers, free to think and talk and act for myself—and I will obey every law. . . ." Here was the American credo of individualism; free labor; liberties of commerce, thought, and worship; and, especially notable to the Nez Perces, the right to move at will, to be "free to travel, free to stop." His people had submitted, Joseph said. Why, then, were they not allowed to live fully the life they had submitted to? An American believed that if somewhere else offered a better life, then "better go there," he told a delegation to the Indian Territory. Why, then, were his people now held in the Heat, "as you keep prisoners, in a corral"? A further implication, a comparison to the recently freed slaves, was obvious.

Others on the reservation cultivated the bands' collective image. They took up the plow, growing wheat, corn, squash, pumpkins, tomatoes, and more. Tribal missionaries from Idaho opened schools and a church. They encouraged visits by reporters, politicians, and religious agents, who pronounced the crowded worship services and flourishing gardens part of a "transformation truly wonderful." Delegations were invited for the nation's two supreme celebratory days, Christmas and July Fourth. At the latter they ate in an arbor hung with patriotic bunting and were greeted by a prayer and a meaningful hymn, "Blest Be the Tie that Binds." Always they were reminded of the mistreatment and betrayals leading to the war and the suffering in exile. As a *New York Times* reporter was shown scores of Nez Perce graves, mostly children's, Joseph suddenly rode up, dressed in white men's clothes, to say he hoped the Great Father would "take pity upon this suffering people."

In 1885 the artful efforts of Joseph and others paid off, and the Nez Perces became one of the rarest of rarities in Indian relations, a removed people allowed to go back. None was allowed to return to the Wallowa, however, and Joseph and more than half were sent to live with other Indians in northern Washington State. There he shed all white trappings, refusing a cabin and living in his lodge, but he continued to try to bring his band fully home. He went back east again in 1897, met with several officials, rode in the parade dedicating Grant's tomb, and attended Buffalo Bill Cody's Wild West show in Madison Square Garden, but although he was permitted two brief trips to his home country to plead his case to locals and to visit his father's grave, he was never allowed to lead his people back to the Land of Winding Waters. He died in 1904, probably from a heart attack, while sitting beside the fire in his lodge. The date was September 21, ninety-nine years and a day after Lewis and Clark had walked off Lolo Pass to set Nez Perce history onto a new course.

As a leader Joseph had a place in that history that was both distinctively his own and part of its longer flow. He led his Nez Perces through the final, painful recognition that independence, as they had known it, was lost. He led them through exodus and into exile. There he found his intuitive brilliance. Drawing on his victorious enemies' very misperceptions of who he was, he called them to their higher values, and by that he finally led his people out of their dark time toward what they valued most, home. In his extraordinary performance Joseph also drew on the best traditions of native leadership, the adaptive gift of finding betterment in a changing world and of plotting the best way out of very bad spots, while still protecting what must not change, the precious irreducibles of identity. To understand and appreciate leadership in the American experience, his story and those of other native leaders deserve our attention and respect.

"WHO'S IN CHARGE HERE?"
Visitors' Guide to Washington
SEAL OF THE PRESIDENT OF THE UNITED STATES
©1979 HERBLOCK

WHEN PRESIDENTS BECOME WEAK

Robert Dallek

—

THE HISTORIAN RICHARD HOFSTADTER SAID THAT AMERICA IS THE only nation in history that believes it was born perfect and strives for improvement. The country's success as the richest and most powerful nation has helped sustain the myth of American perfection at home and exceptionalism in the world. But given the numerous stumbles the country has experienced at home—assassinations, recessions, corrupt public officials, and an inability to master a variety of social problems, including unsustainable medical costs, forty-seven million people lacking health insurance, a flawed system of public education, and millions of undocumented immigrants—it is difficult to imagine that most Americans still see the country as without major defects. As for those who still believe that foreigners everywhere aspire to imitate our way of life, they must wonder why millions in Iraq and Afghanistan, like the Vietnamese, refuse to follow our lead toward democracy.

Domestic and foreign doubts about American exceptionalism have registered most robustly in assessments of the country's chief executives. Although Americans see every presidential election as an exercise in renewal or harbor expectations that a new administration or a second term for an incumbent carries with it the promise of better days, it is an optimism that is invariably disappointed. Despite partisan pronouncements by party chiefs about the achievements of their respective presidents, examples of public frustration with each administration are legion. Only Franklin Roosevelt was able to win more than eight years as president, and his successful bids for third and fourth terms rested on unique circumstances. All other presidents, excluding the seven who died in office, ended their terms under political storm clouds. Some, mindful of their diminished popularity, gave up running for a second term; others—William Howard Taft, Herbert Hoover, Gerald Ford, Jimmy Carter, and George H. W. Bush in the last century—unsuccessfully tested their appeal for additional years in power.

With the possible exception of Theodore Roosevelt, those who retired after more than four years as chief executive departed to the sounds of grumbling about the nation's state of affairs. In the last century Woodrow Wilson was a defeated foreign policy leader unable to convince senators and the public to back the settlement he had negotiated at Versailles; Harry Truman, dogged by a stalemate in Korea, could muster only 32 percent approval ratings; Dwight Eisenhower left behind a country frustrated by an economic downturn, fearful of eclipse by Soviet power, and experiencing a lost sense of national purpose; Lyndon Johnson was in disrepute over the Vietnam War that he seemed incapable of winning or ending honorably; Richard Nixon had to resign or be impeached and convicted of high crimes and misdemeanors for his role in the Watergate scandal; Ronald Reagan suffered the embarrassment of unprecedented deficits and the Iran-contra affair, which threatened administration officials with prison terms; impeachment for personal transgressions shadowed Bill Clinton's departure; and George W. Bush left town hounded by complaints about an unnecessary war in Iraq and the worst economic conditions since the Great Depression.

These downturns in presidential fortunes were not inevitable. While uncontrollable circumstances partly explain these presidential troubles, the presidents themselves contributed to their difficulties by poor policy decisions or stumbling leadership, especially, but not exclusively, in response to foreign crises. Presidential actions during World Wars I and II as well as in the Korean, Vietnamese, and Iraq conflicts fueled contemporary and retrospective concerns that undermined their reputations.

Take, first, the case of Woodrow Wilson. In the thirties Winston Churchill is alleged to have said that if Wilson had kept the United States out of the fighting, the war might have ended in a stalemate. Moreover, a deadlock could have meant not Germany's national frustration, which helped propel Adolf Hitler and the Nazis into power, but a sense of shared loss across national lines that might have produced less passion for revenge and greater eagerness for accommodation. It was certainly a plausible alternative to the miserable one that brought so much destruction to Europe for the second time in a generation.

Two other alternatives might have spared Europe and the world from the second round of suffering. The Allies could have followed Wilson's proposal for a generous settlement that lived up to his advocacy of a peace without victors. But this would have been decidedly at odds with the intense emotions for revenge in the victorious nations. A more likely possibility would have been an Allied occupation of Germany that could have shaped a different future from the one produced by imposing a harsh Versailles Treaty on the defeated powers and expecting rather than compelling them to live up to its clauses. An occupied Germany, as after World War II, would not have taken the turn toward the ultranationalism Hitler dictated—at least not if the Allies had maintained a long-term presence that aimed at the creation of a democratic society. As long as the Allies were unwilling to enforce the treaty directly, they were in no position to control the economic and political developments in Germany that facilitated the rise of Nazism.

But it was not only in Europe that the postwar settlement planted seeds of discontent. In the United States, where disillusionment with Wilson's unrealized peace program revived traditional isolationism, Washington became a helpless observer of the downward spiral toward international disaster.

Wilson's prewar defense of American neutral rights, which he equated with the advancement of international law, was an error that ill served U.S. and international interests. It was not as if no one had seen these dangers; Secretary of State William Jennings Bryan resigned in protest against Wilson's policy. It is a tragic irony that Wilson, America's greatest advocate of international peace, inadvertently involved the United States in unwanted bloodshed and helped create conditions that led directly to a second world war.

The election in 1920 of Warren G. Harding, a Midwestern Babbitt as different from Wilson as any successor could have been, demonstrated the depths of Wilson's personal and foreign policy unpopularity. Harding's unsuitability for the country's highest office was transparent within two years of his election. The corruption of people around him and his obvious limits as a chief executive would have put his reelection in doubt. In the midst of an economic downturn early in his term, he admitted that he didn't have a clue about what to do.

Harding's sudden death in 1923 opened the way for Calvin Coolidge, his very different vice president, to win a decisive victory in the following year. Scrupulous and taciturn, the embodiment of old-fashioned values in a time of rapid social change from a rural to an urban society, Coolidge reflected the current antipathy for federal activism and attraction to isolation from overseas political commitments. While his hands-off policies served him and the country well enough in the short run, they were a prescription for long-term disaster. His decision not to run in 1928 spared him the burden of dealing with the economic collapse that beset Herbert Hoover between 1929 and 1933.

Hoover's rigid economic outlook made him the wrong man at the wrong time in the wrong place. An architect of humanitarian relief during World War I and the Russian Civil War of 1918–21, he ironically left office with a reputation as a rigid ideological conservative more intent on preserving free market principles than easing the plight of his fellow Americans. The designation of shantytowns as Hoovervilles spoke volumes about his standing in Depression America.

Although New York Governor Franklin D. Roosevelt was able to win a decisive victory in 1932 and establish himself as the greatest president in twentieth-century America, he was not without failings. His blunder in 1937 in proposing to increase the number of Supreme Court justices as a way to overcome its conservative bias and rejection of New Deal legislation was not the greatest misstep of his twelve-year presidency. Nor was his turn toward economic caution in 1937–38 that caused a recession or even his relatively passive response between 1941 and 1945 to news of the Nazi Holocaust against Europe's Jews. Although some have described his response to the Nazi killing program as an "abandonment" of the Jews, the extent of what Roosevelt might have accomplished had he been more determined to counter Nazis actions is open to debate.

It was Roosevelt's ill-advised decision in 1944 to run for a fourth term that stands out as his greatest error of leadership. He was in failing health and too frail to serve another four years as president. To be sure, he had the precedent of a Grover Cleveland, who had hidden a surgery for cancer of the jaw at the start of his second term in 1893. Roosevelt could also invoke the analogue of Wilson, who had refused to resign despite being in much worse shape from a massive stroke than FDR appeared to be in 1944. Similarly, Coolidge had not been in full command of his capacities during his presidency after he had fallen into a depression when a teenage son died of blood poisoning. Although encouraged by his doctors to believe that he could manage to lead the country through the end of the war and into the postwar period, Roosevelt died less than three months into his fourth term. Having failed to inform Vice President Harry S. Truman about the atomic bomb or about his postwar plans, Roosevelt left an unelected president to deal with the great end-of-war and post-1945 challenges.

When it became known that he was a dying man who had recklessly run for a fourth time in 1944, Roosevelt came under sharp attack for his performance during his brief last term, especially at the Yalta Conference in February 1945. Although any close assessment of events at this second wartime meeting among Churchill, Roosevelt, and Stalin suggests otherwise, the president's conservative critics impugned his historical reputation by asserting that he gave away Eastern Europe to Soviet control; Stalin allegedly extracted concessions from a frail president unable to defend U.S. interests. As any balanced reconstruction of the Yalta context shows, the Soviets had the military might to impose their will on Poland and its surrounding neighbors no matter what Roosevelt and Churchill said. Nonetheless, Roosevelt made himself vulnerable to the later political attacks on his historical reputation by trying to serve for a fourth term in a weakened state of health. Roosevelt believed he was indispensable to the nation's well-being, but as the French leader Charles de Gaulle later asserted, the graveyards are full of indispensable men.

Few Americans thought that Harry Truman could possibly be a credible replacement for the storied FDR. Initially he gained the public trust by ending the war and arranging the establishment of the United Nations. But daunting postwar economic and international problems—

continuing shortages of consumer goods, strikes, inflation, and rising worries about Communist aggression abroad and subversion at home—convinced most contemporary commentators that Truman could not manage demobilization without an economic collapse reminiscent of the Depression or a peace settlement that kept Germany and Japan at bay and maintained good relations with Soviet Russia. A decisive Democratic Party setback in the 1946 congressional elections, in which the Republicans asked, "Had enough shortages? Had enough inflation? Had enough strikes? Had enough communism?," seemed to foretell a Truman defeat in the 1948 presidential election.

But a series of foreign policy actions in 1947 and 1948 highlighted by the Truman Doctrine to rescue Greece and Turkey from communism, the Marshall Plan to rebuild Western Europe, and the Berlin airlift, which saved the western part of the city from East German Communist control, gave Truman credentials as a strong foreign policy leader. Nevertheless, none of the pollsters predicted a Truman victory in the presidential contest. But a brilliantly designed election campaign that appealed to the Democratic Party's liberal base and endeared Truman to voters as well as his unexciting opponent, New York's Governor Thomas E. Dewey, who ran a low-key campaign that compared poorly with Truman's whistle-stop cross-country tour, produced the greatest upset in presidential history.

Truman's triumph, however, was short-lived. By 1951, two years into his term, his approval ratings had collapsed, and he was a lame-duck president who could neither effectively control foreign policy nor enact his Fair Deal agenda of domestic reforms promised in the campaign.

His problem was a stalemated war in Korea. The initial attack in June 1950 on Syngman Rhee's anti-Communist South Korea by Kim Il Sung's North Korea, a Soviet satellite, had brought the United States into the fighting. Post-1945 Soviet domination of Eastern Europe, including a Communist coup in Czechoslovakia in 1948, joined to Moscow's detonation of an atomic bomb in September 1949, at least five years earlier than anticipated, and the triumph in the following month of Mao Zedong's Communists in a Chinese civil war with Chiang Kai-shek's Nationalists made another Communist conquest politically unacceptable to Washington. By the fall of 1950 the successful defense of South Korea had opened the way to consideration of an invasion of the north and the possible ouster of a Communist regime. After so many Communist advances in the previous five years, the liberation of a country from Soviet control was irresistible.

But unifying the Korean peninsula under a pro-Western government carried risks of a wider war with China and the Soviet Union. Truman had his doubts about reaching for more than the rescue of Rhee's government. In October, at a meeting on Wake Island with General Douglas MacArthur, the highly regarded hero of the World War II Pacific fighting, the architect of Japan's reconstruction, and the organizer of the successful offensive that drove the North Koreans back above the thirty-eighth parallel, Truman asked for reassurances that an invasion of the north would not cause a new, larger crisis. MacArthur promised a quick victory without Chinese or Soviet involvement, predicting that if Beijing entered the conflict, it would result in its decisive defeat.

Truman was only too ready to hear optimistic forecasts of a prompt and successful end to the fighting. Political pressures in the United States made it almost essential for the president to liberate North Korea from Communist control. To stop at the parallel would have been in line with the administration's containment policy of holding the Communists in check until their predicted collapse from internal contradictions. But right-wing critics saw this as a weak response to Moscow's and Beijing's ambitions for world dominance. As 1952 Republican vice presidential nominee Richard Nixon was to say of Adlai Stevenson, the Democratic presidential candidate, who supported the Truman foreign policy, he had a Ph.D. from Secretary of State Dean Acheson's cowardly college of Communist containment. Without rollback or liberation, Truman risked a political attack on his administration that put in jeopardy his political influence and his party's chances in the 1952 elections.

Crossing the parallel, however, produced the consequences it was meant to forestall. Not only did the Chinese enter the fighting in great numbers, but they also proved to be formidable foes whose defeat seemed to require much more power than the Truman administration or a majority of Americans were willing to use. Whereas MacArthur wished to expand the fighting from Korea into China and even to resort to atomic bombs if necessary, neither the president nor the public shared his preference for actions that could lead to another world war.

MacArthur's public advocacy of a wider war was an act of insubordination that ran counter to the tradition of civilian over military authority. Truman could not leave it unchallenged. He abruptly recalled MacArthur from Japan and forced his retirement from the service. His dismissal of the general produced a firestorm of criticism that did as much to undermine the president's public standing as to protect the prerogatives of his office. Opinion polls showed that majorities did not favor MacArthur's wider war solution or his defiance of the White House but took exception to the president's unceremonious dismissal of a military hero people felt deserved better of the chief executive.

The downturn in Truman's political fortunes accelerated as casualties in the fighting increased and victory seemed unlikely without expanding the conflict to the Chinese mainland. Because neither side seemed capable of decisively defeating the other in a continuing conflict confined to Korea, they agreed to begin truce talks in the summer of 1951. But the discussions reached an impasse over exchanging the more than one hundred thousand Chinese and North Korean prisoners of war for the roughly twelve thousand American and South Korean POWs. The Chinese demanded an all-for-all swap, and the United States favored voluntary repatriation. Since the U.S. proposal seemed certain to produce a propaganda victory for Washington, Beijing and Pyongyang denounced the suggested arrangement as entirely unacceptable.

The difference became an insurmountable barrier to a settlement. Determined to have more than the restoration of South Korea's autonomy as the result of the fighting that eventually cost the United States more than thirty-five thousand battlefield deaths, Truman could not reach a peace agreement in Korea. Public frustration with the war drove the president's approval rating to a low of 23 percent and left him powerless to enact his domestic Fair Deal reforms at home or further build NATO defenses in Europe, which critics complained the administration should have been putting at the center of its defense against Communist aggression.

Crossing the parallel was a disaster that destroyed Truman's effectiveness and made his second four years a washout. True, his historical reputation greatly outpaced his contemporary standing. Fifty-six years after he left office he is currently remembered as at least a near great president. His reversal of fortunes rests on America's victory in the Cold War, which most historians agree was the result of the containment policy that held the Soviet Union in check without a direct military conflict until the contradictions in its economic and political institutions caused its self-destruction.

Nevertheless, the decision to expand the fighting in Korea to bring down Kim's Communist regime ruined Truman's last two and a half years in office. An end to the fighting in the fall of 1950 could have been presented as a triumph over Communist aggression, served as a warning against future military adventures by Moscow and Beijing, and left Truman free to work for the domestic reforms he proposed in 1948. In short, crossing the parallel was a blunder that trapped Truman in a disastrous war that played havoc with his presidency.

Could Truman have rejected a policy of invading North Korea and the subsequent conflict with China? Certainly the domestic political pressure on him to act aggressively was compelling and was much more the motive for going north than any national security consideration. A decision to stop at the parallel would have provoked fierce political attacks on his leadership. But a rational explanation of what it would have risked in causing a wider war with China and possibly a military conflict with Russia could have promoted sober second thoughts among millions of Americans, who could have accepted the wisdom of simply rescuing South Korea. Knowing how things turned out, of course, makes it easier to offer this judgment. But clearly, restraint was Truman's better option and would have spared the country and his administration considerable grief. It is not unreasonable to conclude that he exercised poor judgment in behaving as he did.

Lyndon Johnson and Richard Nixon have not been as fortunate as Truman in having their historical reputations boosted by recent events. The failed war in Vietnam continues to dog the presidential standings of both men.

For Johnson, Vietnam was the most dramatic and transparent demonstration of failed foreign policy leadership by a president in the twentieth century, though Wilson's aborted peace program is an unenviable rival. The backdrop to Vietnam was the riots in the inner-city ghettos that critics blamed on Johnson's overindulgent treatment of minorities; the stumbling War on Poverty that conservatives complained created a generation of welfare cheats and allowed Ronald Reagan to joke: "We fought a war on poverty and poverty won"; and Johnson's affinity for exaggerated claims, which produced a "credibility gap" and made Johnson vulnerable to comedians, who asked, "How do you know when Lyndon Johnson is telling the truth? When he pulls his earlobe, rubs his chin, he's telling the truth. But when he begins to move his lips, you know he's lying."

Despite Johnson's incomparable record of groundbreaking domestic reforms, led by civil rights and Medicare, he seems unlikely ever to overcome the many poor decisions he made between 1963 and 1969 about the Vietnam War. Within days of becoming president he told American Ambassador to Saigon Henry Cabot Lodge, "I'm not going to be the first president to lose a war." Instead of judiciously weighing the advantages and disadvantages of fighting in Southeast Asia, Johnson jumped to the conclusion that he could lead the United States to victory. Never mind that the French with a long history of involvement in the region could not control events there or that Truman's experience in Korea should have been a cautionary tale giving Johnson pause. His instincts told him that superior American military power would defeat the Communist insurgency promptly and certainly before the war became a politically crippling source of frustration to most Americans, as it had in Korea.

His miscalculations about the dangers to the United States from losing Vietnam skewed his judgments or inhibited him from giving closer scrutiny to the unlikely effectiveness of U.S. forces fighting in jungles ten thousand miles from Washington. He shared President Dwight Eisenhower's assumption that the countries of Southeast Asia were like a series of dominoes that would fall to the Communists if South Vietnam were not defended against Soviet-Chinese–North Vietnamese–inspired aggression. Moreover, Johnson saw the defense of Saigon as equal to avoiding the Anglo-French error in appeasing Hitler at Munich in 1938. Johnson believed that losing South Vietnam would embolden the Communists and possibly lead to a world war. He intended to fight in Vietnam in order not to risk a larger nuclear conflict.

There were domestic political dimensions as well to Johnson's initial actions on Vietnam. Memories of Republican attacks on the Truman administration for having "lost" China to the Communists haunted Johnson. He imagined a similar onslaught against his leadership if South Vietnam fell. He believed it would become a distraction from the Great Society reforms he hoped to enact and would ruin his chances of becoming a great president.

In addition, he thought that setbacks in Vietnam could jeopardize his prospects in the 1964 presidential election. Consequently, in the summer of 1964, in the midst of his campaign against Republican Barry Goldwater, a superhawk, an alleged attack on U.S. destroyers in the Gulf of Tonkin became a chance to blunt Republican complaints about weakness in meeting the Communist threat. Johnson extracted a resolution of support from the Congress to counter acts of Communist aggression in Vietnam. He believed that the congressional endorsement would not only immobilize conservative complaints about a weak foreign policy but also assure him against future political criticism should the fighting require greater commitments than he anticipated. Privately, he crowed: "The resolution was just like grandma's nightshirt, it covered everything."

In February 1965, after Johnson had decisively defeated Goldwater, a Communist assault on Pleiku in Vietnam's Central Highlands killed eight U.S. military advisers and wounded dozens more. With the election out of the way, Johnson's concern remained to mute a foreign policy problem that could shift the focus from domestic reforms, which were his highest priority. Still seeing a passive response as encouraging additional acts of aggression in Vietnam and elsewhere, Johnson decided to use American air power against the North to raise morale in Saigon and discourage Hanoi from supporting further attacks. He ordered a sustained bombing campaign, Rolling Thunder, on the mistaken assumption that Hanoi would respond to air strikes on its military facilities by limiting or even ending support for the Vietcong insurgency in the South. The *New York*

Times now reported that the United States had begun "an undeclared and unexplained war in Vietnam."

By the summer of 1965 it was evident that air power would not assure South Vietnam's autonomy and that some greater military pressure would be necessary to defeat the Communist campaign in the south. The limited results of the air war frustrated Johnson. He complained to his press secretary that there was no light at the end of the tunnel from the bombing. "Hell," he said, "we don't even have a tunnel; we don't even know where the tunnel is."

The only alternative he saw to a long-term conflict that seemed likely to test domestic patience and result in a Communist victory was a commitment of substantial ground forces that he hoped could produce a quick end to the fighting. In July 1965 he announced that one hundred thousand combat troops would be sent to Vietnam. His decision now rested on two erroneous judgments. First, he mistakenly believed that one hundred thousand infantrymen could make a quick end to the war, and second, he thought he could mute the importance of the commitment by announcing it at a news conference in which he also revealed that he was filling a Supreme Court vacancy with Abe Fortas, a distinguished jurist and old friend, and that one of his daughters was pregnant.

By the beginning of 1966 both assumptions had proved false. The war was not being won and was daily front-page news, agitating an antiwar movement on college campuses. In January, Johnson concluded that he needed to deploy another 120,000 troops, but to hide his decision, he told advisers that he would announce an increase of 10,000 a month over the next twelve months. The ploy was ineffective; opposition to a conflict that dissenters in the United States complained was a civil war, which did not threaten the national security and would be interpreted as the actions of a Western imperial power seeking to maintain a colony in Southeast Asia, made Vietnam a domestic controversy that threatened to ruin Johnson's presidency. It was a distressing irony: while he believed that inaction in Vietnam would destroy his credibility and undermine his capacity to win passage of Great Society reforms, the military action was producing just that result.

Yet the more antiwar opponents challenged Johnson's policy, the more determined he became to prove them wrong. By 1968 he had sent 545,000 troops to South Vietnam despite clear indications that the war was a stalemate or could not be won without an invasion of North Vietnam. But fears that such an expansion of the fighting would bring China and the Soviet Union into the conflict persuaded Johnson to resist advice either to use "battlefield" nuclear weapons against the Communists or to send ground forces north of the seventeenth parallel to topple Hanoi's Communist government.

In the spring of 1968 Johnson found himself in a political trap of his own making. On March 31, after a North Vietnamese Tet offensive at the start of the year refuted Johnson's claims that the United States was winning the war, he announced his intention to begin peace talks. Also recognizing that the war had destroyed his domestic political standing, Johnson revealed that he would not seek another presidential term. Secret promises from Republican presidential candidate Richard M. Nixon to South Vietnam's president Nguyen Van Thieu that he would get a better deal from a Nixon administration than from Johnson in any peace agreement convinced Thieu to resist Johnson's pressures to discuss a truce.

By every count, Johnson's Vietnam policies were a failure. Not only did more than thirty thousand U.S. troops perish along with hundreds of thousands of Vietnamese during his presidency, but the fighting did nothing to advance Johnson's domestic agenda or promote America's national security. To the contrary, the war destroyed Johnson's political hold on the country and undermined its credibility with allies and foes. From the perspective of 2009, twenty years after the Cold War ended, it is apparent that fighting in Vietnam was entirely superfluous to winning the struggle with Soviet communism. The North Vietnamese takeover of the south in 1975 had zero impact on the larger Cold War struggle. As both Secretary of Defense Robert McNamara and John Kennedy's and LBJ's first national security adviser McGeorge Bundy freely admitted after they had left office, the Vietnam War was a mistake; its only retrospective value was as an object lesson in what a president and the country should not have done.

Richard Nixon and Henry Kissinger, despite their vaunted reputations as foreign policy realists, did not fare any better with Vietnam than

Johnson. They were convinced from the start of Nixon's presidency in January 1969 that acknowledging American defeat in the war would undermine the confidence of allies in America's defense commitments and encourage the aggressive ambitions of Communist adversaries.

At a minimum, Nixon and Kissinger believed that they needed to convince the world that they had achieved "peace with honor" in Vietnam. Initially, they thought that increased military pressure on Hanoi could force it into an acceptable settlement. Specifically, in April and May 1970 they authorized a combined U.S.–South Vietnamese invasion of Cambodia that aimed to cut North Vietnam's supply lines to the south. In a nationally televised speech defending the "incursion," Nixon offered an apocalyptic view of America's stake in holding the line in Vietnam: "If, when the chips are down, the world's most powerful nation, the United States of America, acts like a pitiful, helpless giant, the forces of totalitarianism and anarchy will threaten free nations and free institutions throughout the world." He concluded by declaring, "We will not be humiliated. We will not be defeated."

Nixon's defense of the Cambodian attack was an exercise in hyperbole that provoked renewed antiwar protests on campuses across the country: Students at Kent State in Ohio and Jackson State in Mississippi lost their lives, and turmoil on other campuses forced the early end of spring terms at several colleges and universities.

The invasion did little, if anything, to halt Hanoi's assault on the South or to assure peace with honor. Because it was politically essential for Nixon to withdraw American ground troops from Vietnam if he was to win a second term and because he had no way to compel a peace agreement that assured Saigon's future autonomy, he announced a program of Vietnamization, the transfer of military security in South Vietnam from U.S. forces to South Vietnamese troops. Despite the questionable ability of Saigon's army to keep the country safe, especially when a 1971 offensive in Laos demonstrated its inadequacies, the Nixon White House publicly maintained that Vietnamization was a viable alternative to a continuing U.S. military presence in the country.

It was another false note in the litany of failures that dogged the Kennedy, Johnson, and Nixon administrations in trying to save South

Vietnam from communism. The defeat in Vietnam produced a public relations cover-up: The Nixon administration tried to persuade the world that the sacrifice of more than fifty-eight thousand American lives in the conflict was essential to America's national security and that the peace settlement in January 1973 was based on guarantees that South Vietnam would not become the victim of Hanoi's aggression. The occupation of the South by the North in January 1975 gave the lie to peace with honor and demonstrated that even the most tough-minded foreign policy realists like Nixon and Kissinger could be the victims of self-defeating illusions. Because misjudgments in fighting the war were too painful for most civilian and military architects of the failed policies to concede, they defended themselves by arguing that South Vietnam's demise could be balanced against the "fact" that the defense of South Vietnam had given other Southeast Asian countries time to develop their economic and political wherewithals to resist Communist subversion.

Other failures of presidential leadership dogged the country after the U.S. withdrawal from Vietnam. Foremost among these was Nixon's forced resignation in August 1974, following revelations of his involvement in the Watergate cover-up scandal. The unprecedented decision of a president to leave office before the end of his term was compelled by the understanding that he was vulnerable to becoming the first president to be ousted from office by a Senate trial for high crimes and misdemeanors. Nixon's resignation moved Gerald Ford, his successor, to declare: "Our long national nightmare is over." But not entirely: His pardon of Nixon in 1974 opened Ford to political attacks that underscored his ineptitude in making domestic and foreign policy and contributed to his defeat in the 1976 presidential election.

The national distress at failed presidential leadership continued under the next five presidents: Jimmy Carter's stumbling presidency punctuated by the limitations on oil exports of the Organization of Petroleum Exporting Countries (OPEC) and gasoline rationing in the United States; the Iran hostage crisis, which demonstrated America's powerlessness to control the actions of a weaker Middle East adversary; and domestic economic dislocations, including stagflation, limited him to one term. Ronald Reagan's restoration of national confidence in presidential leadership through his talent for communication with a mass audience and contributions to the successful ending of the Cold War could not entirely eclipse the feelings of distrust toward occupants of the White House generated by past misdeeds and a new scandal involving policy toward Iran and the contras, conservative opponents of a leftist Nicaraguan regime. Reagan's apparent ignorance of the unlawful actions in the Iran-contra affair by some of his closest associates raised later questions about whether his Alzheimer's disease had begun to affect him and about the wisdom of having someone past seventy serve as president.

George H. W. Bush, Reagan's successor, gained initial approval by putting the finishing touches on Reagan's efforts to bring down the Soviet Union. But his ineffective response to a recession that allowed Arkansas Governor Bill Clinton to frame the 1992 presidential election by declaring, "It's the economy, stupid," made Bush another one-term president. Bush's competence as a foreign policy leader and his limited interest in and/or understanding of domestic issues revived doubts about the capacity of any individual to master the multiple challenges of the modern presidency.

Although Clinton managed to serve two terms, winning reelection against Senator Bob Dole of Kansas, another elderly Republican, his presidency also came to grief when he was impeached for having lied about a sexual relationship with Monica Lewinsky, a twenty-one-year-old White House intern. His acquittal in a Senate trial added to sharp divisions between Democrats and Republicans and to the belief that national consensus was beyond the reach of any president. Despite surviving accusations that he had committed perjury, Clinton could not fully repair the damage to either his reputation or the presidency, which once more suffered diminished public regard.

The start of a new century could not reverse a distressing trend toward what seemed like permanent doubts about the integrity and wisdom of the men—and now women—who were putting themselves forward as leaders worthy of elevation to the White House. The disputed 2000 presidential election added to beliefs that the country's political system was badly in need of repair and that the United States might have seen its best days. Governor George W. Bush's victory over Vice President Al Gore reminded many of the 1876 contest between Rutherford B. Hayes and Samuel J. Tilden, which had to be settled by a special commission that satisfied no one. Hayes's critics belittled him as "Rutherfraud," and Tilden supporters had to be discouraged from acting on threats of "Tilden or blood."

The 2000 contest evoked complaints of another undemocratic result: Bush not only lost the popular vote but also had a questionable victory in Florida, the deciding state in the contest, which the Supreme Court put into his column with a sharply divided 5–4 vote that many believed an inappropriate intervention in a state election.

George W. Bush's presidency provoked new rounds of recrimination about a president's competence and honesty. Although winning an initial large tax cut, a major education reform, No Child Left Behind, and a far-reaching revision of the 1965 Medicare law that provided access to drug benefits for seniors, Bush could not sustain his hold on a majority of Americans. True, he reached unprecedented heights of popularity after he rallied the country following the September 11, 2001, terrorist attacks on the World Trade Center and the Pentagon and military action in Afghanistan ousted the Taliban and threw Osama bin Laden and Al Qaeda on the defensive. Moreover, he was able to become only the sixteenth sitting president out of forty-four to win a second term.

But his last four years became a demonstration of Thomas Jefferson's complaint that the presidency was "a splendid misery" or, as Andrew Jackson described it, "a form of dignified slavery." Herbert Hoover said the office was "a compound hell." Bush also could have echoed Harry Truman's grumbles that being president was like riding on the back of a tiger and that the White House was a "great white prison."

Most of Bush's misery was the product of his own misjudgments. To be sure, after the opportunity presented by the crisis of 9/11, circumstances turned against Bush. The Hurricane Katrina disaster in New Orleans and the long history of sectarian hatred in Iraq were conditions beyond Bush's reach. Still, his dilatory response to the Louisiana natural disaster, which was captured so graphically in the photos of his Air Force One flyover of New Orleans, and the stumbling response of FEMA, which he refused to acknowledge by declaring, "Brownie, you are doing a heck of a job," sounded the initial death knell of his presidency.

But it was the misadventure in Iraq that did so much to play havoc with Bush's standing. When White House assertions about Saddam Hussein's weapons of mass destruction and ties to Al Qaeda proved unmerited, it raised questions not only about Bush's gullibility in trusting false intelligence but also his honesty. Did he in fact know that he was peddling myths in order to take the country into a war of choice that he had been committed to from the start of his term? More than forty-three hundred American military deaths and more than twenty thousand wounded, tens of thousands Iraqis killed in sectarian attacks and millions displaced, and the shadow cast across America's reputation for civilized behavior by its torture of prisoners at Abu Ghraib and secret CIA prisons condemned Bush as a president who fought an unnecessary war with unwanted consequences. Even with the 2007–8 "surge" that reduced but did not eliminate Iraq's sectarian violence and gave a hint of credibility to Bush's stated intention of bringing democracy to the Middle East, he could not escape the responsibility for failed policies.

The onset of the worst economic downturn since the Great Depression in the last year of Bush's term added to his reputation as a chief executive with a limited understanding of either domestic or foreign affairs. Fortunately for the country, Bush did not cling to a rigid free market perspective that might have deepened the country's economic problems. He understood that the federal government had to take a central role in providing credit and bolstering economic activity despite substantial deficits that his opponents blamed on his multibillion-dollar tax cuts for the rich. But the atmosphere of deregulation that the Bush administration had fostered promoted speculation in housing and other investments that triggered the Great Recession, as commentators came to call the downturn.

Bush left office with approval ratings in the twenties and low thirties that rivaled Truman's numbers in the last days of his term. Bush hoped that like Truman, he would make a comeback if and when his decision to fight in Iraq was eventually seen as successful and necessary for the country's national security. But the current weight of evidence on Iraq makes this unlikely. Nor will recollections about the response to Katrina or the economy help his reputation. Whether he will be seen as among the worst presidents in the country's history, as most historians have been describing him, is open to question, though it's difficult to imagine that he will ever be seen as more than a mediocre or poor leader. What is currently transparent is that a majority of Americans were demoralized by Bush's stewardship, as suggested by Barack Obama's election on the strength of promises that the country could do better under a president with a decidedly different outlook. "Yes, we can" was as much a referendum on the Bush years as on Obama's unproved qualities of leadership.

Are there any discernible patterns in the various missteps by chief executives recounted in this essay? Uncontrollable circumstances have certainly been one major contribution to their poor performances. Herbert Hoover's bad luck in dealing with the worst economic crisis in the country's history and Jimmy Carter's misfortune in having to overcome a gasoline shortage caused by foreign actions out of his control were instances of presidents poorly served by unanticipated challenges no president could have prevented. The management of their respective crises, however, left something to be desired, as was made evident by the more effective leadership of their successors, FDR and Reagan, respectively, who demonstrated that a crisis can be as much an opportunity for successful governance as a cause of failure.

A more common source of flubbed leadership has been presidential misjudgment stemming from rigidity and arrogance. Wilson's and Roosevelt's assumptions that they were essential leaders whose illnesses would not deter them from performing their presidential duties were miscalculations that cost the country dearly. Truman's misconceptions about what he could carry off in Korea and his refusal to be more flexible in end-of-war negotiations led to results that no one can describe as anything but failure. LBJ's and Nixon's unbending convictions about Vietnam drew them into unwise actions for which they and the nation paid a heavy price. George W. Bush's similar stumbles in Iraq—false assumptions about what would serve the national security and what could be accomplished there—were another example of how bad ideas and an unwillingness to acknowledge any mistakes undermine a president and hurt the country.

Because all presidents, however well intentioned, are vulnerable to the sorts of errors that even the most intelligent and best advised chief executives can make, is there a mechanism for guarding the country from the consequences of their bad judgment? Since impeachment is reserved for high crimes and misdemeanors, the Constitution offers no remedy for unwise presidential performance. To be sure, the congressional and judicial branches were designed to act as checks on arbitrary executive behavior and the Twenty-fifth Amendment to the Constitution provides for the temporary suspension of presidential authority for incapacity. But the amendment was not designed to suspend a president's powers because of unpopular policies. Moreover, most presidential stumbles have come in foreign affairs, and neither the courts nor the Congress have had an effective response to overseas misjudgments, though they may be costing the country lives and treasure. And even where the other two branches might have acted to inhibit a president—crimping his funding for a foreign adventure or declaring his actions in violation of constitutional restrictions, undeclared wars being the most obvious example—challenges to presidents insisting they were defending the nation's safety have been extremely difficult to assert.

The country needs to consider a constitutional amendment that would give voters the power to recall a failing president. Because political opponents would always be tempted to invoke the provisions of a recall procedure, it would need to be both difficult to exercise and a clear expression of the popular will. The process should begin in Congress, where a recall procedure would need a 60 percent vote in both houses. This could be followed by a national referendum on whether all voters in the previous presidential election wished to remove the president and vice president and replace them with the Speaker of the House of Representatives and a vice president of that person's choosing.

To judge from the fact that only two sitting governors were recalled in the twentieth century—in North Dakota in 1921 and in California in 2003—it seems unlikely that such an amendment would get much use. Nevertheless, its availability would act as a check on a lame-duck president in the closing months of his term. It would give voters a way to punish a president pursuing an agenda that was distinctly at odds with the popular will. It would not be a definitive remedy for presidential missteps, which seem likely to define all future presidencies, however smart and wise they may be, but it could place marginal limits on the damage unwise leadership can do to the nation.

THE PHENOMENON: W. E. B. DuBOIS

Annette Gordon-Reed

HE WAS EVERYWHERE; WRITING, THINKING, ORGANIZING, USING ANY tool he could find, any resource within him and available to him, to accomplish one goal: the destruction of the doctrine of white supremacy as it operated in the United States and throughout the world. His great biographer David Levering Lewis explains it best: "In the course of his long turbulent career, W. E. B. DuBois attempted virtually every possible solution to the problem of twentieth-century racism—scholarship, propaganda, integration, national self-determination, human rights, cultural and economic separatism, politics, international communism, expatriation and third world solidarity."

The first prime minister of Ghana, Kwame Nkramah, called DuBois, as he neared the end of his very long life, "a phenomenon." An intellectual who wrote books, coined famous phrases, helped create the academic discipline of sociology, edited magazines, taught classes, and founded organizations—domestic and worldwide, he lived for ninety-five years. By any measure he can be described as having been a leader. But DuBois was a leader of a different sort. One of his contemporaries and admirers, William H. Ferris, pinpointed the nature of his uniqueness:

> There have been many instances in history where men, through their military or political genius, through their gift of speech or the magnetism of a fascinating personality, have forged to the front, challenged the admiration and compelled the homage of their fellows. Such men were Samuel Adams, George Washington, Abraham Lincoln, Frederick Douglass, James G. Blaine, Theodore

> Roosevelt, Daniel O'Connell, Parnell, Cavour, Garibaldi, Mirabeau, Bismarck, Napoleon and Caesar. But DuBois is one of the few men in history who was hurled on the throne of leadership by the dynamic force of the written word. He is one of the few writers who leaped to the front as a leader and became the head of a popular movement through impressing his personality upon men by means of a book. He had no aspiration of becoming a race leader when he wrote his "Souls of Black Folk." But that book has launched him upon a brilliant career.

There is much to ponder in Ferris's view. First is his conception of writers. As he points out, writers (and we may add into this formulation intellectuals of any sort) are not typically thought of as leaders. Leaders are men and women of action, while those who spend time toiling at their desks—writing prose, poetry, and academic articles or espousing theories—are more often seen as thinkers rather than as doers. They are regarded as denizens of the ivory tower, who by the very nature of their work are removed from the rough-and-tumble of the real world. Ferris's male-dominated list of leaders is of his time, but it does support the notion that those who lead typically put themselves before the public as individuals who desire to, and can, make politics run in some fashion. They are elected to office, or in the case of some of the men Ferris names, they took the reins of government by force.

For most of American history, blacks were in no position to exercise that type of leadership. Indeed at the time of DuBois's birth in 1868 the overwhelming majority of blacks were living in the South, having only recently been emancipated from chattel slavery and the males given the right to vote. There was a brief period during Reconstruction, of which DuBois later wrote brilliantly, when a handful of black men rose to formal leadership in state government in the South. Of course the story of how that turned out is well known. By the time young "Willie" DuBois of Great Barrington, Massachusetts, was all of nine years old, the so-called Redeemer governments in the South had put a stop to the progress of Reconstruction and positioned themselves to reassert white supremacy in the region. By the end of the 1880s the process had culminated in the establishment of segregation and legalized second-class status for African Americans. For decades to come, black voting rights were effectively vitiated by the political machinations and outright violence of southern whites.

What kind of leadership could blacks of DuBois's era exercise? There had been black leaders before, in the eighteenth century, people like Prince Hall, who formed the first black Masonic Lodge; Bishop Richard Allen, who founded the African Methodist Episcopal Church in Philadelphia; and a businessman from that same city, James Forten. These men and others stepped outside attending to their own lives and tried to make life better for African Americans as best they could under the tremendous constraints of the society they lived in.

The most important and famous black leader in America before DuBois's birth was Frederick Douglass. The former slave and tireless abolitionist made his mark with the written word, publishing his astounding memoirs detailing his life under the cruelty of slavery, and editing a newspaper, the *North Star*, that inspired many and furthered the cause of black liberation. While Douglass did serve in government for brief periods, this was long after he had established himself as the preeminent black leader of his day through his determined and intelligent efforts to speak on behalf of the millions of blacks who had no voice. Black leadership, in his era and for a long time to come, fell to those who, by their good fortune, managed to escape the systematic oppression under which blacks lived. And for most of Douglass's life that system was legalized southern slavery. Anyone with any pretense of being a "race leader" understood that his or her principal task was to work for the immediate and total elimination of slavery in America. Things could proceed from there. The only tool available to Douglass was moral suasion, speaking out on the question and hoping to bring people to his side. War eventually achieved what moral suasion could not. There was, however, no black Bismarck or Napoleon to make the decision to go to war, although when it came, blacks threw themselves into the conflict energetically.

By the time DuBois arrived on the scene the landscape had shifted. Legalized chattel slavery was dead, replaced for many by debt peonage and vigilante violence that maintained slavery in the South in all but name. Not everything remained the same. For the first time there were organized efforts through the Freedmen's Bureau to provide education for blacks at the primary through college levels. Access to education brought the hope that blacks would one day take their place as full citizens of the United States. These times were perfectly suited for DuBois's singular talents and capacity to become a race leader.

DuBois's New England origins were central to the development of his character and capacity for leadership. His memories of those early days in Great Barrington, perhaps softened by age, were of a period without knowledge of or dwelling upon the issue of what he came to call "the veil," the racism that blighted the lives of black Americans, whether they had been born free or enslaved. DuBois went to public school with white boys and girls and excelled, surpassing his classmates. There was no occasion for him to develop the idea that his descent from African people meant he was inferior to whites. He claimed that the racial idyll came to an end when he was around ten years old. While he was playing a game of cards with his friends, a white girl who was visiting the town refused to accept a card from him because he was black. That, along with later social slights, brought fully home to him the fact that he was different. Being different, however, does not mean that one is inferior. DuBois's early academic success proved the point. Lewis writes of young Willie DuBois's impatience with the other black boy in his school who failed to do well in his studies, reacting as if the young man had let down the side. Early on he believed there was, in fact, a "side" (read "black people") that could be let down when one among their number who had the opportunity to achieve failed to do so. Black students had duties to people and ultimately to an idea (black advancement) that went beyond themselves and their immediate families.

Because he stood out so much in this small late-nineteenth-century New England town, DuBois's teachers encouraged him to stretch himself, giving him books to read and sending the signal that education was a route to advancement. Again, none of this would have had quite the same effect without all the social changes that were taking place at the same time. There were now more black newspapers being published. So a fifteen-year-old DuBois could begin to write regularly for the *Globe,* a

New York–based black newspaper that "spoke for the forward-looking members of the race." With legalized slavery gone, there were now other imperatives to attend to. At an early age DuBois became part of a progressive vanguard, separated from his white classmates who had other interests. He was now self-consciously connected to people like the editor of the *New York Globe*, Timothy Thomas Fortune, who took an uncompromising stance on the question of the rights of black people.

Later observers noted DuBois's tendency to conflate himself with the entire black race. There is no evidence that he ever wholly deviated from this notion, and it appears that this way of thinking began as early as his childhood. Each educational triumph was a triumph for black people. It is easy to see why he would want to think that way. His preternatural confidence in himself translated into confidence about the eventual prospects of blacks overall. That confidence later brought charges of haughtiness, as he was totally convinced that he was part of an aristocracy of talent destined to be in the leadership class of the black community. But how would that leadership be carried out and what would be the animating principle of the effort?

During DuBois's first phase, academic excellence and achievement were the main order of business. He went on to Fisk University and the University of Berlin and became the first black person to receive a Ph.D. at Harvard University. He considered these distinctions to be examples of the ways black people could become leaders in their communities. Through these achievements blacks showed others that such things were possible. If there was a first, there could be a second, third, and so on.

It was DuBois's classic work, *The Souls of Black Folk*, published in 1903, however, that established his place in the forefront of black leadership. He was speaking directly to an audience with a voice unlike any other that had been heard until that point. Throughout the many twists and turns in his thinking about his role as a leader and the direction black advancement should take, *The Souls of Black Folk* stands as the core of his philosophy that never changed. He wrote as if it were eminently clear that black lives contained all the capabilities, promises, and weaknesses of other human beings and that they mattered. Blacks' humanity was on full display with firm conviction and not the barest hint of hesitation. This reflected DuBois's lifelong belief that true progress for blacks, in the United States and abroad, required a full-scale assault on the doctrine of white supremacy. It was not enough—was not even possible—to secure the dreams he had for people of African descent so long as that doctrine held sway. Ameliorating blacks' circumstances, improving whites' behavior toward them, was not the main goal. Those things could be done while the racial hierarchy remained firmly in place. DuBois was demanding far more: that white people adandon both the belief that they were inherently superior to blacks and the social and political system built upon that idea.

It may be difficult from this remove to appreciate how audacious and problematic DuBois's critique of white supremacy was in the early twentieth century. In his time the assumption of white supremacy was so deeply ingrained that few whites questioned it. Even the people who saw themselves as the friends of blacks and supported the interracial organizations and efforts in which DuBois was involved were discomfited by frank, no-holds-barred attacks upon white supremacy. They wanted to help blacks, and some even worked hard to lessen the most egregious forms of racial prejudice. But that did not mean they believed that blacks and whites existed on an equal plane of humanity. It was also significant, and unprecedented, that this message was coming from a man to whom whites could not condescend. He had been born free. He was a college graduate whose classical education was capped by a Ph.D. from Harvard. He had traveled widely and published scholarly works.

There is no question that *The Souls of Black Folk* was a transformative event for black people and therefore for whites as well. But can a book really change a society or alter the course of history? In response people often cite Harriet Beecher Stowe's *Uncle Tom's Cabin* as a work that had a tremendous impact on the politics and ultimately the course of American history. Lincoln, when greeting her for the first time, purportedly said, "So this is the little lady who started this big war." But Stowe is remembered today as an author, not as a leader. After writing *Souls,* DuBois entered the arena in a different, more active way. Because he believed that the doctrine of white supremacy was at the root of the problems blacks faced, he understood early on that racism was a global problem that had to be confronted at all levels. He was among the few African Americans who attended the first Pan-African Congress in London in 1900, and he continued to be a prominent leader of the movement for as long as these congresses were held. Black rights were human rights. What was going on in Georgia was connected to the situation in the Belgian Congo and other places.

DuBois's famous disagreement with Booker T. Washington, which he aired in *The Souls of Black Folk*, about the correct course for black advancement was not merely an argument about the pace of change (gradualism versus more immediate transformation). It was a fundamental disagreement about the nature of the problem blacks were facing. Washington's approach to black leadership suggested that he had no interest in launching attacks upon the doctrine of white supremacy. He described moves for social equality as "folly." Indeed his 1895 address at the Cotton States and International Exposition, which has been called the Atlanta Compromise speech, was his bid to assure whites that neither he nor any blacks under his sway had any intention of challenging the basic racial order of the day. "In all things purely social we can be as separate as the fingers, yet one as the hand in all things essential to mutual progress." That is why the audience of southern white businessmen, many of whom most likely had either personally enslaved blacks or came from families who did, leaped to their feet in thunderous rapture when Washington finished his speech. Blacks could cast down their buckets where they were, form their own organizations, and maintain a largely separate existence in the United States. The fact remained, however, that what was "purely social" covered a lot of territory. Washington was accepting that white Americans could relegate black Americans to second-class citizenship for as long as they wanted.

As with all historical events, it is essential to consider the context. Washington was speaking to members of a society that had shown itself to be willing to use, or acquiesce in the use of, terrorism as a means of social control. During the 1890s only Mississippi topped Georgia in the number of lynchings of black people. There is strong evidence that the prevalence of racially motivated violence and the constant threat of it were at least one of the factors prompting the Great Migration to the

North, which began in earnest in 1910. Consider the numbers. In 1900, just five years after Washington's speech, 90 percent of American blacks lived in the South; 10 percent, in the rest of country. By 1930 those percentages were exactly reversed. In other words, within fifteen years of Washington's announcement of his plan for racial accommodation in the South, blacks began to vote on southern society with their feet. They escaped in droves. There were other reasons for their decision to leave: changes in the economy brought on by World War I, and a boll weevil infestation that devastated farming communities. But those events didn't send everyone fleeing from the South in even relatively large numbers. It was the black outmigration that was the most conspicuous. If Washington's program had brought about a change (an improvement?) in white attitudes, and if he had actually convinced many blacks of the rightness of accepting second-class citizenship until some distant time when they would come to "deserve" better, one doubts if so dramatic a population shift would have occurred. Blacks of the early twentieth century were eager for something more than this vision of accommodation.

DuBois of course was having none of this. He knew that black people in the South were under the gun metaphorically and actually. He attended college in the region and taught in Atlanta. He agonized over the reports of lynchings and other forms of racial violence. The threat of violence whether from official sources or vigilantes required blacks to fear for the physical safety of their families. Too much assertiveness by blacks would come at a tremendous cost. Since the rest of the country, by and large, accepted the white South's marginalization of blacks (and actually had its own ways of doing the same), there was no guarantee that they would be at all supportive if mass violence were to break out.

At the same time, DuBois understood that openly acquiescing to inferiority in any form would only buttress the idea of white supremacy and bring further contempt. That he could not abide. Just as DuBois could not concede that there were many, if any, whites who were superior to him, so he could not concede that whites as a race were superior to blacks. He understood that beliefs about black inferiority centered most often on their supposed mental inferiority. Blacks were not smart enough to create civilizations that could be admired, to invent useful products, to create poetry or beautiful music, all achievements that were said to be the province of Europeans and, perhaps, Asians. As DuBois put it, "Everything black was hideous. Everything Negroes did was wrong." Booker T. Washington's program for black advancement did not address these canards but merely justified and strengthened them. Industrial education would leave the most pernicious and damaging ideas about blacks in place. DuBois was not totally opposed to the Tuskegee model, but he knew it would not be enough. He also came to realize that educational achievement and writing books would not solve the problem of race either. It was much bigger than the life and experiences of any one person; indeed it was bigger than what was going on just in the United States. Washington's program would affect not just blacks in America, but around the world.

For that reason, the "success" of Booker T. Washington's program alarmed DuBois and many others. More specifically it was Washington's influence and support among whites that concerned DuBois. While his chief audience may have been blacks, DuBois was addressing whites as well, hoping to change their minds. To counter the seductive nature of Washington's appeal to whites, DuBois and about thirty other African Americans, including the volatile William Monroe Trotter, decided to organize against it. Another book, another sharply worded essay, was not enough. The group assembled on the Canadian side of Niagara Falls came to be known as the Niagara Movement. Its manifesto, which bears the clear mark of DuBois, was a direct challenge to the doctrine of white supremacy and stated clearly that blacks would never give in to the notion. The chosen location for the second meeting drove the point home: It met at Harpers Ferry, West Virginia, the site of John Brown's raid.

Although the Niagara Movement was short-lived, the core of its founders joined with a number of prominent white liberals in 1909 to create an organization that still exists today, the National Association for the Advancement of Colored People (NAACP). This group, consisting of black and white members, seemed to fulfill DuBois's vision of people of substance and intellect (of all colors) working together for the cause of black advancement and against racism. The organization itself, however, replicated some of the problems of the society as a whole. The first president was white, and DuBois was the sole black person at the executive level of the organization.

So he then turned to another weapon in his arsenal, journalism. DuBois founded the *Crisis* magazine in 1915, and the publication became a vehicle for a very potent form of direct intellectual leadership. It was in many ways the perfect showcase for his talents and interests, another way to lead his community. Not aimed at an academic audience and not bound by scholarly convention, it was nonetheless completely serious and substantive. The *Crisis* published the leading poets and writers of the day, as well as opinion pieces. Most important of all, an increasingly educated and stable black community was ready and eager to hear what DuBois had to say about all subjects that touched on black life and interests and to see the examples of black excellence displayed in the magazine. Using humor when needed, preaching when required, or employing his razor-sharp analytical abilities, DuBois in the *Crisis* became a "must read" for every black person and, broadly, any progressive person between 1915 and 1934. At one point the circulation topped one hundred thousand, making it more widely read than the *Nation* and the *New Republic.* There had never been anything like it, and there has been nothing like it since the heyday of DuBois's editorship.

Just as the postwar years brought greater numbers of people who could appreciate what DuBois offered in the way of leadership, so they also brought new ideas about what was to be done. It is startling to think of it, but by the 1920s DuBois had entered his sixties. A younger generation was seeking new answers to the problems facing blacks; some, particularly those involved in the Harlem Renaissance, were impatient with the somewhat prudish "uplift the race" strategy to which DuBois and older members of the leadership class were wedded. He had already had an earlier, more serious brush with another movement for black advancement, one that was not nearly so well financed and organized as Washington's Tuskegee Machine but that had powerful appeal nevertheless. In the tradition of some black leaders in the eighteenth century, like Martin Delany, who saw no hope for true black equality so long as blacks lived in a predominantly white nation, Marcus Garvey's call for black nationalism and return of blacks to Africa gained enormous attention during the same time that the NAACP was gaining ground between 1915 and 1920. With the reemergence of this back to Africa appeal, the three positions about the best method of advancement were openly competing for adherents.

Booker T. Washington died just as Garvey was arriving on the scene. But Washington's plan for blacks to accommodate themselves to their situation in America was still very much alive. Garvey occupied the opposite end of the spectrum on the question of how American blacks could reach their fullest potential. "Where is the black man's Government? Where is his king and kingdom? Where is his President, his country, his ambassador, his army, his navy, his men of big affairs?" he asked, knowing that they were not in the United States. If they wanted to have these things, blacks would have to leave America altogether, a bit of advice that many refugees from the South were ready to accept. They had come north seeking a promised land and found instead that they were shunted away into northern ghettos. It was better than the South, but it was still not a place where they could feel as though they were free citizens of the country. This was galling after many black men had gone to war in Europe to help "make the world safe for democracy." Now they were home, and democracy wasn't safe for them on 125th Street and Lenox Avenue. DuBois had actively urged blacks to support American intervention in World War I, as if this way of showing patriotism would win support for them and help erase discrimination. That didn't work, and there was never a real reason to think it would. Blacks had fought in every conflict in America since the Revolutionary War, and it had made no difference to their treatment. In addition, to many working-class blacks, DuBois's NAACP was "a snob affair." Although Garvey had gone to college and was very well read, he had more in common with the working class than did the ultrapatrician DuBois.

DuBois did not totally discount Garvey's views. After all, he was sympathetic to the notion of ties between Africans and blacks in the diaspora. By the 1930s he had begun to advocate a form of voluntary self-segregation as a way of developing cultural and economic strength. Many of his colleagues at the NAACP were appalled. They believed the idea ran counter to everything the organization had stood for up until that time. Integration was the goal. But DuBois saw no conflict, saying that leaders had to pursue different strategies as the situation warranted. With blacks suffering disproportionately in the Great Depression, a focus on economic development (shades of Booker T. Washington) made sense. The dispute led DuBois to resign as editor of the *Crisis* in 1934. But his vision of nationalism, a nation within a nation, was very different from Garvey's brand. He simply did not believe that a return to Africa was the answer for the nearly eleven million black inhabitants of the United States. There was no way that any but a fraction of them would ever get on the Black Star Line to start life over again on the African continent. Even if such a thing were possible, DuBois simply did not think that Garvey and his compatriots could pull it off. Then, when Garvey, who had not grown up in America, openly made common cause with the Ku Klux Klan, the group that had murdered and terrorized scores of blacks from the days of Reconstruction on, DuBois became convinced that rather than being a mere nuisance, Garvey had become an actual menace to the black community. In the end Garvey's movement, under attack from whites, DuBois, and other mainstream black leaders, faltered. However, his theme of black nationalism has continued to remain a potent part of the black intellectual tradition even today.

Having decided early on that the destruction of white supremacy was the key to transforming the lives of blacks in America and around the world, DuBois became convinced that this many-headed hydra would not be slain with one sword. His victories had not led to the kind of transformation he longed for. By the 1940s the warrior for black equality had come to realize that his Enlightenment-influenced notion that the diffusion of knowledge would solve the race problem was flawed. The worldwide crisis of capitalism radicalized many people in the 1930s, and DuBois was among those who were led to think deeply about the meaning of the economic collapse. Washington had not been wrong in promoting economic self-sufficiency. The problems lay in thinking that it was even possible in a South where whites were determined to keep blacks down and in proposing that this method of advancement should be pursued at the expense of demanding the rights of American citizenship.

DuBois was not wrong to focus on establishing blacks' civil rights, but a basic level of economic self-sufficiency for blacks was important too. He was led by pessimism to adopt some aspects of Washington's program.

There was another avenue open to him, one that he came to champion until the end of his life: socialism. When DuBois first read Marx, he was not impressed. The German theorist, he wrote, "did not envisage a situation where, instead of a horizontal division of classes, there was a vertical fissure, a complete separation of classes by race, cutting square across the economic layers." At the same time, the international bent of Marxism attracted him. From the earliest days of his involvement with the Pan-African Congress, he had sought to make connections with people all over the world who were interested in human progress. During his final two decades of life, he became ever more an internationalist, adapting his dream of a talented tenth of blacks who would uplift the race to "a World conception of human uplift." Although important, race was no longer at the center of his philosophy. The group to be uplifted was the world's working class, and that included people of every race, creed, and color.

The timing of DuBois's transformation could not have been more unfortunate for him personally. The 1940s and 1950s, with World War II and the beginning of the Cold War, were not a time in the United States to advocate international class warfare to bring about socialism. Already long under the scrutiny of the FBI, DuBois's speeches and participation in international peace conferences made him increasingly suspect during the period of Red hysteria. It was not just the government that recoiled. His ever more strident denunciations of the United States put him in conflict with mainstream black civil rights organizations as they went about the process of dismantling legalized segregation in the United States. People like Thurgood Marshall, who was to help put an end to segregation, DuBois's own cause for decades, had absolutely no use for communism and socialist agitation. They respected all that DuBois had done for blacks. But many suspected that the old man had lost touch.

He was, however, "DuBoisian" until the end. His last years were spent being what he was to his very core, a scholar and a teacher. In 1961 the prime minister of Ghana, Kwame Nkrumah, invited him to Accra to work on his dream project, the completion of the *Encyclopedia Africana.* When the U.S. government refused to give him a new passport, he became a Ghanaian citizen (shades of Garvey). He died in Ghana in 1963, on the day before the fabled March on Washington, when a new generation of black leaders was making its mark in the fight for black equality. It is especially fitting that DuBois's last days on earth were spent working on scholarship that would detail the voluminous contributions that African people had made to the world, and that he would be buried in the soil of the continent whose honor he had defended so assiduously.

Copyright

MR. McGRAW

Kevin Baker

THEY CALLED HIM THE LITTLE NAPOLEON, AN ODDLY REDUNDANT nickname that was nonetheless apt. He led his teams with a passion that might—literally—leave your city razed to the ground before he was done. They called him Mickey Face and Muggsy, names that reflected the America in which he lived and the vast ethnic tides that swept across it. And they called him Mr. McGraw for the immeasurable respect they always had for him.

In the long history of baseball, there has been no one else like John Joseph McGraw. No other great player in the modern game went on to become a great manager. In addition, he was the outstanding scout, general manager, and part owner—all at the same time—during most of his thirty years with the New York Giants. No one else ever ran his team with so much calculation or was so given to uncontrollable rages—until the calculation, and the rages, became all but impossible to tell apart. No one ever got into so many fights, fistfights, with opponents, teammates, friends, fans, sportswriters, umpires. No one ever did so much for his players or rode them so hard and so unfairly. No one ever lived so close to scandal and disgrace for so long yet came away from it all so universally admired.

Ferociously loyal, he was capable of betrayal. Blunt to the point of rudeness, he could dissemble with the best of them. Able to do everything there was to do around a ballpark, simultaneously filling jobs that it would take an entire front office to do today, he played a key role in the blunders that eventually doomed his beloved team.

It is impossible to think that anyone like him would be allowed to walk around free—and unmedicated—today, much less manage a major-league baseball team. He had an anger problem. He had impulse control problems. He had an eating problem and a drinking problem. He liked to bet on anything that moved, and he consorted with gamblers and known underworld figures. All was forgiven, if it was not simply overlooked in the first place.

"The idea is to win," he liked to say, and in the end he did, 2,763 times, more than all but one other man who ever managed. That man was Connie Mack, who also bested McGraw head to head in two of three World Series. Yet Mack himself offered the ultimate tribute: "There has been only one McGraw, and there has been only one manager—and his name [is] McGraw."

IT IS EASY ENOUGH to trace where the demons came from. Throughout his life John McGraw was beset by freak injuries, illnesses, and personal tragedies. He lost most of one season to malaria, another to typhoid. In 1903, when he was not quite thirty, an errant throw flattened his nose, causing a nearly fatal hemorrhage and leaving him plagued by sinusitis for the rest of his life. Later he nearly lost a finger to infection, and he had all but ruined his legs before he was done playing.

His beloved first wife died of a burst appendix when he was twenty-six. Growing up in the little town of Truxton, New York, he lost his mother and four siblings within four days from a diphtheria epidemic when he was just eleven. His father, a Civil War veteran and track worker for the Elmira, Cortland and Northern Railroad, began to knock him around. When John was twelve, his father beat him so badly for the crime of breaking a window with a baseball that John ran away to an inn across the street that was run by a kindly widow.

There he stayed for the rest of his childhood, if one could call it that. He left school and supported himself as a "butcher boy" on his father's road, peddling magazines, newspapers, and refreshments to the passengers. Throughout his life he was embarrassed by his lack of a formal education and did what he could to mitigate it. He took college courses in the off-season and became probably the only manager ever to be given a complete set of Shakespeare by his team. But always the resentment, the feelings of inferiority and abandonment remained. Later in life McGraw owned a series of terriers, each of which he named after his old hometown. At the end of the day he would rouse them with the cry "It's Truxton against the world!"

He obtained another kind of education, playing ball while he waited out the train layover for the trip back. By the age of sixteen he was good enough to sign a professional contract with Olean of the New York–Penn League. In his very first game he had a single—and committed eight errors in ten chances, playing an unreasonable facsimile of third base. Released within a week, he managed to catch on with another minor-league team, and the following August he was brought up to the National League's Baltimore Orioles, informing all who would listen, "I'm as good as they come."

Typically, in his first major-league game McGraw made a run-scoring error but singled and scored what proved to be the winning run. Afterward he told reporters, "It's nice. Just give me a little time and I have got 'em skinned to death."

The man and the team were met. The Orioles of the 1890s became legendary for their hustle and savvy, their brawling and cursing, and their cheating. Their manager, "Foxy Ned" Hanlon, was credited with being one of the inventors of the inside game, a seismic leap forward in the evolution of baseball, in which players forced the action and did the little things necessary to win. The Orioles backed one another up on throws when they were in the field, and at bat they bunted, stole, and hit-and-ran with abandon.

They also assaulted other teams constantly with their spikes, fists, legs, bats, and an endless stream of obscenities. Playing at a time when only one umpire worked most games, they took shortcuts going from first to third, hid baseballs in the high grass of the outfield, tripped and kicked opposing players, and grabbed hold of their belts to slow them down. *The Sporting News* accused Baltimore of "playing the dirtiest ball ever seen in the country."

"They were mean, vicious, ready at any time to maim a rival player or an umpire if it helped their cause," John Heydler, an umpire at the time and later the president of the National League, wrote. "The things they would say to an umpire were unbelievably vile, and they broke the spirits of some very fine men."

Supposedly, McGraw was schooled in this game by Hanlon and his veterans. If so, this was the start of an amazing baseball lineage, extending over a hundred years, with Hanlon's knowledge passed on from McGraw to his pupil, Casey Stengel, and from Stengel to *his* protégé, Billy Martin, under whom the old inside game came to be known as Billyball. And it was true, Hanlon must have been some kind of teacher, producing five pennant-winning managers from among his players.

Yet the suspicion lingers that John McGraw needed little instruction in this sort of baseball. He was already a star at twenty, and over the course of his career he hit .334, stole 436 bases, and scored 1,024 runs in just 1,099 games. To this day he holds the third best all-time career on-base percentage in major-league history. When it comes to getting on base, the primary aim in baseball, there is just Ted Williams, Babe Ruth—and John McGraw.

He could be brilliant. The modern player he resembled most closely was Pete Rose. Never a great fielder, McGraw, like Rose, played wherever he was needed and eventually made himself a passable third baseman. In the batter's box he was in constant motion, fouling off pitch after pitch before blooping a single or driving a Baltimore chop into the hard ground in front of home plate, drawing a walk, or getting himself hit with a pitched ball.

Whatever he may have learned from Ned Hanlon, it seems unlikely he needed any tutelage in the sort of havoc the Orioles liked to let slip on a ballfield. In 1894, McGraw got into a fight with Boston's Tommy Tucker that quickly escalated into a donnybrook involving both teams and many of the Boston fans. Before it was over, a fire in the right field bleachers had consumed the South End Grounds, the most elegant ballpark of the day, along with seventy thousand dollars' worth of equipment, and 170 neighboring buildings. This was the force that was McGraw. Not even the Yankees ever burned Southie to the ground.

—

FIVE YEARS LATER HANLON had departed for greener pastures along with most of the Orioles' stars. Muggsy, still just twenty-six, was put in charge of a floundering franchise. He started at third base, managed, *and* served as the team's general manager and chief scout. That was too the same summer that his first wife died, leaving him devastated and unable to sleep for weeks. Nevertheless, he brought his team in a respectable fourth and had his greatest season, hitting .391, stealing 73 bases, and leading the league with 140 runs scored.

It was also the last time he played as many as a hundred games in a season. Only five-seven, with a playing weight that rarely exceeded 130 pounds, McGraw's frenetic style of play left him exhausted by midseason, his legs aching from frequent spikings and other collisions on the base paths.

He was looking to move up, and now he learned to play the cutthroat world of turn-of-the-century baseball off the field as well as he did between the white lines. Two years after the National League had summarily disbanded its Baltimore franchise, he signed up to own, run, and manage a new Orioles team in the insurgent American League. Once there, to nobody's great surprise, he soon fell out with AL president Ban Johnson, who had built his league around the idea of rejecting the very sort of "rowdyism" McGraw reveled in and making the ballpark safe for respectable middle-class crowds.

McGraw could be ruthless. When he became convinced that Johnson wanted to replace him, the boy from Truxton's instincts for self-preservation—or his paranoia—kicked in. Sent by Johnson to New York to scout out the possibilities of placing an American League team in Manhattan, McGraw connived instead with the owners of the National League Giants. In 1902, they engineered a coup in which McGraw managed to sell his stake in the Orioles at a healthy profit, then skipped town with a lucrative new contract to manage the Giants—and with so many of the Orioles' players that the team had to forfeit its next game.

Thanks to his maneuverings, major-league baseball was dead in Baltimore, and it did not return for more than fifty years. Baltimore was a city that McGraw had come to as a penniless teenager, it was where he had fallen in love and married, where he had opened a thriving café supported by his many fans, where he was one day to be interred. It was a city that had taken him to its heart and that he had professed to love. But on leaving it for New York, McGraw bragged only that he was now going to "the cornerstone of baseball" and that Johnson's American League "is a loser and has been from the start."

Orioles fans were devastated, a writer for the *Baltimore Sun* inveighing, "Loyalty and gratitude are words without any meaning to ballplayers and especially to McGraw." *The Sporting News* compared McGraw to a terrorist, and wailed; "He was and is in the game for loot." All McGraw would ever offer in response was the rationale that Johnson was trying "to ditch me at the end of the 1902 season. So I acted fast. . . . Someone would be left holding the bag, and I made up my mind it wouldn't be me."

IT NEVER WAS HIM. In New York the boy from Truxton was at last on a stage appropriate to his talents. The Giants, once the city's darlings, were stumbling along in last place when he took the reins, and he was not able to move them out of the cellar before the season ended. (The beleaguered Orioles finished last too, making John McGraw, perhaps the greatest manager who ever was, also the only man to manage the last-place team in both the American and National leagues in the same year.) But fans who came to see McGraw's first game, on July 19, 1902, noticed an immediate difference in their Giants. Watching the home team whip through their pregame warm-ups with unaccustomed zeal, a fan yelled out, "They're awake!"

Indeed they were, and they remained awake for the next three decades. Over his twenty-nine full seasons at the helm, McGraw's Giants finished first or second twenty-one times. He won three World Series and ten pennants and finished out of the first division only twice. It is a record that remains to this day unmatched in its consistency, one made all the more remarkable by the fact that he compiled it across distinctly different eras of baseball.

His teams won in the dead ball era of the early 1900s, which he loved, and in the lively ball era of Babe Ruth, which he detested. They won with pitching and by stealing bases and by hitting home runs. They won with raw rookies and grizzled veterans, with superstars and with no-names.

They did more than win. They became *the* sporting event in the greatest city in the country, breaking attendance records and building themselves the biggest, grandest stadium in the majors, at the Polo Grounds in upper Harlem. When the final bell rang, Wall Street brokers rushed uptown to see them in special trains. Broadway's stars flocked there in carriages and plush new automobiles for the late-afternoon games, before hying it back downtown for that night's performance. McGraw soon became their darling, a first-nighter and member of the show business Lambs Club; the friend of stars and powerful politicians and wealthy men.

He was, as baseball historian Steven Goldman wrote, "the father of all baseball managers, and all football coaches too . . . the master, 'the czar,' as he put it, of the New York Giants, the proudest team in professional baseball."

How did he do it? Partly it was desire and pure cussedness. Grantland Rice thought that "McGraw's very walk across the field in a hostile town was a challenge to the multitude." He would fight anyone, anytime, even though he was almost comically bad at it. McGraw, in Damon Runyon's description, "a café gladiator," was even punched out once during a naked fistfight in the showers with his cheerful elfin teammate Wee Willie Keeler, after McGraw cursed Keeler for allegedly throwing to the wrong base.

It didn't matter. At times he seemed driven by the Furies. During a game against a minor-league Chattanooga outfit while still a player-manager, McGraw held a runner by his belt to keep him from advancing on a flyball, spiked the opposing shortstop, and tagged a runner in the face, bloodying his nose. The week before, he had lit into the manager of a Savannah semipro team so furiously the man knocked him down. That was just spring training.

Fans and sportswriters in other cities loathed him. "He has the vilest tongue of any ball-player," a New Orleans scribe once insisted after another exhibition game. "[H]e adopts every low and contemptible method that his erratic brain can conceive to win a play by a dirty trick." They chanted, "Hoodlum!," "Tough!," and "Dirty McGraw!" at him on the road. Even former Oriole teammate Joe Quinn admitted: "I often wonder how McGraw got away with some of the plays he made on and off the field."

Nothing deterred him, especially when he was in a good pennant race. In 1905, his greatest year as a manager, McGraw "twisted the nose" of *New York Evening World* reporter Allen Sangree in a hotel lobby; got himself ejected from three consecutive games; started a brawl in Philadelphia that ended with fans stoning his team's carriages as they fled from the ballpark; started a brawl in Pittsburgh that ended with another stoning and McGraw's Giants holding off eighteen thousand enraged fans with their bats; and got thrown out of a game against the Pirates at the Polo Grounds, after which he climbed into the stands and led the Giants' fans in taunting Pittsburgh owner Barney Dreyfuss as a gambler who welshed on his debts and paid off the umps. When league president Harry Pulliam called to chastise him, McGraw denounced him as "Dreyfuss's employee" and went to court to get an injunction against any fine or suspension. Then, when the Giants had to return to Philly, McGraw saw to it that the players' carriages were filled with rocks, so that they could return fire with the fans who had lined the streets to jeer and throw things at them on their way to the park.

That same season he told the legendary umpire Bill Klem, "I can lick any umpire in baseball, you know," and threatened, "I'm going to get your job, you busher." Umps, even the formidable Klem, into whose face he once hurled a glass of water when the umpire refused to let a suspended Giants player take the field, were a special target. McGraw fought with the umpires in ways that simply would not be tolerated today and that were unmatched even at the time.

He could be brutal. McGraw reportedly drove the saintly former Giants pitcher turned arbiter Timothy Keefe out of the game by calling him a drunk over and over again. He believed in using "judicious kicking" on umpires, and according to one sportswriter of the period, his harassment of the men in blue won his team as many as twenty-five games a year: "[T]he umpires have been afraid to decide against McGraw's men, threatened as they are with physical violence and certainly subjected to foul language that the roughest rowdies in the Bowery would not make use of."

Here again, McGraw himself encouraged the notion that it was all about winning and putting fannies in the seats. "The only road to popularity is to win. The man who loses gracefully loses easily," he liked to say. "Sportsmanship and easygoing methods are all right, but it is the prospect of a hot fight that brings out the crowds."

Yet the evidence suggests that McGraw often really was out of control, almost manic on the field. Christy Mathewson described his antics as manager in the third-base coaching box, where complete with a glove on his hand, he sometimes liked to survey the field: "McGraw leaps in the air, kicks his heels together, claps his mitt, shouts at the umpire, runs in and pats the next batter on the back, and says something to the pitcher. . . ."

If his "judicious kicking" intimidated some umpires, it only made others his open enemies. While he was still playing and managing back in the American League, umpire Jack Sheridan watched Boston's Bill Dineen hit McGraw *five times* in five at bats without letting him take his base, insisting that Muggsy had not tried to get out of the way of the ball. After being plunked for the fifth time, McGraw simply sat down in the batter's box and refused to move until Sheridan ejected him. When the game ended a few minutes later, the fans predictably rushed the field, nearly mobbing the umpire.

This was not an anomaly. McGraw drew constant suspensions and almost every year saw at least one game when he worked himself into such a rage that he refused to leave the field even *after* being ejected, usually resulting in a forfeit by his team and a near riot by the fans. This was not particularly good for his club. McGraw just could not always help himself, a condition that became more and more obvious over the course of his career.

Always his sense of being wronged shone through. He protested vociferously whenever he was punished for even his most flagrant transgressions, insisting that umpires, league presidents, and opposing owners all had it in for him and his team. There was constantly present the abused boy who had been forced to go out in the world and fend for himself from the age of twelve.

THE ONLY REMEDY was control, control over everything to do with his domain, on the ballfield. "Players, to him, were little beyond automata who batted and ran bases as he pulled the strings," F. C. Lane wrote in *Baseball Magazine* when McGraw finally retired. This was an exaggeration, but not much of one.

"I think we can win it all, if my brain holds out," he liked to say, and he told his players, "Do what I tell you, and I'll take the blame for mistakes."

In this, much like Joe Torre on Steinbrenner's Yankees, nearly a century later, he was the perfect manager for New York. He provided cover for his players from the city's pack of rabid sportswriters, who tended to adore him and hung on his every colorful quote. Throughout his career he lost big games in exasperating, agonizing ways, and while this might leave him raving against umps, league presidents, opponents, and even his own coaches, John McGraw never took his biggest losses out on his players.

He lost the madcap 1908 pennant race when an umpire decided, on his own and without warning, to call the Giants' rookie first baseman Fred Merkle out on an obscure baserunning rule that had not been enforced for decades. When Merkle sobbed afterward to McGraw, "Lose me, I'm the jinx," Muggsy gave him a three-hundred-dollar raise, praised his "gameness . . . through all this abuse" in the press, and told him, "I could use a carload like you. Forget this season and come around next spring."

He made Merkle his chief lieutenant on the bench and even a regular bridge partner. When Fred Snodgrass dropped an easy fly to help lose the 1912 World Series, McGraw gave him a thousand-dollar raise, telling reporters, "It could happen to anyone. If it hadn't been for a lot that Snodgrass did, we wouldn't have been playing in that game at all."

In 1924, McGraw lost the seventh and decisive game of the World Series, the very last World Series game of his career, in twelve innings, after his veteran catcher tripped on his own mask while chasing a pop foul, and not one but *two* ground balls hit pebbles on a badly groomed

Washington infield and skipped over the shoulder of the Giants' third baseman. This might have been a bit much for any man. But when they got back to New York, Muggsy invited his players and their wives to a gala party at the Hotel Biltmore, where he himself led the singing, along with George M. Cohan and other Broadway stars.

"All I want to know is that they are honestly trying to do what I tell them," he said of his Giants. "If they haven't the ability it is my fault if I keep them." He never punished them for physical mistakes: "I wouldn't have a man on my team who doesn't make errors. It shows he doesn't go after the ball."

Mental errors or, God forbid, disobedience were another matter. On at least two occasions, he fined players who hit game-winning home runs; both had been ordered to bunt. Chastisement could be even more severe, including fines and tirades that sometimes devolved into still more fist-fights. But even then his players tended to respect him.

"I liked him, and I liked playing for him," conceded Al Bridwell, who once knocked McGraw down the dugout steps after being on the receiving end of a particularly vituperative harangue. Frankie Frisch, the great second baseman, whom Muggsy derided almost ceaselessly as "cement head" and "dumb Dutchman" before trading him to St. Louis, still maintained, "I always thought McGraw was sort of on the genius side."

He worked his men hard, and he had a hand in every detail of their preparation. McGraw had the first primitive spring training complex constructed in little Marlin, Texas, a town of no more than five thousand, where he hoped his players would be isolated from the usual diversions of ballplayers. Each day they walked the two miles from the hotel to the ballpark and back along the railroad tracks, but it was about more than just exercise.

"When you train under most managers, you merely get yourself in good physical condition," claimed Rogers Hornsby, the great, ill-tempered slugger whom McGraw traded Frisch for and who wanted to steal Muggsy's job. "When you train under McGraw, you learn baseball."

On the field, McGraw innovated constantly, flashing signs from the bench by blowing his nose or using the sign language all his Giants learned when deaf pitcher Luther "Dummy" Taylor was on the team.

He loved the game of the "dead ball" era best because of the premium it put on every run, the control it gave the manager in deciding when to bunt and steal and hit-and-run, the sort of ball he had come up on. But he understood any kind of baseball and adjusted easily to the lively ball introduced after 1919, much as he disliked it. McGraw conducted some of the earliest experiments in platooning hitters and employing full-time relief pitchers and replaced his speedsters with power hitters.

"A manager would look foolish not to play the game as it is, meet the new situation with new tactics," he conceded. "[T]here is no use in sending men down on a long chance of stealing a bag when there is a better chance of a batter hitting for two bases, or, maybe, out of the lot."

He won an unmatched four straight National League pennants at the start of the live ball era from 1921 to 1924. And once again he found a way to take the reins into his own hands, winning the 1921 and 1922 World Series, when he personally called every pitch that his hurlers threw to Babe Ruth.

Critics questioned such tactics, claiming that McGraw's control was so complete it left his players unable to think for themselves in the midst of the action. Even Christy Mathewson, Mac's golden boy, wrote (or allowed to be ghosted) an article attributing New York's three consecutive World Series losses from 1911 to 1913 to how Muggsy made the Giants "a team of puppets worked from the bench by a string."

Others disagreed. Fred Snodgrass insisted: "Most of the time we were on our own . . . we were supposed to *know* how to play baseball, and were expected to do the right thing at the right time." Decades later McGraw's players were still raving about him, in encomiums solicited for Lawrence S. Ritter's oral history of the early game, *The Glory of Their Times*: "What a great man he was! The finest and grandest man I ever met!" "What a great man he was! We held him in high esteem. We respected him in every way." "He was a fine man, Mr. McGraw was. I really liked him." "It was really a lot of fun to play for McGraw."

JOHN MCGRAW UNDERSTOOD BALLPLAYERS. He understood what their strengths were and where they should play. While his predecessor on the Giants experimented with Christy Mathewson at first base, McGraw immediately put him back on the mound and left him there. He did just the reverse with his Hall of Fame first baseman and successor Bill Terry almost thirty years later. He saw that Roger Bresnahan was a catcher. He kept Mel Ott with him when Ott was a seventeen-year-old rookie, personally converting him from a catcher to an outfielder and making him a great slugger.

He always recognized talent, no matter how raw or how young it was. No other man in the history of American professional sports—not just baseball but *all* sports—both discovered *and then also developed* so much outstanding talent as did John McGraw. Over twenty years into the job, deep in the 1920s, he was still signing and molding one top star after another: Frisch, Terry, Ott, George "Highpockets" Kelly, Fred Lindstrom, Irish Meusel, Ross Youngs, Hack Wilson, Carl Hubbell. It was all the more impressive considering that McGraw's scouting work was done mostly by himself, on the fly, slipping away from the team when he could for a few days to look over a player that one of his many contacts around the country had written him about.

He tried to search in more exotic locales as well. Throughout the twenties McGraw, like the managers of the other New York teams, was eager to develop a Jewish star, and he signed, among others, the inimitable Moe Berg and the power-hitting outfielder Mose Solomon, quickly dubbed "the Rabbi of Swat" by the tabloids. (The rabbi, alas, had an iron glove and was soon sent down.)

Much more daringly, McGraw attempted to slip the superb black second baseman Charlie Grant onto the Baltimore roster during his sojourn in the American League, passing him off as an Indian called Chief Tokahoma. White Sox owner Charles Comiskey saw through the ruse, and McGraw was forced to leave Grant behind when spring training ended and the team came north. Muggsy had played a winter in Cuba, where he was affectionately called *El mono amarillo* (the yellow monkey), and he brought his Giants back repeatedly for spring training games against the likes of "the Black Diamond," José Mendez, a splendid pitcher of color whom McGraw openly salivated over, saying he would pay fifty thousand dollars for his contract. He had no more luck with this than he had had with Grant. Baseball's color line was too strong even for Muggsy to break.

MORE THAN SIMPLY drilling them in the fundamentals or writing in their names at the right positions, though, McGraw made his men *feel* like ballplayers. He saw to it that they were better cared for than any other players in the game, putting the Giants up in first-rate hotels during the regular season. He went so far as to redesign their uniforms, taking off the collars players had worn since the earliest days of the professional game. He dressed them all in black because, he claimed, he had "heard army officers say that the snappiest dressed outfit is usually made up of the best fighters."

He was a master clubhouse psychologist, taking each man individually, getting what he could out of him. His most unlikely alliance was with his greatest star, Christy Mathewson, who seemed to be his polar opposite. Mathewson was the *beau ideal* of turn-of-the-century American sports, Frank Merriwell incarnate, a tall, clean-cut, clean-living college man, considered such an appropriate role model that his likeness was installed in a stained glass window at the new Cathedral of St. John the Divine.

Yet Matty's and Muggsy's respect for each other was immediate and unshakable, founded on the intelligence with which they both approached the game. They and their wives got on so well that the two couples even shared an apartment for a couple of years, leaving Mathewson biographer Frank Deford to ask, incredulous, [D]id ever any other manager and star player in any sport room together with their wives?" Yet they did, in perfect harmony: the refined, college-educated, Protestant, Anglo, Republican Mathewsons and the rough-edged, self-made, Catholic, Irish, Democratic McGraws. But Matty, one of the greatest pitchers ever to play the game, was the least of his manager's challenges.

"It was an important part of McGraw's great capacity for leadership," Heywood Broun wrote, "that he could take kids out of the coal mines and out of the wheat fields and make them walk and chatter and play ball with the look of eagles."

This was a more important skill than it may seem today, back in an age when a player might move directly from an industrial team or even a sandlot to the majors. Yet there was another, less heartwarming side to guiding a ball club in the early years of the twentieth century, as Steven Goldman pointed out: "Just as often, though, it wasn't coalminer kids who [*sic*] McGraw was trying to turn into eagles but hard-core alcoholics, gamblers, and thieves." Baseball in the first decades of the twentieth century was still a marginal profession, like most entertainment enterprises in the United States, its players often men used to scraping by however they could, even on the wrong side of the law.

McGraw was always confident he could turn them around, to the point where it became an axiom: "If you have a bad actor, trade him to McGraw." This meant out-of-control drunks, such as "Turkey Mike" Donlin, who might do anything when on a bender, including pulling a pistol on a crowded train or belting a popular actress in the face at the theater. It meant Arthur "Bugs" Raymond, a spitballing alcoholic, of whom it was said he need only *breathe* on the ball to make it wobble. Raymond was so desperate for money to drink with that he stole tips from tables in the team's hotels. Sent out to the Polo Grounds' distant bullpen to warm up, he was just as likely to keep going all the way out of the park and to a saloon across Eighth Avenue. McGraw tried to reform him through every method he knew how, sending Raymond to a sanatorium, sending his paycheck straight to his wife, even trying to administer an admonitory beating (and failing completely, with his usual comic ineffectiveness at fisticuffs).

There was another category of McGraw's special cases. These were men accused of "laying down," a broad term of the time that came to cause some confusion. A player who "laid down" might be one who was simply lazy or accused of not hustling, or he could be engaged in something considerably more sinister. Again and again McGraw hired on men whose careers were shadowed by accusations of fixing games, men such Buck Herzog, or Heinie Zimmerman, or Hal Chase, a flashy first baseman who was one of he shadiest characters ever to play the game. McGraw's confidence that he could turn even these hard cases around devolved into a sort of hubris. He could not stop thieves from stealing any more than he could stop drunks from drinking, and his refusal to acknowledge this blotted the edges of his legacy and almost drew him into much deeper trouble.

For the 1919 season, McGraw went so far as to assemble a veritable rogues' gallery of players, an all-star team of game fixers, chiselers, and petty criminals, a cast so extreme that it almost seemed as if he were setting a challenge for himself. The Giants' roster included not only the notorious Chase but also an outfielder who was later banned from organized baseball for life for consorting with gamblers and taking part in a stolen-car ring; an infielder who would be blackballed by McGraw himself for his gambling connections; three future Hall of Famers who were accused but acquitted of trying to fix a game; two pitchers who were later banned from the game for the same offense; another pitcher who had shot and killed a hunting partner he supposedly mistook for a cougar; and still *another* pitcher who hung around with gamblers when he could but who had taken a breather from them the previous off-season, having spent most of it in jail for draft evasion *and* violating the Mann Act.

This team of scoundrels got off to a fast start, but everything came predictably apart down the stretch. The Giants finished a distant second, and Hal Chase spent the last half of September helping Arnold Rothstein fix the World Series. McGraw ended up before a Chicago grand jury, later admitting, "In my opinion Chase deliberately threw us down. I never was more deceived by a player than by Chase."

YET THE FACT was that McGraw, like so many others in baseball at the time, was already well steeped in the sporting life. When he wasn't at the ballpark, he spent most of his waking moments at the racetrack. He was known to have won four hundred dollars betting on his team to win the 1905 World Series, and around the same time he offered the manager of the Yankees a five-thousand-dollar "side bet" on an exhibition series between their two teams. He was actually arrested one off-season in the wide-open resort town of Hot Springs, Arkansas, after he and a friend, pitching coins in a hotel lobby, had skinned some suckers for twenty-three hundred dollars. At other times he owned a stake in a horse track and casino in Cuba and a pool hall in Herald Square with partners who included Rothstein himself.

Even for the time this was playing it close to the edge. McGraw made no secret of owning his pool hall. The culture of baseball was such that no one batted an eye, even though this meant that McGraw, along with every other pool hall operator in Manhattan, made a three-hundred-dollar payoff every month to his local police precinct. That was simply business.

Rothstein was another story. The biggest, most nefarious figure in the gambling world, bankroller of the mob, he was supposedly a silent partner in McGraw's pool hall, but he made a very loud, very deliberate noise there over the course of two nights and one day in November 1909. Rothstein, an expert with the stick, took on an out-of-town ringer, a Philadelphia stockbroker named Jack Conway, in a pool-shooting contest that began at five in the evening on a Thursday and went on until four in the morning on the following *Saturday*, drawing mobs of sporting men off the street and running up dizzying amounts of action, until at last McGraw called a halt and packed both men off to a Turkish bath, growling, "I'll have you dead on my hands. And if you don't want to sleep, some of the rest of us do."

It was an epic match, one that was talked about for years afterward and may have served as the inspiration for the game between Paul Newman and Jackie Gleason in *The Hustler*. It supposedly made Rothstein four thousand dollars, along with his reputation, and thereafter he was never far from McGraw's orbit. It was Rothstein's longtime lawyer Billy Fallon, "the Great Mouthpiece" (and the inspiration for the defense lawyer in *Chicago*), who defended McGraw after the worst scrap of his life. It was another Rothstein mark, the gambler and Wall Street bucket shop operator Charlie Stoneham, who came to own the Giants and made McGraw a major partner in the team.

There is no hint that McGraw ever bet against his own team. There *is* the curious fact that the Giants' team physician tried to bribe the umpires before the tumultuous makeup of the Merkle game back in 1908, but McGraw was never connected to this effort, and at worst he may have been trying simply to steal back a game he felt he had been robbed of in the first place.

His greater sin was that he, along with almost all the rest of baseball, failed to see the corrosive effect that organized gambling had on the sport, even after the World Series was fixed practically under his nose. Hal Chase was dumped, but McGraw remained friends with Rothstein, who frequently shared the owner's box at the Polo Grounds with Stoneham until Commissioner Kenesaw Mountain Landis put an end to it for propriety's sake.

McGraw also failed to see the gambler's mentality that Stoneham brought to his team. The new owner treated Muggsy well, giving him the shares to become a partner, eventually upping his salary to an unheard-of seventy thousand dollars and thereby making him the second highest-paid man in baseball, after only Babe Ruth. But throughout the 1920s Stoneham also declared frequent dividends for himself and his investors, fellow sports like Rothstein, or Tammany clubhouse hacks. At the same time, the Yankees, who were sharing the Polo Grounds and paying the Giants a lucrative rent for the privilege, reinvested most of their profits back into their organization, outdrawing McGraw's club and making themselves into an indomitable rival.

Stoneham's response was a gangster's play, ending the Yankees' lease and forcing them to seek out and build their own stadium, way up in the Bronx. McGraw egged him on, eager to get out of his ballpark Babe Ruth, the man who had single-handedly ended the style of baseball Muggsy loved the most and whom he liked to call "the big monkey."

"They are going to Goatville, and before long they will be lost sight of," McGraw gloated when the Yankees left. What he and Stoneham had done was to force their rivals to build an enormous new state-of-the-art stadium in the middle of the fastest-growing, most middle-class borough in the city, a stadium they could also rent out for countless football games, boxing matches, and mass meetings, while no longer paying a fat rent to the Giants.

It was a colossal mistake, one that ensured the Giants' long eclipse in the town they had once owned and their eventual exit to California. But McGraw did not seem to grasp it, just as he didn't grasp how other teams were outflanking the Giants by systematically building farm systems of minor-league teams. He continued to rely on his own acumen and connections to identify and sign new talent, even as he aged and became less and less up to the rigors of running a major-league team both on and off the field, his judgment slowly clouding with the years.

Drinking clouded it more than ever. McGraw was often an intemperate, belligerent drunk. He made some of the worst mistakes of his life while in his cups, such as publicly blaming his loyal friend and coach Wilbert Robinson for losing a World Series. McGraw had been bosom buddies and business partners for years with "Uncle Robbie," a rotund, amiable ex-teammate, whom McGraw had left holding the bag as acting manager when he abruptly departed from Baltimore with half the Orioles' team.

When the franchise folded, Robinson had to go work for years as a butcher. Muggsy brought him back to baseball as a pitching and base coach, in which role he proved invaluable, but then fired him in the midst of a drunken party for supposedly messing up a steal sign during the Series. Robbie responded by emptying his glass of beer over McGraw's head and walking out all the way to Brooklyn, where he managed the Dodgers and cost the Giants a couple of pennants. The two old friends did not talk again for another seventeen years.

During the disappointing 1920 campaign Muggsy came almost all the way apart. On one especially bibulous evening McGraw started a fistfight in the Lambs Club, then inexplicably slugged a fellow member who was helping him home, knocking the man to the sidewalk and fracturing his skull. Muggsy escaped trial only with the vigorous intervention of Billy Fallon, but his treasured ties to Broadway were ruptured for good. He was kicked out of the Lambs and retaliated by revoking all its Polo Grounds passes.

He could be intransigent. McGraw recovered some of his equilibrium and came back to have some of his finest seasons as a manager, but he seems to have learned nothing from the Lambs Club debacle. During a sordid lawsuit between his fellow Giants partners a few years later, the wife of one of them reported seeing Muggsy "so intoxicated that . . . he had to be carried to his room by players." Asked if he had been conscious or unconscious at the time, she gave one of the great one-word answers in the history of American jurisprudence: "Semi."

Increasingly, as the years slipped away and the Giants fell just short of winning again, McGraw became more and more impatient, leaving his team for days and even weeks at a time to play the ponies, and involving himself in a typical Florida land deal of the period that cost him much of his savings and nearly an indictment for mail fraud. Now he hastily dealt away players when they did not win him another pennant, including some of those who had been closest to his heart. Throughout his career the childless McGraw had adopted surrogate sons from among his ballplayers, including Frisch and a loquacious, bandy-legged outfielder who came to the Giants near the end of his playing career in the early 1920s.

Casey Stengel idolized McGraw, adopting many of his strategies, such as platooning, and even aping his mannerisms during his own long career as a manager. The bachelor Stengel often went back with McGraw to his apartment after a game, where the two champion spielers swapped baseball tales long into the night.

"What on earth they gabbed about I never learned . . ." McGraw's remarkably indulgent second wife remembered. "Of course, it was just an excuse to stay up all night. They spent most of the time in the kitchen, because it was nearer the food. Casey liked to cook bacon and scrambled eggs, which he did two or three times a night, and John liked to eat them."

Stengel, like Frankie Frisch, had his best years for McGraw. Yet when he thought he could do better, McGraw traded both men away—and after unfairly maligning Frisch to anybody who would listen. He could be callous.

AWAY FROM THE FIELD and a bar rail, he was better: a loving husband and "the kindliest, most generous and most sympathetic of men." He was renowned as a soft touch for former teammates down on their luck, once giving away an estimated two thousand dollars in a single year. Branch Rickey found him "quiet spoken, almost disarmingly so" when out of uniform. His second wife remembered that he liked to simply sit and watch her close family interact; he had what she described as "a sort of gnawing hunger" to belong.

He could be gentle, as when he heard the news of Christy Mathewson's tragic death from tuberculosis, at just forty-five. "I do not expect to see the likes of Matty again . . ." he told reporters. "Matty was my close friend. His passing is one of the great sorrows of my life. God rest his soul." He had been just as sweet in his eulogy for Giants owner John T. Brush, the closest thing he ever had to a surrogate father, more than ten years before:

"He was as tender as a dear girl, as resourceful as a man in the fullest of grand health. . . . What a wonderful—what a beautiful character—was John T. Brush."

The boy from Truxton had picked up a little erudition along the way, and his affection for Brush and Matty was repaid many times when he died, less than two years after finally retiring, in 1934: He was "far and away the greatest baseball manager of all time," "He had a baseball mind that was in a class by itself," and "He treated me as though I were his son and I have also looked on him as a second father. . . . I have lost the best friend I ever had" were some of the things his players said about him.

Yet the best tribute he ever received had come more than ten years before, at the pinnacle of his managing career, just after his Giants had swept the hated Yankees for McGraw's last World Series win. A giddy crowd waited for him outside the Polo Grounds, eager just to touch him, patting his back and kissing his cheeks, stealing the hat from his head. McGraw thanked them, and then one elderly woman came forward to shake his hand, then told the others, "I can go home now. I've seen the greatest manager in baseball."

He could be loved.

HOOVER AND ROOSEVELT
Two Approaches to Leadership

Alan Brinkley

—

THEODORE ROOSEVELT LAMENTED DURING HIS PRESIDENCY THAT circumstances had prevented him from achieving true greatness. He was a very successful president, to be sure, and an exceptionally popular one. But fate, he believed, had denied him the kind of leadership of which he dreamed. "If during the lifetime of a generation," he once said, "no crisis occurs sufficient to call out in marked manner the energies of the strongest leader, then of course the world does not and cannot know of the existence of such a leader; and in consequence there are long periods in the history of every nation during which no man appears who leaves an indelible mark in history. . . . If there is not the war, you don't get the great general; if there is not the great occasion, you don't get the great statesman; if Lincoln had lived in times of peace, no one would know his name now."

Herbert Hoover and Franklin Roosevelt had abundant opportunities to achieve the kind of greatness Theodore Roosevelt sought. Their presidencies coincided with one of the greatest crises in the nation's history. Only one of them is remembered as an extraordinary leader. But in 1928, when Hoover was elected president and Roosevelt was elected governor of New York, almost no one would have predicted history's verdict.

Hoover in 1928 was one of the most admired people in America. His extraordinary management of relief efforts in Belgium during World War I; his eight years as secretary of commerce helping corporations adapt to modern times; his unchallenged brilliance: All made him something close to a national hero and an obvious candidate for president. People who interacted with him routinely referred to him as "the great man."

Franklin Roosevelt, on the other hand, was a man whose public reputation rested mainly on his aristocratic family's connections and background. His movement to the New York legislature in 1910, then to the Navy Department in 1913, and in 1920 to nomination as vice president was more a result of the power of his distant cousin Theodore Roosevelt's name than of anything Franklin Roosevelt had done on his own. He could boast of no great achievements (although he occasionally invented some), and he had few obvious convictions. He was known as a reliable and charming party man, but few people took his intellect very seriously. In 1921 he was paralyzed by polio and never walked again, and he was all but invisible to the world for almost six years after his affliction. In 1928 he was persuaded to run for governor by Al Smith, who believed that Roosevelt would be too weak and disabled to be a political rival. Even after he had won the nomination for president in 1932 and been elected by an impressive majority, few people had high expectations of him. Walter Lippmann famously wrote not long before the inauguration that Roosevelt was "a pleasant man who, without any important qualifications for the office, would very much like to be president."

In the end, however, Herbert Hoover left the White House thoroughly discredited, repudiated, even hated, while Franklin Roosevelt was revered by much of the world when he died in office in 1945 after slightly more than three terms in the White House. "Men will thank God on their knees, a hundred years from now, that Franklin D. Roosevelt was in the White House," the *New York Times* proclaimed shortly after his death.

WHY DID THESE TWO leaders fare so differently in their battles against the Great Depression? Hoover confronted a crisis that almost no one anticipated and few understood. Like most presidents, he tried to be optimistic, a stance that only made him seem ridiculous as the economy continued to unravel at an accelerating pace. Nothing Hoover did—and he did more than most previous presidents had ever done in response to a recession—seemed to make any difference. The crisis outran even his most ambitious efforts. But Hoover was not just a victim of circumstances. He was also a victim of his convictions, convictions that seemed to him close to absolute and that contributed mightily to his failure. Hoover was not a believer in laissez-faire economics, and he believed that the government had a role in facilitating the orderly rationalization and development of the economy. But he also believed that the government could not itself become an actor in the marketplace. It could not compel; it could not direct; it could do nothing that would interfere with the rights of individuals. Walter Lippmann, the same columnist who derided Roosevelt's capacities in 1932, wrote caustically of Hoover's view of government late in 1931: "[He] spends his energies lavishly in fields where under our political system the President has no powers and no responsibility; he is unable to use his energy successfully on the major political tasks where he alone has the power of leadership and the consequent responsibility. This is the reason why he has fallen under the double criticism that he is both inactive and meddlesome."

Hoover's unshakable principles shackled him time and again in his effort to deal with the Depression. He believed in maintaining a balanced budget, a view that almost everyone in politics, including Roosevelt, shared. But for Hoover, balancing the budget was not just a preference. It was an irrevocable commitment, closely tied to his belief in the need to maintain public confidence. If the government could not keep its own house in order, he liked to argue, how could it expect others to believe they could restore order to theirs? After 1929, Hoover never succeeded in balancing the federal budget, but that only reinforced his belief that he had to work harder to do so.

He was not an opponent of using government spending as a way to stimulate the economy. In fact during the first year of the Depression he significantly increased government spending on public works, even though Andrew Mellon, his treasury secretary, and others were urging him to retrench. (Mellon was known as a liquidationist, who believed in letting the Depression run its course and drive weak businesses out of the market.) Hoover, in contrast, encouraged state and local governments to continue spending just as he tried to increase federal spending. But because his first concern was always the fiscal health of the government itself, he was never willing to do enough to make more than a tiny dent in the problems of the Depression. Public works spending in 1930, the first year of the Depression, rose by four hundred million dollars and included all levels of government: federal, state, and local. (The federal share was the smallest of the three.) In that same period, private spending on construction alone fell by three billion dollars. After 1931, when the Depression began seriously to erode the government's revenues, Hoover refused to consider any further increases in public works spending. Instead, he retrenched. Hoover understood that public works spending could provide a useful stimulus to the economy, but he was not willing to purchase that stimulus at the price of an unbalanced budget.

One essential quality of leadership that Hoover seemed to lack was political skill. He was an extraordinarily talented manager, and he was very effective when he was working with other managers—hence his great success in the Commerce Department working with business leaders—but he had little capacity to communicate with the public and came to seem to many Americans to be a remote elitist with no understanding of how ordinary people were experiencing the crisis. Hoover was a presentable figure when things were going well. He was cool, efficient, hardworking, serious, intelligent, dignified. But even before the Depression he showed signs of the political problems that, in darker days, were to plague him. He seemed unable to convey compassion, or warmth, or cheer. One of his biographers has written: "He had conditioned himself . . . to perceive human society from the standpoint of the entrepreneurial engineer." He had little interest in, or understanding of, individual human lives.

He did not really like politics and admitted as much. "I have never liked the clamor of crowds," he once said. "I intensely dislike superficial contacts." He did not like Congress very much either. One of his contemporaries said of him: "He has never really recognized the House and Senate as desirable factors in our government." Hoover himself often called the Congress "that beer garden up there on the hill," and he made blunt, sarcastic comments about members that often came back to haunt him. He called the Republican Senate majority leader (a fellow Republican) a man of "spasmodic loyalties and abilities." He described another important Republican committee chairman as "the only verified case of a negative I.Q." He was a wooden public speaker. He rarely smiled for cameras. Oddly enough, for a man who believed in the importance of inspiring confidence and who was (in private contacts with businessmen and business organizations) a great exhorter and encourager, he had no conception at all of how the president could use the force of his own personality to shape public attitudes and promote public confidence.

Above all, perhaps, he was insensitive. He refused to express sympathy for the poor or the unemployed, fearing that to do so would damage public confidence by acknowledging that poverty and unemployment existed. When asked once about the unemployed who were peddling on street corners, he commented: "Many people have left their jobs for the more profitable one of selling apples." When confronted with the real problem of hunger, he replied, falsely, "No one is actually starving. The hoboes . . . are better fed than they have ever been." *Fortune* magazine, a relatively moderate publication, called this statement a lie. It is hard to know whether Hoover actually believed these things; but whether he believed them or not, they were disastrous political statements.

The clearest evidence of Hoover's political insensitivity and the most important event in destroying his public reputation was a single episode in the summer of 1932, the Bonus March in Washington. Hoover's response to it revealed the limits of his talents as a leader more clearly than anything else he did as president. In June 1932 veterans from all over the country gathered in Washington to demand that the government pass a bill authorizing immediate payment of a service bonus voted several years before for World War I veterans. The bonus was scheduled to be paid in 1945; the veterans wanted it at once, when they needed it. About twenty thousand veterans (many homeless and unemployed, many with their families) gathered in Washington at the height of the campaign. But their effort failed. Congress passed the bonus bill. Hoover vetoed it, and the veto was not overridden. Most of the veterans left the city after that, but about a thousand stayed on through the summer, some living in empty government buildings near the Capitol, others in a makeshift shantytown just across the Anacostia River. To Hoover, they were a constant embarrassment. He refused to see the marchers. He increased security around the White House. He banned picketing, closed off streets, and came to view the veterans as dangerous revolutionaries. Finally, in mid-July, he ordered the veterans evicted from the abandoned government buildings they were occupying. When the Washington police tried to enforce the order, some rocks were thrown, some shots were fired (by the police), and two veterans were killed. Hoover interpreted the episode as evidence of anarchism and radicalism and of the inability of the police to control it. And so he called out the U.S. Army and ordered it to clear the building, under the command of General Douglas MacArthur.

The soldiers attacked the veterans with the flat sides of their bayonets. They hurled tear gas and rode their horses at full speed into the crowds. In the shantytown in Anacostia, where many of the veterans were camping, soldiers burned the tents and makeshift shanties and established machine-gun posts on the bridge to keep the veterans from returning to the city. More than one hundred people were injured. The remaining bonus marchers fled the camp and scattered out across Virginia and Maryland.

Hoover had not ordered and had not wanted anything like this massive use of force. But his cold technocratic instincts—his decision to disperse peaceful protesters whom a more astute politician might have tried to placate—helped guide his actions after the fiasco as well. He did nothing to disassociate himself from the melee in Washington, and in fact he supported MacArthur's claim that the veterans had been a dangerous radical mob. His own Veterans Administration publicly disputed him. He had shown dramatically what he had been revealing in many small ways for many months before: that he had no real empathy for those who were suffering and no sense of the public image a leader needed to gain the support and confidence of a troubled people.

FRANKLIN ROOSEVELT HAD weaknesses of his own as he approached the task of dealing first with the Great Depression and then with World War II. He was a complicated, elusive, at times even devious figure and a consummate defender of his own political self-interest. He could be vindictive, petty, and deceitful. He had few real friends, and even those closest to him knew only a small part of his carefully concealed inner self. He had powerful critics, most notably among the wealthy and powerful. Many of them hated him with a passion seldom seen in his time, a passion so great that some of his enemies could not bear to say his name and referred to him as "That Man." Henry Luce, the powerful publisher of *Time, Life,* and *Fortune,* so despised Roosevelt that even after his death he said that it was "my duty to go on hating him."

But Roosevelt had strengths that made him a much more effective leader than Hoover had been, strengths that first became visible in the greatest ordeal of his life. For six years after he contracted polio in 1921 he did virtually nothing but work to recover. He spent much of his time at a rehabilitation center for polio patients he helped found at Warm Springs, Georgia, trying to learn to walk again. He never did. Instead, he learned how to stand for public occasions by using an elaborate system of braces and canes, and he learned how to appear to walk, swinging his paralyzed, braced legs in front of him by moving his hips, supporting himself by holding a cane in one hand and the arm of an aide (often his son) in another. His return to public life was a feat of incredible will, made possible by his ability to hide his paralysis from the public. Most people never realized that he could not walk. Eleanor Roosevelt argued that it was this ordeal that changed Roosevelt, that turned him from a genial, shallow politician into a man of depth and compassion. That may be true, although there were few signs of it at the time. But his struggle with paralysis certainly strengthened Roosevelt's determination. It also reinforced his natural inclination to dissemble, to hide behind an aggressive public geniality. Almost to the end of his life, Roosevelt went to extraordinary lengths to hide his paralysis, lengths so extraordinary (aided, once he was in office, by the resources of the Secret Service and other government agencies) that perhaps the most photographed man of his time was virtually never photographed sitting in his wheelchair. In the process, he hid much of the rest of himself as well.

Roosevelt won the 1932 Democratic nomination for president largely because as a Roosevelt and as governor of New York, he was an obvious choice. Unlike other leading Democrats, he had not spent enough time in office or in the public eye in the 1920s to have antagonized any of the warring factions that had divided the Democratic Party so badly for the previous decade. He campaigned for president in 1932 largely by denouncing Hoover for excessive government spending and for expanding the federal bureaucracy.

It could probably safely be said that Franklin Roosevelt had no real political philosophy beyond a basic commitment to capitalism that he shared with virtually everyone else. Roosevelt's writings and statements prior to 1933 consist of a lot of obvious, romanticized convictions and platitudes. Even as president he never gave much evidence of ideological clarity. He was famous in fact for his evasiveness. (Senator Huey P. Long of Louisiana visited Roosevelt in the White House in 1933. He said later that the president responded to Long's suggestions by saying, "Fine, fine, fine." He learned later that Senator Joseph Robinson of Arkansas, one of Long's political enemies, heard Roosevelt say the same thing. "Maybe he says 'Fine' to everyone," Long complained.) Only rarely did anyone get a straight answer out of Roosevelt. His ideas were so flexible, his ideological commitments so few that it was easy for him to juggle many different, even contradictory positions at once.

How, then, did this man who had risen to prominence on the basis of so few real accomplishments earn a reputation as the champion of the common man and as the symbol of modern, committed liberalism? Part of the answer lies in Roosevelt's personality. What seemed in 1933 to be weaknesses often turned out to be strengths. What seemed like liabilities Roosevelt turned into assets.

Roosevelt's privileged, insulated background may have limited his understanding of common people to some degree. There was always a certain naiveté in him (as when he talked about his own experiences as a gentleman farmer in Dutchess County as evidence of his understanding of the problems of American agriculture). But Roosevelt's background also gave him a remarkable sense of self-assurance, an ease in dealing with people, what one of his college classmates called "an air of effortless command." And that confidence may also have contributed to his ability to question his own beliefs and orthodoxies without feeling (as Hoover apparently did) that he was questioning the basis of his existence.

Roosevelt's smooth, genial public image and his boyish enthusiasm and optimism led many people to think of him as superficial and glib. But his personal style itself became an integral part of his political program. Roosevelt was charming and witty and eloquent; he was almost always smiling, always vigorous. He also transmitted his own self-assurance to the nation—nowhere more clearly than in the first desperate days of his administration, when his confident inaugural address, his cheery public optimism, his fireside chats over the radio, his personal magnetism were of crucial importance in stemming what had been a growing panic throughout the country. He was the first president to make extensive use of the radio, and he made effective use of it throughout his presidency. He cultivated the press so successfully that he managed to set all the ground rules on coverage, including no reporting of his paralysis and no photos of his wheelchair. Another, more indirect result of his social background was his sense of something like noblesse oblige. That sense was reinforced by Eleanor Roosevelt, for whom an aristocratic background had been a route to social activism. She was active in the settlement house movement, and she became an important force in influencing her husband by bringing social problems to his attention, despite their troubled personal relationship. Franklin was less committed to such causes, but he championed them when they served his purposes.

But perhaps Roosevelt's most important quality, the one that separated him most decisively from Hoover, was his pragmatic, experimental nature. To be sure, it produced much ideological fuzziness and prevented the New Deal from achieving any real consistency (a frequent criticism of Roosevelt to this day). The New Deal was characterized by the clash of many different ideas, by trial and error. The historian Richard Hofstadter once called the New Deal a "chaos of experimentation." Raymond Moley, Roosevelt's onetime adviser, wrote in a sour memoir published after his falling-out with the president: "To look upon these programs as the result of a unified plan was to believe that the accumulation of stuffed snakes, baseball pictures, school flags, old tennis shoes, carpenter's tools, geometry books, and chemistry sets in a boy's bedroom could have been put there by an interior decorator."

But it could also be argued that this absence of a clear ideology was responsible for much of whatever success the New Deal achieved and that it saved him from Hoover's fate of being wedded to rigid, unshakable philosophies that impeded recovery. In the midst of an unprecedented catastrophe, a crisis without obvious solution, the lack of a consistent philosophy was almost certainly better than a philosophy that had failed. Roosevelt was deliberately experimental, openly pragmatic. He liked to say, "Take a method and try it. If fails, admit it frankly and try another."

The achievements of the New Deal owed a great deal to Roosevelt's pragmatic nature. His first Hundred Days broke dramatically with Hoover's dour orthodoxy and produced an unprecedented wave of legislative innovations. Not all of them were successful. The National Recovery Administration (NRA), created by the National Industrial Recovery Act, was the most ambitious of Roosevelt's efforts. It was a broad program of reform designed to revive industrial prosperity by allowing businesses to collude in raising prices and setting wages. It also declared the right of workers to unionize and bargain collectively with employers, although it did not include any enforcement provisions. For a time it was the most popular government program in the country, saluted by parades and rallies and by decals in store windows everywhere, saluting the symbol of the NRA, the Blue Eagle. But the NRA did not help the economy revive, despite its bold innovation. Instead, it contributed to the greatest problem of the Depression: deflation. Raising prices and lowering wages, which were what the NRA essentially did, was a recipe for reducing economic activity. When the NRA was struck down by the Supreme Court in 1935, some New Dealers were relieved.

But Roosevelt's experimentation had more successes than failures. The Agricultural Adjustment Administration (AAA) set out to reduce agricultural production so as to raise farm prices, and over its first two years it succeeded significantly in helping end the declining value of crops. To make it work, the government offered subsidies to farmers for keeping some of their land fallow and for destroying livestock, to avoid surpluses that would drive prices down. Higher food prices were not of course good news for urban consumers. But given the sizable agricultural population in the 1930s, the rising incomes of farmers more than compensated for increases in food prices. Simultaneously, the New Deal created programs to strengthen the banking system, to insure individual bank deposits, to regulate the securities markets, to protect homeowners and farm owners from foreclosure, and to provide jobs for the unemployed. The almost frenetic pace of the New Deal in its first weeks was itself a remarkable change from the Hoover years and indeed from most other administrations in American history.

The energy and innovation that Roosevelt brought to government earned him enormous popularity and support. But within a year of his inauguration, it was becoming clear that these ambitious programs had not succeeded in bringing real recovery. "It simply has to be admitted," Roosevelt's aide Rexford Tugwell later wrote of the New Deal in 1934, "that Roosevelt was not yet certain what direction he ought to take." But the idea of choosing a "direction" and sticking to it was not in Roosevelt's nature. He was always ready to change course when circumstances required it. And changing course was certainly necessary in early 1935. Business leaders and other powerful and wealthy Americans had turned on the New Deal with unusual bitterness. Dissident populists from all over the country began to mobilize on behalf of a wide range of proposals to restore prosperity, many of them implausible, some of them radical, few of them attractive to Roosevelt and his colleagues. As his reelection campaign approached, he began to use an incendiary rhetoric that pilloried the "economic royalists," who he claimed were undermining his efforts at recovery. In the summer of 1936, he spoke of "all my old enemies . . . monopoly, speculation, reckless banking . . . war profiteering," and he went on to a remarkable climax: "Never before in all our history have these forces been so united against one candidate as they stand today. They are unanimous in their hate for me—and I welcome their hatred. . . . I should like to have it said of my first Administration that the forces of selfishness and of lust for power met their match. . . . I should like to have it said of my second Administration that in it these forces met their master." Even many of Roosevelt's own allies were appalled by what one former aide called "the violence, the bombast, the naked demagoguery" of his words. But for most Americans struggling through the Depression, his rhetoric was a rallying cry and helped ensure his reelection.

Roosevelt's incendiary rhetoric was just that—rhetoric. He pursued no significant policies designed to punish the "economic royalists"—to the relief of many of his colleagues in government. But there was a switch in policy. Having failed to solve the Depression in his first two years, he began in the next two years not only to deal with immediate problems but also to create lasting reforms that would, over time, protect citizens from catastrophe and help increase consumption. Among the most significant of these new initiatives was the Social Security Act. It created old-age pensions, unemployment insurance, aid to the disabled, and support for needy families with children. Equally important was the National Labor Relations Act (known as the Wagner Act after the New York senator who sponsored it). It restored to workers the right to organize unions and bargain collectively with employers, which had been part of the NRA before it was invalidated by the Supreme Court. But the new bill went further than the NRA labor policies. It created a mechanism to enforce union rights, through the National Labor Relations Board. Roosevelt was skeptical of both these programs at first, fearing they were too radical. But he championed both in the end, partly because he understood their political benefits. At about the same time, he and his intimate aide Harry Hopkins created the Works Progress Administration, the largest jobs program ever created by the federal government. It hired three million people in its first year and more than eight million in its eight-year life.

In the aftermath of Roosevelt's stunning reelection, one of the largest landslides in American political history, the New Deal began to unravel. Roosevelt's pragmatic eclecticism could do damage as well as good, and the president's postelection hubris contributed mightily to new efforts that did his administration lasting harm. Enraged at the conservatism of the Supreme Court, which had invalidated a number of New Deal programs already, Roosevelt, fearing even greater Court defeats, proposed a reform of the judiciary. Cloaked in moderate rhetoric, he was in fact proposing an increase of the number of justices on the Court that would allow him to change its ideological balance. It became known as court packing, and its unpopularity not only defeated the bill but did lasting damage to Roosevelt's political power.

A year later Roosevelt stumbled again. The economy, at long last, seemed to be recovering from the Depression in early 1937. (The relevant word was "seemed," because the economy was a great deal more fragile than Roosevelt and his orthodox secretary of the treasury, Henry Morgenthau, believed.) At Morgenthau's urging, Roosevelt agreed to cut spending to help achieve the shibboleth of a balanced budget. The result was a severe recession within the Depression that began in mid-1937 and continued for a year, plunging the economy into a decline nearly as bad as in 1932. Once again Roosevelt, never one to stick with failure, changed course and authorized new spending on job creation and public works of five billion dollars, a sum that grew even larger over the next several years and that helped undo the damage that the recession had caused. This shift also marked the emergence of the ideas of the British economist John Maynard Keynes as a force in American economic policy. Roosevelt and Keynes had met once in the White House, and neither man had been impressed by the other. But the president was willing to try anything that he thought might work, and his first excursion into Keynesianism seemed to work very well. Shortly after launching new spending, Roosevelt supported a new bill to stimulate the economy, the Fair Labor Standards Act, which established a forty-hour workweek (with overtime pay for those who worked more), a minimum wage, and a prohibition of child labor. It was also an effort to increase mass purchasing power and thus to stimulate economic growth.

By the end of 1938 Roosevelt was only about halfway through his presidency, but the New Deal he had created was already close to completion. In retrospect, it has sometimes seemed as significant for the things it did not do as for the things it achieved. The New Deal did not end the Great Depression and the massive unemployment that accompanied it; only the enormous public and private spending for World War II finally did that. It did not transform American capitalism in any fundamental way. Except in the fields of labor relations and banking and finance, corporate power remained nearly as free from government regulation or control in 1945 as it had been in 1933. The New Deal did not end poverty or significantly redistribute wealth. Nor did it do very much, except symbolically, to address some of the great domestic challenges of the postwar era, among them the problems of racial and gender inequality. Despite the commitment to civil rights of Eleanor Roosevelt and such New Deal officials as Secretary of the Interior Harold Ickes, the president consistently shied away from issues that he feared would divide his party and damage his ability to work with Congress.

Even so, the domestic achievements of the Roosevelt administration rank among the most important of any presidency in American history. The New Deal created new state institutions that significantly and permanently expanded the role of the federal government in American life, providing at least minimal assistance to the elderly, the poor, and the unemployed; protecting the rights of labor unions; stabilizing the banking system; building low-income housing; regulating financial markets; subsidizing agricultural production; and doing many other things that had not previously been federal responsibilities. As a result, American political and economic life became much more competitive, with workers, farmers, consumers, and others now able to press their demands upon the government in ways that in the past had usually been available only to the corporate world. Hence the frequent description of the government the New Deal created as a "broker state," a state brokering the competing claims of numerous groups. Roosevelt also produced a political coalition, the "New Deal Coalition"—of farmers, workers, the poor and unemployed, African Americans in northern cities, traditional progressives, and committed new liberals—that made the Democratic Party the majority party in national politics, a position it retained for more than a generation. Finally, the Roosevelt administration generated a set of political ideas, known to later generations as New Deal liberalism, that remained a source of inspiration and controversy for decades and helped shape the next major experiment in liberal reform, the New Frontier and the Great Society of the 1960s.

The New Deal sputtered to something like a close in Roosevelt's second term in part because the political tides were turning against him. In 1938 and again in 1942, Democrats suffered considerable losses in congressional elections; the emerging conservative coalition of Republicans and southern Democrats was now capable of blocking almost anything liberals proposed. But the New Deal faded as well because of the president's growing preoccupation with the greatest catastrophe of the twentieth century, the spiraling global crisis that led Europe, Asia, and ultimately the United States into World War II.

ROOSEVELT'S PRAGMATIC and ever-shifting approach to leadership was particularly visible as he began slowly to engage with the international crisis. To the frustration of many people who wanted a clear and decisive position on the crisis, Roosevelt continued on his enigmatic path. He was evasive when asked whether he would run for an unprecedented third term, even though he was privately committed to being a candidate again. Only at the Democratic convention in 1940 did it become clear that he would run again, and not until a carefully orchestrated "draft" had been arranged by the president and his political aides. Shortly before the balloting, some Democrats constructed a seven-foot-high papier-mâché model of a sphinx, on its head the smiling face of Roosevelt, a cigarette holder clasped jauntily between his teeth. It was an apt symbol not only of his behavior in 1940 but of his personality throughout his life. He won his third term easily over the attractive Republican candidate, Wendell Willkie, and then skillfully persuaded Willkie to work with him on the war effort. Earlier in the year he had appointed two eminent Republicans to his cabinet. Henry Stimson, former secretary of war under William Howard Taft and secretary of state to Herbert Hoover, became Roosevelt's secretary of war. Frank Knox, a newspaper publisher who had been the Republican vice presidential candidate in the 1936, election, became secretary of the navy. Roosevelt was shifting course again, this time to make his wartime administration at least appear to be bipartisan.

Roosevelt understood the precariousness of public opinion on the war: strong support for Great Britain once World War II began in 1939, but equally strong opposition to sending American troops into the conflict. For more than two years he struggled to balance the political obstacles to intervention against the urgent need to support Great Britain and prepare for America's possible entry into the war. He increased support for the embattled British. The 1939 cash-and-carry law, overturning the Neutrality Acts that had forbidden American firms from selling arms to belligerents, allowed the British to purchase armaments from the United States. A year later Roosevelt embraced an unusual proposal to trade American destroyers to Britain in exchange for new American bases in the Caribbean. In the spring of 1941 he introduced the lend-lease program, which provided direct aid to Britain and, later, other American allies. Also early in 1941, he secretly began to allow the U.S. Navy to defend British convoys as they crossed the Atlantic, eventually allowing American ships to fire on German submarines. Throughout this slow march to war he was assuring Americans that the United States would not join the fighting. A few days before the 1940 election he disingenuously assured a crowd in Boston that "your boys are not going to be sent into any foreign wars," even though he knew that he was unlikely to keep that promise. This deft, if somewhat deceptive, strategy was typical of his leadership: hiding his real intentions and making steady steps forward along with occasional steps backward.

Despite Roosevelt's belief, shared by most Americans, that the greatest danger to the nation was Nazi Germany, it was Japan that finally pushed the United States into the war. Roosevelt cut off Japanese access to American oil and froze Japanese assets in the United States in the fall of 1941. There had been controversy for years on whether Roosevelt and Stimson were acting deliberately to provoke a war with the Japanese. It is unlikely that these seasoned leaders really believed that the Japanese retreat from China they had demanded would be the result. They almost certainly knew that the steps they were taking would probably lead to war. Roosevelt and his aides did not, however, expect an attack on American soil. They assumed that Japan's next step would be to seize the oil-producing British and Dutch possessions in the Pacific. Instead, on December 7, 1941, a wave of Japanese bombers struck the American naval base in Pearl Harbor, Hawaii, killing more than two thousand American servicemen and damaging or destroying dozens of ships and airplanes. American intelligence had broken the Japanese codes and knew an attack was coming. But because no one anticipated that the Japanese would (or could) launch so bold a naval effort so far from home, no one predicted what they actually did.

Roosevelt may not have anticipated Pearl Harbor, but he knew how to use it once it happened. The attack galvanized the American people and created overwhelming support for the war—and for Roosevelt's leadership. Three days later Germany and Italy, Japan's European allies, declared war on the United States, and the American Congress quickly and unanimously reciprocated.

Even before Pearl Harbor, Roosevelt was maintaining an intense relationship with Churchill, who spent months at a time in the White House working with the president on strategy and goals while also sharing cocktails and meals. The two men disagreed on many things—notably the fate of Britain's colonies after the war. Churchill was determined to retain the empire. Roosevelt was increasingly committed to decolonization. But Roosevelt's ability to evade and dissemble prevented any open conflicts with his British partner, and their relationship remained strong. Indeed their partnership was one of the most important relationships of the twentieth century.

Roosevelt was also moving toward a statement of war aims. In August 1941 he met with Churchill aboard an American cruiser off Newfoundland, where they signed what became known as the Atlantic Charter. It included "the right of all peoples to choose the form of government under which they will live . . . the final destruction of the Nazi tyranny . . . [and] a peace which will afford all nations to dwell in safety . . . [so that] all men in all the lands may live out their lives in freedom from fear and want." The document both cemented the alliance with Britain and provided the American public (and the world) with an idealistic argument for war. Roosevelt reinforced this idealistic vision of what victory could bring with his inspiring Four Freedoms speech in 1941 and his highly progressive Economic Bill of Rights in 1944, which suggested to Americans—and to much of the world—that an Allied victory would enhance democracy and progress.

But Roosevelt's idealism went only so far. He was not very receptive to the demands of the many Americans who sought to harness the war effort to great moral causes. In 1940, largely because of heavy pressure by African American leaders, Roosevelt created the Fair Employment Practices Commission to enhance black employment opportunities in war industries. It was the first federal agency since Reconstruction that was actively engaged in the effort to promote racial equality. But he did not respond to many other demands for racial equality despite his own discomfort with segregation and his wife's very public support of civil rights. The armed forces remained segregated throughout the war, and while African American leaders promoted the idea of the Double V—a simultaneous commitment to victory in the war and victory over racism—there was little progress toward such goals before 1945.

In 1942, shortly after the attack on Pearl Harbor, the president acquiesced to one of the most egregious violations of civil liberties in American history. Military officials on the West Coast, supported by the War Department, proposed "interning" the thousands of resident Japanese Americans in California, even though there was no evidence to suggest that they were in any way disloyal. Attorney General Francis Biddle strongly opposed the relocation of the Japanese Americans, but Roosevelt deferred to the War Department, which supported officers in California, who had proposed the plan. Thousands of families were transferred from their homes to internment camps, most of them in the deserts. Few were released until 1944.

To many Americans, at the time and since, the greatest moral failure of the United States in the war years was its seeming unwillingness to take forceful action against the Holocaust. The United States did little to save the Jews in Europe, who, beginning in 1941, were being systematically exterminated by Nazi Germany. Six million Jews, and two million others, died in this unparalleled act of genocide. In fairness, there was little the United States could have done to save most of the Jews imperiled by the Holocaust after 1939, other than win the war. But the United States gave little help to Jews attempting to escape from Europe before the war began and offered refuge to very few of those imperiled people on the edges of the Nazi empire who might have been rescuable. Early in 1944, Roosevelt, increasingly alarmed about the reports of the Holocaust that had been flowing into America since 1942, created the War Refugee Board, which provided authority and funds to help refugees escape from Europe. In the end, however, it managed to remove fewer than a thousand Jews from danger. In a gesture that had little impact on the war but had a significant impact on its aftermath, Roosevelt, with the support of

Churchill and Stalin, promised to create tribunals to try "war criminals" after the war, a step that led to postwar trials in Nuremberg and Tokyo.

In the last months of his life he struggled to sustain the wartime alliance that he, Churchill, and Stalin had built to win the war. At the famous, and to some people notorious, Yalta Conference in the Crimea in early 1945, Roosevelt struggled to reach an agreement that would keep Stalin in the alliance without giving up too much to the Soviet Union in return. In the end, the Yalta Accords proved futile in the face of Stalin's obduracy and the Soviet Union's preexisting occupation of most of Eastern Europe. Yalta was not a betrayal, as many critics have maintained over many years. Roosevelt had little power to create a better agreement. But he continued until his death in April 1945 to believe, somewhat naively, that his combination of charm and guile might keep Stalin in the fold.

IN THE FIRST YEARS of the twentieth century two great philosophers helped lay out competing paths for thinking about morality, politics, and leadership. One was Josiah Royce, a Harvard philosopher who was a champion of idealism, the belief that there must be some "absolute truth" or "absolute knowledge" behind any legitimate moral claim. The other was Royce's friend and colleague at Harvard, William James, who was one of the founders of pragmatism, perhaps the first major philosophical innovation to have emerged from American thought. James was skeptical of the idea of absolute knowledge and argued instead that ideas had value only to the degree that they "worked." Every idea had to confront the test of its relevance to its time and circumstances. There could be no easy recourse to an absolute truth—either from religion or from ancient texts or from contemporary philosophy. People and nations must live with the knowledge that even their deepest beliefs could be challenged and, if necessary, rejected.

No one—not even Royce and James—could live wholly successfully on the basis of an unchallengeable idea of truth; nor could one live wholly successfully entirely for the moment, without at least some reference to tradition and community standards. But the contrast between Herbert Hoover (a man not without flexibility but hobbled by strong principles) and Franklin Roosevelt (who was not without principles but was a master of pragmatic experimentation) suggests that leadership cannot succeed through ideals and strong convictions alone. The world is a complicated and ever-changing place, and a great leader must be capable of adapting to change and understanding the diversity of the ideas and principles that shape history. By ordinary standards, Herbert Hoover was an admirable man—more so, perhaps, than the elusive and often deceptive Roosevelt. But by the standards of global leadership, Roosevelt was the far more successful at guiding the United States through the two greatest crises of the twentieth century. He did so in part because his values were appropriate to his time but also because he understood that values must reflect the realities of his age.

U.S.

THE QUALITIES OF LEADERSHIP
Dwight D. Eisenhower as Warrior and President

David M. Kennedy

—

FEW LEADERS ARE MEN FOR ALL SEASONS. THE QUALITIES THAT DEFINE an effective leader in one circumstance may be useless or even mischievous in another. Ulysses S. Grant provides a notorious example of this disjunction. Gloriously successful as a military commander, he was embarrassingly inept as president. His malfeasance in the White House mounted to such proportions that he formally apologized to his countrymen in his final State of the Union message. Americans took the point. They had elevated five generals to the presidency in the Republic's first century.* They waited nearly another century before they so honored another professional soldier, Dwight D. Eisenhower.

Both Grant and Eisenhower were obscure Midwestern-bred career military officers, of modest achievement and unspectacular promise until war suddenly thrust great responsibilities, and opportunities, into their hands. Before he met Lee in triumph at Appomattox, Grant had tasted battle in Mexico, served a few routine tours of duty at desolate outposts, and resigned from the army out of boredom in 1854.

Like Grant's, Eisenhower's capacity for leadership long languished in latency. A fifty-one-year-old freshly commissioned brigadier general when the Japanese attacked Pearl Harbor, Eisenhower had yet to see combat. He had spent World War I training tank troops in a stateside

* George Washington, Andrew Jackson, William Henry Harrison, Zachary Taylor, and Grant. Franklin Pierce attained the rank of general in the Mexican War, as did Rutherford B. Hayes, James A. Garfield, and Benjamin Harrison in the Civil War, but none was a professional soldier in the mold of the earlier presidents.

camp, attended several advanced military colleges in the ensuing decade, and served on Douglas MacArthur's staff in the Philippines in the 1930s. In December 1941 he was attached to Third Army headquarters in San Antonio, Texas, when Army Chief of Staff George C. Marshall summoned him to Washington to head the Pacific and Far Eastern Section of the War Department's War Plans Division.

Marshall valued Eisenhower's familiarity with the Far Eastern situation, particularly in the Philippines, but he wanted more than his subordinate's regional expertise. Amid the chaos of war-girding Washington, Marshall needed assistants who would shoulder heavy responsibilities and act decisively without constantly coming to him for consultation. Eisenhower did not disappoint. Within hours of his arrival he drafted a plan to use Australia as a base of operations against the Philippines. Characteristically, he justified his proposal for swift and heavy military effort with an appeal to considerations of morale: "The people of China, of the Philippines, of the Dutch East Indies will be watching us. They may excuse failure but they will not excuse abandonment."

Eisenhower's next assignment was to draw up a letter of instruction for a still-unnamed "supreme commander" of American, British, Dutch, and Australian land, sea, and air forces in the western Pacific. This was a formidable task, envisaging the virtually unprecedented coordination of traditionally discrete services from several sovereign states. Eisenhower submitted his draft on December 26, 1941. He later noted in his diary that "the struggle to secure the adoption by all concerned of a common concept of strategical objectives is wearing me down. Everybody is too much engaged with small things of his own, or with some vague idea of larger political activity, to realize what we are doing, rather, not doing. . . . [W]hat a job to work with allies."

Allies, Napoleon once said in exasperation, were his preferred enemies in war. Eisenhower at times shared the sentiment. Yet the ability to work productively with allies, however frustrating, proved to be Eisenhower's special genius. In June 1942, Marshall sent him to England as the head of American forces in the European theater of operations. By the end of the year he was commander of the Allied expedition in North Africa. During the invasions of North Africa and Italy in 1942 and 1943, he developed a command structure that integrated the several services of various nationalities under three British subordinates directly responsible to him. Assembled in full uniform, Eisenhower's biographer Stephen Ambrose wrote, these men "looked the personification of British tradition and habit of command." They might have intimidated a Kansas boy on his first combat assignment, but Eisenhower determined "to work with them, not by imposing his will but through persuasion and cooperation." By those means, Eisenhower demonstrated a remarkable capacity for coordinating British, American, and French air, naval, and ground forces. His reward came at Cairo on December 6, 1943, when President Roosevelt named Eisenhower supreme commander of the Allied Expeditionary Force in Europe, responsible for planning and executing the invasion of northwestern Europe that eventually took place in Normandy on D-day, June 6, 1944.

The Allies might have shared the common objective of defeating Hitler, but Eisenhower never took inter-Allied cooperation for granted. Indeed he considered its careful and deliberate cultivation to be among the highest priorities of his command. "The seeds for discord between ourselves and our British allies were sown," he wrote to Marshall, "as far back as when we read our little red school history books. My method is to drag all these matters squarely into the open, discuss them frankly, and insist upon positive rather than negative action in furthering the purpose of Allied unity."

Immediately on his arrival in England in June 1942, he ordered his staff to cultivate an attitude of enthusiasm and optimism. He specifically encouraged friendly relations with the British. Officers who publicly criticized the British he sent home. When General George Patton demanded an apology for British criticism of his corps, Eisenhower forcefully suppressed this call "for the last pound of flesh." He would not tolerate "any criticism couched along nationalistic lines," he admonished Patton, so that "every subordinate throughout the hierarchy of command will execute the orders he receives without even pausing to consider whether that order emanated from a British or American source."

Eisenhower instinctively felt that the gossamer tissue of personal relationships counted for far more than the formal architecture of his table of organization in determining the success or failure of his command. "The problem of establishing unity in any allied command," he explained to Lord Louis Mountbatten, "involves the human equation." The British-American Combined Chiefs of Staff might issue carefully crafted written directives on the structure of an allied command, but the command's "true basis lies in the earnest cooperation of the senior officers assigned to an allied theater. Since cooperation, in turn, implies such things as selflessness, devotion to a common cause, generosity in attitude, and mutual confidence, it is easy to see that actual unity in an allied command depends directly upon the individuals in the field. . . . Patience, tolerance, frankness, absolute honesty in all dealings, particularly with all persons of the opposite nationality, and firmness, are absolutely essential. . . . *[T]he thing you must strive for is the utmost in mutual respect and confidence among the group of seniors making up the allied command* [Eisenhower's italics]."

Eisenhower practiced what he preached. No matter how wearing his duties or how grim the military outlook, by act of will Eisenhower as supreme commander "firmly determined that my mannerisms and speech in public would always reflect the cheerful certainty of victory." His British colleague and sometime rival Bernard Montgomery conceded that Eisenhower's "real strength lies in his human qualities. . . . He has the power of drawing the hearts of men towards him as a magnet attracts the bits of metal. He merely has to smile at you, and you trust him at once. He is the very incarnation of sincerity." Omar Bradley noted more succinctly that Eisenhower's smile was worth twenty divisions.

It would be mistaken to discount the importance of Allied unity in the winning of the war or to undervalue Eisenhower's techniques of willed optimism and cultivated trust for achieving that unity. World War I, with its costly lack of liaison among national armies, as well as its protracted bickering about what use to make of American troops, provided an object lesson about the human toll that lack of concerted military effort could exact. The stakes were even higher in the vastly larger conflict of World War II, especially in the dauntingly complex operations that culminated in D-day and the race for the German frontier. One observer at a meeting before the Normandy invasion wrote that "it seemed to most of us that the proper meshing of so many gears would need nothing less than divine guidance." Eisenhower's guidance may not have been divine, but it was surely inspired. Most important, it worked, and historians rightly give him major credit for providing the kind of concerting leadership that ultimately crowned the Allied effort with success.

Eisenhower defined the ability to nurture optimism and elicit cooperation as the essence of leadership. He believed that such ability was not an innate but an acquired characteristic, the acquisition of which resulted from serious psychological study. "The one quality that can be developed by studious reflection and practice is the leadership of men," he wrote to his son in 1943. "The idea is to get people working together, not only because you tell them to do so and enforce your orders but because they instinctively want to do it for you. . . . Essentially, you must be devoted to duty, sincere, fair and cheerful. You do not need to be a glad-hander nor [*sic*] a salesman, but your men must trust you and instinctively wish to win your approbation and to avoid things that call upon you for correction." Conspicuously absent from this list of a military leader's qualities was any mention of the need for aggressiveness or initiative, or steely resolve in the face of a threatening enemy, or any of the bravura theatrics or pugnacious posturing that one associates with figures like Douglas MacArthur and George Patton. Here, clearly, was no ordinary military commander.

By war's end Eisenhower had not only masterfully completed the acquisition and deployment of his chosen leadership techniques but succeeded in projecting their appeal to wide segments of the American public. Both political parties sought him as a presidential candidate. Americans might have been tired of war in the late 1940s, but they had not wearied of this war hero. Significantly, their high regard for Eisenhower rested on a perception that he was not in fact a "militaristic" personality, as Columbia University sociologist Robert Merton demonstrated in an analysis of some twenty thousand letters written to the general in 1948. Similarly, much of his later popularity in the nation's highest political office owed to the notion that he was not an ordinary "politician." Eisenhower, in short, had perfected the art of playing against his assigned role, first as a nonmilitary general and later as a nonpolitical president. This deliberately cultivated style had proved enormously successful in war. How would it work in the White House?

Among those urging a presidential candidacy on Eisenhower in the immediate postwar years was the former New York governor and two-time Republican presidential candidate Thomas E. Dewey. Visiting Eisenhower's home in July 1949, Dewey outlined his reasons for wanting Eisenhower to run. The general, now president of Columbia University, reflected at length in his diary on the conversation with Dewey. He wrote:

> The governor says that I am a public possession, that such standing as I have in the affections or respect of our citizenry is likewise public property. All of this, though, must be carefully guarded to use in the service of all the people. . . . The governor then gave me the reasons he believed that only I (if I should carefully preserve my assets) can save this country from going to hades in the handbasket of paternalism, socialism, dictatorship. . . . His basic reasoning is as follows: All middle-class citizens have a common belief that tendencies toward centralization and paternalism must be halted and reversed. [But] no one who voices these views can be elected. . . . Consequently, we must look around for someone of great popularity and who has not frittered away his political assets by taking positive stands against national planning, etc., etc.

Three years later this political strategy paid handsome returns, lifting Eisenhower to the presidency with one of the largest popular majorities in the century. Carefully striking a nonpartisan pose during his campaign, he entered office with his truly remarkable assets of public affection and respect fully intact. Those assets had been painstakingly accumulated and conscientiously conserved for more than a decade. Now, if ever, was the time to spend them.

OF ALL THE ISSUES confronting the new president in 1953, none seemed more appropriately to call for the investment of his great moral capital than the historically vexed problem of racial equality. Nearly a hundred years after Ulysses Grant had conquered the slave power on the battlefield and helped direct the reconstruction of the South as president, black Americans were still not fully free. Most still dwelled in the eleven states of the former Confederacy. There they attended segregated schools, held the least desirable jobs, and were denied all political power. Only about 20 percent of eligible southern blacks were registered to vote in the election that brought Eisenhower to the White House.

Yet the low number of southern black voters represented a dramatic improvement over the situation just ten years earlier, when only about 5 percent of eligible blacks were registered to cast ballots. Thanks to the Supreme Court's 1944 decision in *Smith v. Allwright*, outlawing the restriction of Democratic Party membership to whites, and to the raised consciousness and rising militancy of returning black war veterans, the winds of change were beginning to sweep through the musty structure of race relations in the South. They gathered further force in 1954, when the Supreme Court declared in *Brown v. Board of Education of Topeka* that segregated schools were unconstitutional. But even then those winds were only beginning to stir. To become a real driving force or to avoid swelling to a destructive typhoon, wise leadership was needed.

For blacks and whites alike, the 1950s marked a moment when old patterns of thought and behavior started to swing loose from their traditional moorings, a moment when the culture's official values of equality and fairness were thrust abrasively against the base realities of discrimination and prejudice. Alternatives to segregation now opened up. As the philosopher Sidney Hook observed in his study of the hero in history, "insofar as alternatives of action are open, or even conceived to be open—a need will be felt for a hero to initiate, organize, and lead."

Psychological research has confirmed Hook's intuitive insight. In experiments studying schoolchildren in new situations, they were found to be more susceptible to guidance "during the period of initial ambiguity." The 1950s witnessed the first element of ambiguity in American race relations in nearly a century. It was an unusually opportune time for the effective exercise of leadership, a rare historical moment when the path lay open to what James MacGregor Burns has called "transforming leadership," leadership that "can exploit conflict and tension within persons' value structures" and lift them to higher levels of moral development.

Dwight Eisenhower, who had organized and led the Western Allies in the liberation of Europe from Nazism, was an authentic hero. Few figures could have been more fit to lead Americans out of their ancient enslavement to racism. To Eisenhower fell a unique opportunity to assert "transforming leadership." That he did not grasp it constitutes perhaps the greatest failure of his presidency. It also raises questions about the particular qualities of leadership that Eisenhower embodied.

To be sure, Eisenhower had little personal taste for this task. He had grown up in an all-white town and served out his military career in a segregated army. As supreme commander in Europe he had allowed black troops to volunteer for combat duty during the sharp crisis of the Battle of the Bulge in late 1944 but swiftly returned them to their all-black noncombat units when the crisis passed. He had advised against integrating the armed forces in testimony to the Senate Armed Services Committee in 1948. During his presidential campaign in 1952 he had criticized Democratic proposals for a permanent Fair Employment Practices Commission to curb job discrimination by the federal government and government contractors. All his life he had lived, without evident discomfort to his conscience, under the segregationist regime sanctioned by the Supreme Court's doctrine of separate but equal, enunciated in the notorious *Plessy v. Ferguson* decision of 1896.

Yet Eisenhower was no bigot. Though he shared many of the prejudices about African Americans common to his caste and generation, they were tempered by his authentic commitment to values of equality and fair play. He worked to end segregation in the District of Columbia and faithfully saw through to its completion President Truman's program to desegregate the armed forces. He also moved to stop discrimination in several federally operated facilities in Virginia and South Carolina and to integrate schools at southern military bases.

But those measures marked the limits of Eisenhower's disposition to alter the state of American race relations. When in 1953 South Carolina Governor James F. Byrnes expressed his fears about the impending Supreme Court decision that was to upset forever the separate but equal doctrine, Eisenhower reassured him that "improvement in race relations is one of those things that will be healthy and sound only if it starts locally. I do not believe that prejudices, even palpably unjustified prejudices, will succumb to compulsion."

Events soon dramatically tested the viability of the sentiment. On May 17, 1954, the U.S. Supreme Court handed down its epochal decision in the case of *Brown v. Board of Education of Topeka.* The justices unanimously concluded that separate school facilities were inherently unequal, hence unconstitutional. The following year the Court ordered integration of the nation's schools to proceed with "all deliberate speed." This was the very development that Byrnes and other white southerners had anticipated and dreaded. They reacted in ways reminiscent of the era before the Civil War. The Alabama senate passed a resolution of "nullification," and Virginia asserted its right "to interpose its sovereignty" against the Court's decision. Virtually the entire southern congressional contingent in 1956 signed a "Southern Manifesto" announcing their intention to resist the Court's order by all lawful means.

In the *Brown* decision the Court had sharply prodded the most conflict-laden issue in American life, the volatile truce between the black and white races as defined by the separate but equal formula in the *Plessy* case. Eisenhower accurately described the *Brown* decision as upsetting "the customs and convictions of at least two generations of Americans." To reform those mores in this uniquely malleable moment was the challenge now facing him. Regrettably, he refused to accept it. Indeed, on the eve of the Supreme Court's announcement, Eisenhower had spinelessly remarked to Attorney General Herbert Brownell that he hoped the justices "would defer it until the next Administration took over."

Even before the official announcement of the *Brown* decision, Eisenhower thus began to chart a course of avoiding the race issue, a course to which he held throughout the remainder of his presidency. Despite repeated pleas from civil rights leaders, he resolutely refused to declare his approval of the Supreme Court's ruling, claiming that "it makes no difference whether or not I endorse it" and that "if I should express, publicly, either approval or disapproval of a Supreme Court decision in one case, I would be obliged to do so in many, if not all, cases."

He similarly refused, again ignoring the supplications of his sole black aide, publicly to condemn the murder of Emmett Till, a fourteen-year-old black Chicagoan whose mutilated body was found in a Mississippi river after he had allegedly "wolf-whistled" at a white woman. Nor did he protest when the University of Alabama defied a federal court order and expelled a black student, Autherine Lucy, on racial grounds. When at last in 1956 Eisenhower endorsed the idea of a civil rights commission to investigate what he called "allegations" of discrimination in voter registration and employment, he did so, wrote his biographer Stephen Ambrose, in the hope "that such a commission would act as a buffer to keep the race issue out of partisan politics and reduce tension."

In the same vein, when Brownell finally persuaded him to endorse civil rights legislation in 1956, Eisenhower assured Senate Majority Leader Lyndon Johnson of Texas that the initiative represented "the mildest civil rights bill possible." The bill originally embraced four provisions, creating an independent civil rights commission, forming a civil rights division in the Department of Justice, establishing new safeguards for voting rights, and facilitating access to the courts for preventive relief in civil rights cases. But Eisenhower wavered in his support of the last two of these measures, stalling the legislation until nearly the end of 1957. Moreover, his support for the bill, never strenuous in any event, owed in large measure to his belief that if there must be federal pressure brought to bear in the civil rights area, it was greatly preferable to apply it to the formal issue of the franchise than to the far more troublesome matter of school integration.

The ultimate and unavoidable test of Eisenhower's leadership in the civil rights area came with the eruption at Little Rock's Central High School in September 1957. Arkansas Governor Orval Faubus ringed the school with national guardsmen to prevent several black students from matriculating. In a typically conciliatory gesture, Eisenhower received Faubus at the presidential vacation retreat in Newport, Rhode Island, and accepted the governor's assurances that he would direct the Guard to cease preventing the black students from entering the school. When Faubus then failed to change the Guard's orders and rioting broke out, Eisenhower sent in one thousand paratroopers from the 101st Airborne Division to maintain order. He also cut short his vacation to return to Washington for a nationally televised address to the nation on the events in Little Rock.

Yet even in the face of this crisis, the president offered no judgment on the question of integration itself. Instead, he justified his actions as mandated by his duty to maintain order and respect for the directives of the federal courts. "My biggest problem," he wrote to a friend, "has been to make people see . . . that my main interest is not in the integration or segregation question. My opinion as to the wisdom or timeliness of the Supreme Court's decision has nothing to do with the case. . . ." Later, reflecting on the episode in his memoirs, he carefully cited legal and historical precedent for his armed intervention but still offered no opinion on the substantive issue of integration and, beyond it, the whole knotted topic of racial justice that had provoked the incident in the first place.

Eisenhower, in short, took a narrowly proceduralist approach to the subject of civil rights. He exerted himself minimally and repeatedly forswore opportunities to use his vast personal influence—what Dewey had called his enormous "asset" of possessing "the affection or respect of our citizenry"—on behalf of equality for African Americans. Even Stephen Ambrose, his usually sympathetic biographer, sadly concluded that "on one of the great moral issues of the day, the struggle to eliminate racial segregation from American life, he provided almost no leadership at all. His failure to speak out, to indicate personal approval of *Brown v. Topeka*, did incalculable harm to the civil-rights crusade and to America's image."

HOW TO EXPLAIN the striking contrast between Eisenhower's sweepingly successful leadership of the Allied cause in Europe during World War II and his disappointing failure to provide leadership to the cause of civil rights as president? His personal sentiments about race relations no doubt restrained him in part, but they seem insufficiently formed and too weakly held to constitute a full explanation. James David Barber accounts for what he sees as war hero Eisenhower's mostly lackluster presidential performance by noting the inherently different contexts in which military and political authority are exercised. "In the invasion of Europe," Barber wrote, "Eisenhower's brand of coordination went forward in a context of definite authority. . . . In an Army at war, coordination takes places behind the advancing flag: the overriding purposes are not in question. In the political 'order' the national purpose is continually questioned, continually redefined as part of the game."

This important distinction compels a further question: Exactly what attributes of leadership served Eisenhower so well in the one situation and so badly in the other? As psychologists Dorwin Cartwright and Alvin Zander put it, "the skills possessed by a designated leader or the holder of an office may make him well-qualified to perform important group functions under certain conditions and poorly qualified under others. . . . The specific requirements of the group's tasks demand that members possess certain skills in order to serve the appropriate functions. If the task changes, different behaviors are required, and the same person may or may not be able to perform in the new way."

Here it is important to introduce a further distinction between those leadership skills that are conducive to the definition and achievement of a specific goal, on the one hand, and those that contribute to the maintenance of a group's sense of its own integrity, shared identity, and common purpose, on the other. This distinction has been described as differentiating task-oriented and process-oriented leadership attributes. The identification of these discrete components of leadership has been empirically documented in laboratory studies of group behavior by psychologists Robert F. Bales and Philip E. Slater.

Bales and Slater gave each of several experimental groups, all composed of male Harvard undergraduates, an "administrative problem" whose resolution required a "group decision." After each group meeting, individual members were asked to name the member who had contributed the best ideas, the member who had done the most to guide the discussion and keep it moving, and the member they had liked best. At the conclusion of the fourth and final meeting, individuals were asked:

"[W]hich member of the group would you say stood out most definitely as a leader in the discussion?"

A striking result of this experiment was the consistency with which the subjects differentiated the roles of task specialist and socioemotional specialist (or process specialist). The task specialist typically took the initiative in conversation, defined the nature of the objective, and kept the discussion focused on the requirements of the task. His success might be measured by the extent to which he devised a viable plan of action and elicited sufficient agreement (not necessarily unanimity) within the group to realize that plan. The socioemotional specialist typically listened and responded more to others, endorsed their suggestions, encouraged their participation, and sometimes relieved tension with jokes. He was usually better liked than the task specialist. His success might be gauged as a function of the group's ability to maintain a sense of corporate identity and purpose. Virtually all groups expressed these distinct functions, and significantly, they were nearly always performed by different individuals.

Bales and Slater also gave all their subjects a test of personality characteristics known as the California F-scale, which measures attitudes of rigidity and absolutism associated with the characterological structure that T. W. Adorno described as "the authoritarian personality." Among the items about which the test inquired was the degree to which each subject liked or disliked his peers. Not surprisingly, perhaps, the men identified as "best liked" in the various groups were those who made the fewest distinctions about whom they themselves liked. They said, in effect, "I like everyone." But that lack of differentiation correlated significantly with a high F-score, indicating "a certain rigidity in the attitudes of many best liked men toward interpersonal relationships. They may 'have to be liked' and may achieve prominence in this respect because of the ingratiating skills they have acquired during their lives in bringing this desired situation about. Their avoidance of differentiation in ratings may be an expression of the compulsive and indiscriminate nature of this striving."

By contrast, the person who emerged in the various groups as the task specialist was rarely the best liked and, in turn, made more distinctions of his own about those whom he liked. This evinced his ability "to be able to face a certain amount of negative feeling toward him without abandoning his role." Some negative feeling toward the task specialist, Bales and Slater concluded, was inherent in the very nature of his role:

> The task specialist tends to arouse a certain amount of hostility because . . . his suggestions constitute proposed new elements to be added to the common culture, to which all members will be committed if they agree. Whatever readjustments the members have to make in order to feel themselves committed will tend to produce minor frustrations, anxieties, and hostilities. . . . Unfortunately, the very person who symbolizes the demands of the task, and presses for the extension of the common culture in a previously uncharted direction, is in a sense a deviant—a representative of something that is to some degree foreign and disturbing to the existing culture and set of attachments.

THESE TYPOLOGIES CAN contribute to an understanding of the particular leadership qualities of Dwight Eisenhower. He was at his best when the goal was defined for him, at least in broad outline, as in his assignment to win the war in Europe. In that context he could assume at least a rough measure of agreement among his followers on the objective to be achieved. His job was to orchestrate the energies of his subordinates, sustain their sense of shared and realizable purpose, and extract from each of them maximum contributions to the common effort. As Bales and Slater's results suggest, those functions are necessary to the effective operation of any group, and Eisenhower's brilliant provision of them as supreme Allied commander evidenced a commendable capacity for leadership on that crucial dimension.

But on the dimension that required the definition of a goal and the ability to face sometimes ferocious hostility among followers in the effort to accomplish it, Eisenhower proved woefully deficient. His deficiencies derived from deeper causes than differences between the military and political realms. They stemmed from the limitations of his own character.

Some of those limitations were evident even during Eisenhower's ultimately triumphal performance as supreme commander in Europe. Many of his wartime associates criticized his indecisiveness when caught, as the military historian B. H. Liddell Hart put it, "in the uncomfortable position of being the rope in a tug of war between his chief executives." The most notable example of this paralysis of leadership occurred during the drive to the German frontier following the breakout from the Normandy beachheads in late 1944. At this moment in a rapidly unfolding battle of pursuit, Eisenhower, as the commander in the field, probably had more strategic discretion than at any other moment in the war, and his immediate subordinates noisily tried to push him in different directions.

British Field Marshal Bernard Montgomery pleaded with Eisenhower for sufficient fuel and munitions to strike swiftly parallel to the Channel and North Sea coasts to Berlin. The American generals, Omar Bradley and George Patton, urged that those same resources be put at their disposal to support a massive, broad frontal push into the German industrial heartland of the Ruhr. Eisenhower ultimately settled on the broad frontal strategy, but only after weeks of hesitancy and futile efforts at compromise. Patton angrily claimed that Eisenhower had put harmony before strategy, and he called the resultant delay "the most momentous error of the war." Bradley later commented that though Eisenhower "was a political general of rare and valuable gifts . . . he did not know how to manage a battlefield." Montgomery echoed this sentiment when he said that Eisenhower "knew nothing about how to fight a battle." Alan Brooke, chairman of the British chiefs of staff, concurred: Eisenhower was "a past-master in the handling of allies, entirely impartial and consequently trusted by all. A charming personality and great co-ordinator. But no real commander."

Eisenhower, in short, was by both inclination and experience a superb process specialist, expert at orchestrating the efforts of his colleagues. He was considerably less gifted as a task specialist, whose function was to give decisive definition to a goal and to absorb the hostility that resulted from necessarily divisive choices. He naturally fastened on the requirements of group harmony as his premier objective and indeed frequently defined the essence of leadership in terms that excluded all else.

During the war he had advised Mountbatten, first and foremost, to cultivate "mutual respect and confidence among the group of seniors making up the allied command." Nearly twenty years later Eisenhower elaborated on his conception of the leader's role in a letter to New York Governor Nelson Rockefeller. Touching on the relation of moral principles to leadership, he wrote: "In almost every field of thought and action, humans seem to distribute themselves almost according to a natural law, from one extreme to the other. . . . [W]hat might be called the compatible group is about two-thirds of the aggregate." The dictates of moral principle might cast issues in black and white, he continued, but "the task of the political leader is to devise plans along which humans can make constructive progress. This means that the plan or program itself tends to fall in the 'gray' category. This is not because there is any challenge to the principle or to the moral truth, but because human nature is itself far from perfect."

That frank rumination vividly illustrated Eisenhower's temperamental commitment to moderation. It also conspicuously demonstrated his belief that the power to lead was exclusively confined to people already compatible. Here in its amplest form was the mentality of the process specialist, devoted above all to group maintenance.

Like Bales and Slater's process specialists, Eisenhower showed a deep need to be liked. Whether in the privacy of his diary or the pages of his published memoirs, his descriptions of other individuals typically open or close with a statement of his warm regard for the person in question. "A leader's job," he told a friend in 1954, "is to get others to go along with him in the promotion of something. To do this he needs their goodwill." But as Thomas Dewey had warned him, taking positive stands on issues—especially an issue as volatile as race relations—would rapidly deplete that stock of goodwill. Here perhaps, at a deep level of personality and character, lay the explanation for Eisenhower's failure to expend the enormous goodwill he enjoyed on behalf of civil rights. Simply possessing goodwill was far more important to him than actually using it for political purposes. The public affection that Dewey correctly labeled Eisenhower's greatest asset was, in the last analysis, not a means for the achievement of particular goals, but for Eisenhower an end in itself. He is unimaginable in the posture of Franklin Roosevelt in 1936, acknowledging that his opponents were "unanimous in their hatred for me, and I welcome their hatred!" Indeed Eisenhower's principal criticism of the Democrats under Roosevelt and Truman was that they had fostered class conflict in American society.

This was not a temperament well suited to dealing with the unavoidably conflictual issue of civil rights. When it came to race relations, there was no naturally "compatible group" that needed simply to be orchestrated in pursuit of a consensual goal. There was instead the historic hostility of two races, reconcilable only by the exercise of "transforming leadership," able to embrace conflict and exploit it creatively. That sort of leadership Dwight Eisenhower was characterologically incapable of providing.

"[T]here are different ways to try to be a leader," Eisenhower acknowledged at the beginning of his presidency, when many people were urging him to assume an assertive role. "I simply must be permitted to follow my own methods, because to adopt someone else's would be so unnatural as to create the conviction that I was acting falsely." His own methods remained those that had served him so well as supreme commander: "fair, decent, and reasonable dealing with men"; avoiding "the false but prevalent notion that bullying and leadership are synonymous"; and "the use of methods calculated to attract cooperation." At the end of his presidency he summed up: "In war and peace, I've had no respect for the desk-pounder, and have despised the loud and slick talker. If my own ideas and practices in this matter have sprung from weakness, I do not know. But they were and are deliberate or, rather, natural to me. They are not accidental."

Eisenhower's ideas and practices with respect to leadership were remarkably consistent over his career. They suited him admirably in war, when he need not define the goal to be accomplished and could take as essentially given a disposition to cooperate on the part of the people he was called upon to lead. But when it fell to him as president to define the very agenda of American life, especially in the contentious arena of civil rights, he could not do it. Specifying a task of such magnitude and facing the hostility that its designation and pursuit entailed were simply beyond him.

Paradoxically, the man who had distinguished himself in history's greatest military conflict harbored a deep characterological aversion to conflict among his military colleagues as well as in the civil society over which he eventually presided. Ironically, the very skills of process leadership that gained Eisenhower such immense popularity and thus uniquely positioned him to transform his countrymen's values on the race question evidenced a personality incapable of embracing the necessarily divisive role that civil rights leadership required.

These were Eisenhower's personal strengths and weaknesses as a leader, but they perhaps also reflected values deeply rooted in the very culture that had nurtured him. "Eisenhower's beliefs, and his expression of them," concluded Ambrose, "were those of Main Street." The famed British philosopher and historian Isaiah Berlin said of Eisenhower at the end of the war that the American public had the "conviction that he symbolizes something essentially American." That essential something perhaps included the need for social comity and tranquillity, even at the expense of social justice. That need may have been especially acute in the 1950s, after two decades of depression and war. In that limited sense and without blinking at the price of justice delayed for African Americans, Eisenhower as warrior and as president may indeed have been an American for all seasons.

CIAL

THE IMPLAUSIBLE WENDELL WILLKIE

Leadership Ahead of Its Time

David Levering Lewis

IN A RATHER UNSETTLING INTRODUCTION TO HIS *AMERICAN POLITICAL Tradition and the Men Who Made It*, historian Richard Hofstadter found the national belief system sorely in need of renewal a mere three prosperous years after the end of the Second World War. "A new conception of the world" was needed, he wrote in 1948, one that replaced "the ideology of self-help, free enterprise, competition, and beneficent cupidity upon which Americans have been nourished since the foundation of the Republic." Hofstadter saw the once grand but now expended paradigm of American exceptionalism undergoing replacement by a leadership model based merely on personal appeal. From Franklin Roosevelt's unconsummated New Deal had come a stillborn American liberalism that was, he lamented, "rudderless and demoralized."

Wendell Lewis Willkie, the Republican candidate against Roosevelt in 1940, died four years before the appearance of Hofstadter's book, and many of its informed readers must have thought that he had anticipated the author's summons to a progressive "new conception of the world." *One World*, the visionary credo that Willkie wrote with his companion Irita Van Doren, literary book editor of the *New York Herald Tribune*, had sold two million copies by the end of 1943, its first year. "No book in the history of book publishing has been bought by so many people so quickly," Simon & Schuster's press release boasted.

The extraordinary impact of *One World* in its many translations once seemed potent enough to instigate an international movement for the betterment of the world's peoples. John Gunther, the renowned global investigator, praised Willkie as "one of the most . . . forward-looking Americans of this—or any—time." This great bear of a lawyer from Elwood, Indiana, presided over the country's largest utility holding company at age forty, wrenched a fabulous monetary settlement from the Tennessee Valley Authority (TVA) after a six-year judicial slugfest, and sauntered away from a crushing repudiation of a second presidential run in the 1944 Wisconsin primary, after which there is credible evidence of secret discussions with FDR for a realignment of the frequently dysfunctional two-party system. Had he taken better care of himself and curtailed the consumption of scotch, Willkie would almost certainly have continued to exercise a significant role in the unfolding drama of postwar politics in America. If he had lived five or so more years, there would have been many more pages in the history books, perhaps a page relating one of the most intriguing and possibly productive collaborations in the history of twentieth-century American civil rights. Dead, in his prime, at fifty-two, Willkie quickly dwindled in prominence from a notable profile in Irving Stone's contemporaneous *They Also Ran* to that of a once significant public figure for whom no neat category is readily found.

Willkie was a dynamic work in progress and a principled egoist who seldom allowed categories to stand in his way. His well-publicized conflict with New Deal economic policies elicited plaudits from big business, yet his conception of responsible markets was more compatible with John Maynard Keynes's than with Adam Smith's. His farm boy haircut, hayseed manners, and sartorial indifference bespoke common man straightforwardness—"grass-roots stuff," said a wary FDR. But this businessman turned politician possessed a supple intellect, a remarkable fund of knowledge, and a concealed disdain for parochial ideas. Indeed he was constantly to surprise many admirers and bitterly disappoint more than a few intimates who mistook Willkie's small-town Hoosier origins and big business success as the sum of the inner man.

Willkie's maternal and paternal grandparents migrated to the United States in 1861 after their radical politics had brought unwelcome scrutiny from the Prussian authorities. His Indiana parents, Herman and

Henrietta, were conspicuous reformers. Herman Willkie refused the customary free pass available to lawyers from the railroad companies. He took up the cause of local striking iron and steel workers for a nominal compensation after the price of the great Clarence Darrow's services had left them without legal representation. He organized Elwood's public school system, raised money for the local library, and became a principal player in Madison County Democratic politics. Son Wendell never forgot the evening his first political hero, William Jennings Bryan, was a guest in the family's new three-story house on Elwood's fashionable north side.

Henrietta, the first woman admitted to the Indiana bar, was also the first to smoke in public. She practiced law as Herman's full partner and presided as sovereign in matters familial. Herman supplied the overt affection in the household. Henrietta gave the marching orders. Both parents agreed that rambunctious Wendell needed the stiffening of a summer stint at Culver Military Academy after his junior year in high school. It was Henrietta who decided that Wendell should settle down elsewhere after college rather than in comfortable, provincial Elwood.

Willkie's German American family values stood him in good stead at Indiana University. He distinguished himself by superior grades and enhanced the undergraduate curriculum after convincing the dean that he could find ten students to sign up for a course on socialist theory. He made a display of his familiarity with *Das Kapital* and John Spargo's primer, *Socialism.* Later his apt characterization of those undergraduate years was that any man "who is not something of a socialist before he is forty has no heart," then concluded that "any man who still is, has no head."

He graduated from Indiana at twenty-one, a popular leader of the class of 1913 in no hurry to enter law school. Instead, Willkie tried teaching high school and coaching basketball and track for a year in the Kansas border town of Coffeyville. He was good at both. His classroom dramatics left an indelible memory of the battle of the Marne with a former student who described the impact years afterward in a fan letter. The lure of adventure and a higher salary as a laboratory chemist in Puerto Rico the next year exposed the Hoosier to his most different cultural experience. Herman Willkie's son reacted in true family tradition to the abject poverty and harsh exploitation. Appalled by the seeming indifference with which some American associates listened to his concerns, Willkie headed for home and law school at Bloomington in the fall of 1915. The Puerto Rican experience stayed with him a lifetime, he told close friends: an un-American example of the kinds of unnecessary and corrigible wrongs that he resolved to help put right at the first opportunity. Up to that point it appears that Willkie's contact with African Americans had been virtually nonexistent. Two years of law school in no way inhibited a penchant for crusading. The prizes for oratory, moot court, and thesis preparation that came Willkie's way afforded him a graduation bully pulpit from which to preach institutional overhaul not only of the state's premier law school but of the state's lax regulations of banks and businesses along with the Indiana constitution. The Elwood Jacobin's diploma was withheld two days until trustees, legislators, and eminent jurists were finally placated by the dean's extraction of a formal apology.

Willkie's 1917 law school graduation controversy revealed a susceptibility to principled pugnacity. Officer Candidates School several months later exposed another signature proclivity, a freewheeling audacity that put Second Lieutenant Willkie in a balloon from which he parachuted unrehearsed and on a dare from fifteen hundred feet. Edith Wilk, Elwood's slim, shy new public librarian and brand-new Mrs. Willkie, would have been better off as a widow, in the opinion of her new officer husband, than as the spouse of a coward. In the event, Willkie's courage under fire was never tested. His artillery unit disembarked at Le Havre in mid-September 1918, too late in the war to see action against the Germans. Promoted to captain on the eve of demobilization, he returned to Elwood where Madison County family and law school connections opened doors to a position as legal chief of the personnel division of the Firestone Tire and Rubber Company in Akron, Ohio. Captain Willkie (he favored his army title) reentered civilian life ready to enroll in the great peacetime battle for Woodrow Wilson's League of Nations. Willkie's conviction that the Great War must be atoned for by a peace of the just in which the United States participated as principal guarantor remained powerful enough that he claimed it "almost reaches the point of religious conviction." The Firestone company's formidable trial lawyer also established himself as one of the city's leading Democrats, provoking Harvey Firestone's caustic remark that Willkie would never "amount to much" because of his party affiliation.

In 1929 the ailing tycoon Bernard Capen Cobb, founder and president of the Commonwealth & Southern Corporation, reeled Willkie into New York from the provinces to apply his well-reputed organizational skills on behalf of the nation's largest utility holding company. The stock market crashed just as Willkie installed himself in a Fifth Avenue apartment. His savings vanished along with those of hundreds of thousands of middle-class citizens in the rolling bankruptcies of traction combines and electrical monopolies built on watered stock.

When Cobb retired in early 1933, Willkie became the youngest president of the largest utility corporation. Two months later Franklin Roosevelt took office as president and assured the American people that they had nothing to fear but fear itself. Among his first acts was the creation of the Tennessee Valley Authority (TVA). A favorite Chamber of Commerce boast of Willkie's ran that although he and FDR had taken office at the same time, "only my company is running at a profit while his company is running at a loss." In reality, Commonwealth & Southern's stock had fallen from twenty-two dollars to less than two dollars a share since the 1929 crash. The TVA was an extraordinary intervention into the private utilities market, a public entity financed by the federal government to supply cheap electricity throughout seven southern states drained by the Tennessee River. Constructed on an Ozymandian scale, the authority's dams and hydroelectric power stations were to irrigate and light up the South, lifting the region from preindustrial socioeconomic stasis into rough parity with the rest of the nation.

The TVA signaled imminent death by reduced electricity rates for Commonwealth & Southern's Tennessee, Mississippi, and Alabama operations. Willkie's characteristic response combined pugnacity with imagination. Tall, efficient David Lilienthal, who became known as Mr. TVA, reported, some years after their first meeting at the Century Club, in New York, of leaving "somewhat overwhelmed" by Willkie's "cocksuredness." To show what efficient private enterprise could do, even faced with the resources of a government Leviathan, Willkie devised an ingenious "objective rate" for electricity consumption (lower rates tied to increased use) that reduced his corporation's rates 27 percent under the industry average. He hired five hundred salesmen to pitch new electrical appliances purchasable on credit, with a quadrupling of sales. New power lines were strung into remote towns and settlements whose astonished denizens gratefully signed up with C&S ahead of the cheaper service offered by the advancing TVA grid. The authority was bedeviled by mysterious severings of numerous power lines. At the end of the year Willkie and Lilienthal crafted a compromise. Commonwealth & Southern agreed to sell its Mississippi, Alabama, and Tennessee properties to the TVA; the TVA agreed not to compete with Willkie's company in other locations.

Up to that point, relations between the utility holding company and the government remained civil. The Oval Office meeting between FDR and Willkie one week before Christmas 1934 was marked by superficial jollity as the two outsize egos jousted. "[Mr. Willkie,] I am one of your customers," the president bantered. "We give you good service, don't we?" the Commonwealth & Southern chief needled, as he cast the TVA's ultimate elimination of market competition in energy as an overreach of federal power. When it was revealed that the attorney for the stockholders contesting the TVA–Commonwealth & Southern compromise agreement had received a fifty-thousand-dollar retainer from a fictitious Edison Electric Institute set up by Willkie, the White House took full measure of its adversary. FDR called for the "abolition of the evil of holding companies" in his January 1935 State of the Union address. Three weeks later a tight-lipped Willkie left his second Oval Office conference with a virtual company death sentence rendered. "It is futile," FDR declared unambiguously when Willkie demanded to know whether it was possible to resist "any further efforts to avoid the breaking up of utility holding companies."

FDR's 1935 Public Utility Holding Company Bill and Secretary Harold Ickes's Interior Department proposed to make the New Deal world uninhabitable for the likes of Commonwealth & Southern executives. The utility holding company bill containing a so-called death sentence (forced liquidation within three years) passed the Senate by a single vote.

While the House prepared to debate the administration's holding company legislation that summer, Willkie mobilized the full resources of the private utilities industry for a life-and-death counterattack.

Willkie lived on Fifth Avenue and worked a block from Wall Street, but his Hoosier ways, the flat vowels, the loping gait, the brown shock of hair over the right temple, and the self-effacing bonhomie made him studio-cast as an ingenuous opponent in an uneven combat, the David of his industry, a role none of his peers could have filled as resourcefully—and as attractively. "It was an asset to my business to look like an Indiana farmer," he confided to associates. Harold Ickes claimed to see right through the pose and called Willkie "a simple, barefoot Wall Street lawyer." Willkie counted on the public's being more gullible, however, and it soon became clear that people found some justice in Willkie's protest against unfair government competition and bureaucratic intransigence. Hadn't his industry made a good-faith offer of selective rural divestiture in exchange for retention of key urban markets? Willkie's testimony before the sympathetic House Military Affairs Committee bolstered his cause on Capitol Hill.

The fight threatened to undermine the New Deal's mandate in the 1936 election. Upgrading the stakes, Willkie conceded that big business had been the problem before the New Deal, but he contended that now a new threat of domination had arisen. "Power is just as destructive on Pennsylvania Avenue as it is on Wall Street," he warned in written speeches and country club talks. Hard-boiled Sam Rayburn, still a few years away from becoming Speaker of the House, told FDR that Willkie's was the "richest and most ruthless lobby congress has ever known." Republican-owned newspapers and magazines spoke of executive highhandedness and carried well-crafted underdog ads from bogus citizens' groups and organizations financed by the utilities cartel. "Subsidized government competition established in one industry threatens all industry" was one of the messages they used. Eight hundred thousand telegrams and letters called on the House of Representatives to vote down the public utilities holding bill, which it partly did that July by attenuating the death sentence by a seventy-vote margin.

Willkie's public relations campaign helped spare utility holding companies from immediate congressional dissolution, but they were now regulated under the 1935 Public Utility Holding Company Act and allowed to operate only in a single state or required to divest multiple utilities ownership in order to operate as regionally integrated systems. Willkie regarded the reprieve from death provided by the act to be tantamount to a life sentence in prison. "While a strait-jacket will keep a man out of trouble," he wisecracked, "it is not a suitable garment in which to work."

Willkie still considered himself a good Democrat. He was a member of Tammany Hall, New York City's Democratic patronage trough, having been elected the previous year to membership in the same class with James Farley and Bernard Baruch. But he believed that the nation had experienced more than enough of Franklin Roosevelt's paternalism. New Deal policies had rescued the country from economic collapse and political crisis, but Willkie warned of cures that might become worse than the malady. He kept rhetorical company with another alienated Democrat, who had expressed similar fears at the beginning of the year. Al Smith skewered FDR's creeping socialism in an American Liberty League keynote speech in Washington. Willkie's message on NBC and CBS radio networks and from country club to business forum in the months before the November election reiterated that "the abuses that corrupted the 1920's have been transferred from Wall Street to Washington." Millions of Americans saw a rumpled-suited, tousled-haired Willkie for the first time in Henry Luce's new *March of Time* movie series, a twenty-minute feature on the TVA. *The March of Time* appearance marked Willkie's debut as a favorite of the *Time, Life, Fortune* empire.

Willkie was one of the first attractive public figures during the early New Deal to assimilate traditional critiques of government power, streamline them, and package them in Hoosier homilies that have since become conservative boilerplate. His evolving prescience about the dangers of big government served him poorly, nevertheless, in the political reality of the moment. He voted in 1936 for Republican Alf Landon, the governor of Kansas, who lost to Roosevelt in a crushing landslide.

After the election the TVA's David Lilienthal made Willkie's Commonwealth & Southern a fifty-five-million-dollar settlement offer. Most corporation heads would have readily accepted. Instead, Willkie raised the stakes with a ninety-five-million-dollar counterproposal, and he authorized the Alabama Power Company to sue the Interior Department for negotiating contracts with towns served by Commonwealth affiliates. Willkie promised his stockholders he would fight big government until it either conceded the right of utility holding companies to compete in a fair market or agreed to indemnify them satisfactorily. He had to fight several more years before he achieved what he considered to be an equitable settlement.

Willkie's apotheosis as the straight-shooting cracker-barrel loner ready to face down FDR and his phalanx of brain trusters and technocrats truly began during the early months of the second New Deal. A large, celebratory Willkie feature, replete with handsome color photos, appeared in the May 1937 issue of *Fortune* magazine. Willkie's dedication to private ownership merited praise for its uniqueness, said the magazine. "He knows all the arguments. They are persuasive . . . not because they are new, but because he frames them intelligently, and hence he makes them sound new." America's *Town Meeting of the Air*, the popular weekly radio broadcast forum, hosted a debate between Willkie and Robert H. Jackson, head of the Justice Department's Antitrust Division. Three million citizens heard Willkie trounce one of FDR's favorite officials in a bravura performance. The source of their dispute was obvious, Willkie explained to the federal enforcer: "Government officials and business men fail to understand each other . . . because one thinks and speaks the language of politics and emotionalism, while the other thinks and speaks the language of economics and realism."

The political climate became less congenial to the New Deal after the 1938 off-year elections. Roosevelt had pledged to "purge the obstructionists" from his party in a defiant June fireside chat, but these southern Democrats were returned in full force, and they were joined in their opposition to the New Deal by eighty-one newly elected Republicans in the House and eight in the Senate. Negotiations between the TVA and Willkie's company resumed, and they concluded in February 1939 with Willkie's winning close to the price he had been demanding.

The final act was staged with flair before newsreel cameras in the offices of the First National Bank at 2 Wall Street. Lilienthal looked like the dutiful, overworked federal official that he was as he handed the Commonwealth & Southern president a blowup of a check for $78.6 million, roughly equivalent in 2010 to $1.3 billion. Willkie hammed the scene with the practiced lack of sophistication of a lucky hayseed. "Thanks, Dave," he drawled. "That's a lot of money for a couple of old Indiana boys to be handling." Already acclaimed in the February issue of the *Saturday Evening Post* as "The Man Who Talked Back," the Hoosier wonder continued speaking out to a rapidly widening audience as writing and talking invitations poured in. In a *Saturday Evening Post* article, "Idle Men, Idle Money," Willkie summed up what he charged was most inexcusable about the New Deal economic policy. Banks were holding four billion uninvested dollars, he wrote. "Can we cause our great reservoir of free capital to flow into the channels of industry? If we can, our democratic system will be preserved. If we cannot, then our democracy will vanish in the chaos of national bankruptcy."

In that same month the June *Atlantic Monthly* carried the high-decibel "BRACE UP, AMERICA," Willkie's evocation of the people's rugged individualist roots and a call for repeal of New Deal paternalism. In Washington, later in the week, he spoke emphatically of the "New Fear"—no longer FDR's "fear itself" but the legitimate fear of government. Little wonder that General Hugh S. Johnson, FDR's alienated former NRA administrator, speculated in his syndicated column that the utility executive would make a formidable Republican presidential candidate. Asked for his reaction, Willkie served the reporter a thigh-slapping quote. "If the government keeps on taking my business away," he chortled, "I'll soon be out of work and looking for a job. Johnson's offer is the best I've had." Henry Luce was inclined to think Johnson's was the best offer for both Willkie and the country. *Time* placed a handsome, slightly jowlish Wendell Willkie on its July 31, 1939, cover. "The New Deal is going to be on trial again," Willkie opined. If Roosevelt decided to try a third term, the two of them might have "a great discussion."

David Lawrence, the powerful syndicated conservative columnist and Washington insider, identified Willkie as precisely the kind of presidential candidate that "nine out of ten Republicans really want but do not venture to ask for." The authoritative Arthur Krock of the *New York*

Times concurred. Willkie was not quite ready to believe that life after Commonwealth & Southern could lead to the Republican candidacy for the presidency of the United States. "Really, from my standpoint, it cannot constitute more than a joke," he wrote to a friend. How could the American people "even consider the election of a utility executive with an office in the precincts of Wall Street for constable, not alone president?"

Yet he kept company with new admirers who encouraged him to believe that the Republican Party and the nation urgently needed his leadership. One such admirer was the literary book editor of the *Herald Tribune*, Irita Bradford Van Doren, a brainy Alabama belle who had abandoned her Columbia Ph.D. studies to marry fellow graduate student and literary golden boy Carl Van Doren. Sophisticated women found Willkie immensely appealing, if bumptious. "Actually, he has the well-organized balkiness of a healthy bear, and singularly brilliant eyes" was a typical Rebecca West assessment. Willkie met Irita Van Doren sometime in 1937, two years after her divorce. Almost instantly she became his great passion. William Shirer, the correspondent whose knowledge of the Third Reich was unsurpassed, described Irita as "not pretty, but she was beautiful." FDR, who made certain to learn about Willkie's personal affairs, described her as an "awful nice gal, writes for the magazine and so forth and so on."

It was an open secret that Wendell spent more time with Irita than with wife Edith. She was her lover's passport to a circle of sophisticated types who gave smart dinners and frequented the Algonquin Hotel. A friend of Irita's, the novelist and biographer Marcia Davenport, described Irita's effect on Willkie. "Before they met, he was just a big businessman," she decided. From her he learned pronunciation, new terms, literary style. "She brought him into a world where his intellect was stimulated." Those surprisingly polished, thoughtful contributions in the *Atlantic Monthly* and the *Saturday Review of Literature* were Van Doren's work. She helped him write better and think out his ideas.

Van Doren found herself sharing Willkie's mind with the managing editor of *Fortune*, Russell Davenport. Son of a Bethlehem Steel vice president, Yale Skull and Bones, awarded the Croix de Guerre for service with the AEF, and a major figure in Henry Luce's empire, Davenport was a man of vaulting intellectual pretensions, a published poet, and the prospective author of a large book on American politics. Willkie was a guest at the *Fortune* Round Table run by Davenport. He "took the whole group by storm," Davenport expostulated, "put into words that day the things I've been thinking for years." As of that day he committed himself to Willkie's political future as he raced home to tell his wife he'd met the man "who ought to be the next President of the United States. . . . It's spontaneous. You see him and you know it."

Davenport and his wife entertained Willkie in August 1939 at their country place in Saugatuck Harbor, Connecticut. That weekend became part of the conspiracy lore surrounding Willkie's political career. The historian Harry Elmer Barnes told colleagues that Ogden Mills Reid, publisher of the *Herald Tribune*, and Thomas Lamont, head of J. P. Morgan, engineered Willkie's meteoric rise shortly after the Davenport weekend. The whorl of strategic dinner parties at the Davenports' fashionable Manhattan East Side apartment that summer and into early fall and the marshaling of writing talent and expert opinion behind his public statements added credence to claims of a collaborative manufacture of Wendell Willkie. After Willkie and Luce met face-to-face at the Davenports', the publisher decided that his initial confidence had been well placed. Henceforth Willkie had behind him the full resources of *Time*, *Life*, and *Fortune*.

The grounds for optimism among some members of the eastern establishment seemed well founded as the 1940 national elections approached. FDR declined to say whether or not he would seek an unprecedented third term. There was feral hostility from the business community to the "traitor to his class" in the White House, widespread disenchantment in the middle classes to taxes and presidential intimidation of the courts, and deep disaffection on the left with the administration's recourse to conservative economics. The disastrous spike to 18.9 percent in unemployment caused by the 1937 budget-balancing policy had started downward with the resumption of deficit spending, but 15 percent of the national workforce was still unemployed. A Memorial Day march of steelworkers and sympathizers was bloodily crushed by the Chicago police. And as war clouds formed over Europe, the GOP leadership and most of the party regulars geared up for a fight to enforce the letter of the just enacted Neutrality Act.

Willkie's dedicated cabal helped him prepare a call to action in the April 1940 issue of *Fortune.* His essay bore the portentous title "We the People: A Foundation for a Political Recovery." It spoke powerfully to liberal Republicans and disaffected Democrats, to business interests and conservative midwestern farmers, as well as to a fair number of the putative "Sixty Families"—reviled by FDR as plutocratic parasites—that were ready to risk supporting an unknown against the confiscatory terrors of a third New Deal. "You have separated 'business' and 'industry' from the ordinary lives of the people and have applied against them a philosophy of hate and mistrust," Willkie wrote. "Therefore, abandon this attitude of hate and set our enterprises free." The essay promised a New Deal devoid of class animus and faithful to the Great Depression reforms, a new New Deal with its budgets balanced (gradually) and bureaucratic waste and duplication eliminated. *Reader's Digest* reprinted the full text of Willkie's essay.

Three weeks after his *Fortune* essay, on May 11, 1940, Willkie pitched himself to five hundred GOP regulars for the first time in Des Moines. He was all for FRD's budget for American military readiness. "We double-damn Hitler," he thumped with coat removed, "but what about the $60 billion you've spent and the ten million persons who are still unemployed?" *Life* featured an eleven-page Willkie profile, which called him "by far the ablest man the Republicans could nominate." Until *Life*'s pronouncement, only the *New York Sun* had noted that Willkie had switched his party registration from Democrat to Republican.

Ten days later the Wehrmacht surrounded retreating British and French forces at Dunkirk. The "blood, toil, tears, and sweat" speech of Britain's new prime minister to the House of Commons stirred men and women on both sides of the Atlantic. Americans were deeply divided, however, about involvement in the war. The Republican leadership, overwhelmingly isolationist, spoke for the party's majority in favoring strict nonintervention. Thomas Dewey, Manhattan's thirty-eight-year-old crime-busting district attorney, firmly opposed intervention. The Gallup poll accorded Dewey a 67 percent lead in May over his main rivals for the Republican nomination, Ohio's Senator Robert Taft and Michigan's Senator Arthur Vandenberg.

Willkie came to Washington on June 12 to speak to the National Press Club. Indiana Congressman Charles Halleck, serving his second congressional term, was there to hear him. Willkie spoke quickly to Halleck and gained his agreement before addressing the audience. "Gentlemen, this is on the record," Willkie announced from the podium. "I'm going to be a candidate for President of the United States. And my good friend Charlie Halleck from Indiana is going to place my name in nomination."

There were twelve days to go before the opening gavel fell at the Republican National Convention meeting in Philadelphia. The last Gallup poll had given Willkie a 3 percent favorable rating among Republican voters. Three days before the convention Gallup caught up with Willkie, who had jumped in less than one month to 29 percent, with Dewey leading by 47 to Vandenberg's 14 percent and Taft at 12. Speaking from the House floor a few days after the National Press Club bombshell, Republican Usher L. Burdick of North Dakota warned that the Willkie boom was an "artificial" product of money and media and that the time was right "to find out whether the American people are to be let alone in the selection of a Republican candidate for the Presidency, or whether the 'special interests' . . . are powerful enough to dictate to the American people." Willkie's explanation of Willkie was characteristically breezy yet portentous. He told the press that his rising support might mean that he was "a hell of a fellow . . . but I think it means . . . I represent a trend, or am ahead of a trend."

The Republican Party's regulars needed help in catching up with Willkie's trend. But a barrage of thousands of telegrams crashed down upon the national committee as delegates arrived in Philadelphia. There was no "possible way this great spark of enthusiasm can be manufactured," Connecticut's wealthy Sam Pryor, head of the convention's key Committee on Arrangements, insisted. A keen Washington political observer, Joseph Alsop, also thought so and told Alice Roosevelt Longworth that Willkie's support was grassroots. She thought not. "From the grass roots of ten thousand country clubs," she retorted famously.

Willkie's Philadelphia advent on Monday, June 24, was pure Jimmy

Stewart in *Mr. Smith Goes to Washington*, the Frank Capra box-office success released the previous year. Leaving the Thirtieth Street Station, a relaxed Willkie jawed with a swarm of congenial reporters. "Ask me any damn thing in the world. Nothing is off the record," he guaranteed. "So shoot, ask me anything you want." The easy, breezy access of a contender who admitted "usually" to sleeping on Sundays, smoking three packs a day, and drinking heavily contrasted with Dewey, Taft, and Vandenberg. He opined darkly on a possible third Roosevelt term, asking rhetorically, "[S]ince he won't discuss the principles of a third term, what does [FDR] think about a fourth term?" He said he would keep much of the New Deal legislation. The problem was FDR and his army of bureaucratic parasites. The other problem, Willkie made clear, was the foreign policy choices incumbent upon the Republican Party in the face of a Nazi-occupied Europe.

Delegates pledged to Dewey, Taft, and Vandenberg found guest tickets in suspiciously short supply. Sam Pryor's Arrangements Committee had allocated free balcony passes in a ten to one ratio in favor of young Willkie supporters. Harold Stassen delivered a lengthy keynote address on Monday afternoon, the first televised convention speech in history, transmitted by NBC cameras. The Minnesota governor then joined Halleck and Davenport as a Willkie floor manager amid deafening decibels from the hall's Willkie supporters–packed balconies. With more than two-thirds of the thousand delegates nonpledged, the uncertain outcome of the first ballot generated a level of excitement unusual for a Republican convention. Despite Dewey's crime-busting celebrity, his youth and national inexperience troubled many in the party. Harold Ickes's demeaning remark that Dewey had "thrown his diaper in the ring" was well known among the delegates. Dewey's 360 votes were an unpromising augury. Willkie's first ballot count was an impressive 105 votes, behind Taft's 189, with Vandenberg trailing at 76.

The momentum to Willkie continued on Tuesday, with Willkie rising to 171 and more slippage for Dewey. Two developments that day had long-term significance. News reached America of the imminent surrender of the mighty French Army to the German high command in the Forest of Compiègne. With the full might of the German war machine about to fall on Britain, the next president of the United States would face decisions of unprecedented magnitude. The second development was indicative of shrewd ethnic politics, yet also of Willkie's civil liberties sensibility that was to evolve into a singular commitment to the advancement of full citizenship for people of color. On that issue, the party's "Negro Plank," pledging an end to discrimination in the army, navy, civil service, "and all other branches of the government" together with "effective universal suffrage," read splendidly. By contrast, the appalling segregationist policies of the New Deal were roundly denounced by the black publishers of the *Baltimore Afro-American* and the *Pittsburgh Courier*. Willkie's afternoon open house for African American delegates in his hotel rooms made unusually good press for the candidate. He recounted a successful fight with the Akron, Ohio, Ku Klux Klan and pledged that his White House would be responsive to African American rights and interests.

The convention's fourth and unprecedented fifth days, Thursday and Friday, proceeded with frenzied deal making on the floor and in hotel rooms and the rising and falling or persisting stubbornness of contenders until, at one tense stretch after the fourth ballot, Willkie predicted a Taft victory. William Allen White, a strong Willkie backer and chair of the Committee to Defend America by Aiding the Allies, failed to persuade Alf Landon to throw the Kansas delegation behind Willkie. He believed he had lost, Willkie told a friendly publisher, "but it has been a grand fight," and it was better not to win "by making any deal." Dewey, trailing Willkie badly, telephoned Hoover, urging him to throw his support to Taft, but the former president stubbornly held on to his handful of delegates. In fact the crucial fifth ballot put Willkie 429 votes out front, with shouts from the balconies splintering the rafters.

At 12:20 A.M. on Friday, as the roll call proceeded, Vandenberg's campaign manager approached the podium with an urgent message. Convention chair Joseph Martin broadcast the Michigan poll to a momentarily silent hall. "The chairman of the delegation has asked me to announce the result as follows: for Hoover, one; Taft, two; Willkie, thirty-five." On the sixth and final ballot, the dark horse utility company candidate for the Republican nomination held 499 votes, 2 short of the necessary total. The Pennsylvania delegation then put him over. In keeping with the amazing developments of the week, the nominee-elect broke precedent and came to Convention Hall to address the delegates.

Had the Republicans selected a different leader in Philadelphia, it is virtually certain that the party would have fought the 1940 presidential election on a noninterventionist platform. Taft would have assailed FDR as a warmonger ready to waste American boys' lives in a European civil war. Dewey would have pandered to the isolationist sentiments of the majority of Americans. With Willkie as the GOP's charismatic leader, the eliding of noninterventionism was assured, as were the fundamentals of the New Deal. As Socialist Party leader Norman Thomas had the wit to observe, the GOP presidential contender "agreed with Mr. Roosevelt's entire program of social reform and said it was leading to disaster."

By the time the twelve-car Willkie Special steamed out of Rushville, Indiana, heading round-trip for the Pacific coast on September 12, the candidate had talked nonstop on and off the record during his Colorado Springs vacation. Sam Pryor claimed that "every screwball" came to Colorado and that Willkie was "mentally fagged out" and never really recovered from his improvisations and undisciplined exertions. Much of this was a boon for FDR because as historian Herbert Parmet itemized, Colorado yielded "virtually a point-for-point" endorsement of the New Deal, with statements about the need to regulate the "force of free enterprise," "collective bargaining for labor and wage and hour standards, federal regulation of interstate utilities, securities markets and banking as well as pensions, old-age benefits and unemployment allowances." The "rich man's Roosevelt" (more Ickes) had acquitted himself even better only days before the start-up of his campaign in pressing enough reluctant House Republicans to vote (51 of 112) the passage of the Selective Service Act. Earlier he had sent word unofficially condoning FDR's executive action trading fifty destroyers for leases to bases in the British Empire, but the resulting intraparty firestorm forced Willkie to reach for protective rhetoric and condemn the exchange as "the most dictatorial action ever taken by any president."

The Willkie Special with GOP notables, thirty staffers, forty reporters, and Edith Willkie traveled a thirty-thousand-mile circuit in seven weeks, generating more popular passion than the Great Depression election of 1932. Gallup had put the candidate ahead of FDR in August in twenty-four states representing an electoral college majority. Willkie announced that he would "talk in simple, direct Indiana speech," and he kept his promise more often than not. His native élan and at least four campaign managers and two speechwriters (Davenport and sometimes Luce) inevitably made for great confusion on the trail, as when Willkie, told that he was in Cicero, not Chicago, shouted to the crowd, "Then to hell with Chicago!" He was hit by working-class eggs in Chicago, but the *Chicago Defender*, the country's largest black newspaper, praised Willkie's superior ability to inspire the common man, in contrast with FDR. Ten thousand African Americans in Chicago's Negro American League's Chicago baseball park cheered his promise of an antilynching statute, an end to segregation in government, and abolition of poll tax disabilities in voting. Major black newspapers—the *Baltimore Afro-American*, *New York Age*, and *Pittsburgh Courier*—endorsed him. For the time being, Colonel Robert McCormick's fiercely isolationist *Chicago Tribune* had warmed to the candidate.

The campaign sustained its momentum in the polls until late September, drawing huge crowds, whom the irrepressible candidate (regularly abandoning the microphone to speak directly) inspired, amused, and sometimes confused. An unimpressed Taft snorted that "wisecracking which keeps the nominee on the front page every day [may] really get results, but I rather doubt it." Willkie was adroit at sidestepping or publicly disclaiming embarrassing endorsements by the German American Bund, the Order of the Sons of Italy in America, the American Communist Party, and Father Charles Coughlin's powerful National Union for Social Justice. As for Coughlin's movement, Willkie announced he didn't have to be president, but he did have to keep his ideas clear "in order to live with myself." The new America First Movement of strange bedfellows such as Norman Thomas, the Socialist leader, and Burton Wheeler, the isolationist senator, posed a trickier problem. Its hundreds of thousands of members in thrall to the magnetic Charles Lindbergh necessitated a certain amount of campaign doublespeak. Willkie served up mixed messages to good effect in California, where he praised that state's venerable isolationist senator Hiram Johnson, and in the Northwest, where he pledged to complete the gargantuan electricity-generating Grand Coulee Dam. For good measure, he lambasted FDR for imposing "state socialism" but reaffirmed his commitment to an efficient, budget-balanced New Deal.

Willkie lost his voice along with his poll numbers in October. The more he extolled the salvageable virtues of the New Deal and the existential dangers to America of a defeated Great Britain and Fascist-dominated Europe, the more irreplaceable an unresponsive Roosevelt became in the public mind. The October Gallup poll revealed Willkie's electoral college count had dropped from states with seventy-eight to those with only thirty-two. The projected popular vote count, with some 11 percent undecided, still remained close. Hoarse and frustrated from lambasting his unresponsive opponent, Willkie became reckless on the hustings and even charged FDR with having agreed to "sell Czechoslovakia down the river" in a phone conversation with Hitler and Mussolini. Backing down from outrageous falsehoods, he made a calculation in the vintage tradition of transactional politics that dismayed William Allen White, Walter Lippmann, Arthur Krock, Dorothy Thompson, and his many internationalist supporters. The candidate commenced a series of fierce attacks against FDR as a warmonger. Elect me, Willkie shouted on stops across the Midwest, and "when I am President I shall send not one American boy into the shambles of a European war." In St. Louis he told the crowds the choice was peace with Willkie or "your boys will be sent overseas" with Roosevelt.

The war scare tactics worked. Willkie's poll numbers climbed in the last two weeks of October. Burton Wheeler and Hamilton Fish III paid lavish tribute to the candidate in the Senate and House. Taft, Dewey, and Landon spoke on his behalf, as did the embittered Al Smith and other well knowns of the Democrats for Willkie variety. Lindbergh and eight hundred thousand American Firsters were buoyed by the assumption that the candidate would enforce the amended 1935 Neutrality Act, as were Communists and fellow travelers obedient to the realpolitik of the Molotov-Ribbentrop Pact. Historian Charles Beard and University of Chicago president Robert Maynard Hutchins publicly applauded. The *New York Times* editorialized euphorically: MR. WILLKIE ON THE UPSWING.

The narrowing polls instigated sharp attacks from the *Nation*, the *New Republic*, and other progressive publications. The *New Republic*'s Willkie special called Willkie "a Wall Street insider as slick as they come" and blamed the Great Depression on his ilk. Finally, the president emerged from his White House cover as commander in chief to rebut the existence of secret war plans in Philadelphia's Shibe Stadium. There were none, FDR declared on October 23, nor would the United States participate in foreign wars "except in the case of attack."

On the same day, however, the Willkie machine countered with public meeting responses to what it labeled "Anti-Third Term Day." Willkie spoke before the annual Forum on Current Problems sponsored by the *Herald Tribune* at the Waldorf-Astoria, where, again, he challenged FDR to a debate. Simultaneously, Al Smith, speaking to a Brooklyn Academy of Music audience, shared "a general belief among people that the New Deal is trying to get us into war." The following morning, the *New York Times* ended its quadrennial support of Roosevelt and endorsed Willkie, declaring the president's fiscal policies "disastrous failures" and his executive powers alarming. A day later John L. Lewis, the most powerful labor leader in America, endorsed the GOP presidential contender over the three national radio networks. Seething over FDR's alleged ingratitude and third-term arrogance, the CIO founder and perpetual United Mine Workers president (publicly vouchsafed a labor leader as secretary of labor in a Willkie cabinet) summoned his unionized legions in his distinctive Welsh baritone to forsake the Democrats for a better New Deal. Although the publicity value of Lewis's October 25 endorsement was considerable, it remained to be determined in a few days if organized labor's response would be more than lukewarm. That a shady Texas oilman with Nazi connections had paid the networks the eighty-thousand-dollar Lewis broadcast fee was unknown until after the election results.

Another headline endorsement miscarried at the last instant as Henry Luce's reception team awaited the arrival from London of Ambassador Joseph Kennedy's plane at La Guardia Airport on the twenty-seventh. Kennedy's assessment of British survival prospects had reached rock bottom after Churchill's defiant determination to continue fighting after the fall of France. A Kennedy diary entry secretly communicated to

FDR predicted that the war would show the world "what a great service Chamberlain did to the world and especially for Britain." Even though ordered by his president to remain at his post, the ambassador flew home, intending to make a dramatic endorsement of Willkie. Instead, Kennedy was escorted by government officials from the airport to Washington after speaking briefly to FDR by telephone.

Years later Lyndon Johnson, then a second-term congressman, recalled witnessing FDR draw a finger across his own throat at the conclusion of his telephone exchange with Kennedy. Speculation on what precisely transpired in the Oval Office runs from disclosure of compromising British intelligence reports to promises of political support for Joseph Kennedy, Jr. In any case, Kennedy praised the president on purchased radio time on CBS the night before FDR spoke in Boston. Roosevelt's Boston address on the thirtieth drove a stake through the heart of Willkie's war scare appeal. He had said it before, an adamant FDR intoned, but he would repeat it "again and again and again. Your boys are not going to be sent into any foreign wars."

On November 5, 50 million Americans voted, a record turnout in a population numbering 132 million. The major newspapers and Gallup conceded an edge to FDR yet considered the results too close to predict confidently. Willkie's election eve denouement obviously benefited from the deep pockets of GOP donors. He spoke to the nation from New York City on the three national networks twice during the day and once that night. From other parts of the country, Taft, Stassen, and Al Smith for Democrats for Willkie made radio appeals for the Republican standard-bearer. Boxing phenomenon Joe Louis joined Clare Boothe Luce and John L. Lewis at Madison Square Garden to hear a hoarse Willkie shout that the reelection of Roosevelt would mean "the destruction of our democratic way of life. Help me, help me, help me save it!"

FDR's 449 electoral college result swamped Willkie's 82. Thirty-eight of the forty-eight states decided for the Democrats, but the Democratic victory margins were close in seven states, even closer in Illinois, New York, New Jersey, and Wisconsin. FDR's popular vote count of 27,308,000 was almost 5,000,000 more than Willkie's 22,321,000, still an impressive GOP presidential record unexcelled until Dwight Eisenhower's 1952 election. Joseph Martin, the postwar face of the GOP in the House, summed up the election in his memoir with the flat statement that no Republican could have won in 1940—"once France fell. That was the thing that beat Willkie." Yet it was the fear of involvement and the deep isolationism of millions of Americans that gave the Willkie campaign its surprising eleventh-hour surge. Moreover, the candidate's war scare strategy resulted from a realization that he, like Alf Landon in 1936, was trapped by the paradoxical necessity of representing himself as an improved version of Roosevelt in order to defeat Roosevelt. A great many Americans, however, found the genuine specimen more satisfying in comparison.

Six days after the election Willkie reconceived the meaning of political partisanship. With a fine sense of occasion, he spoke from Manhattan's Hotel Commodore on Armistice Day, offering an eloquent statement of the role of the party out of power. His was a powerful party, Willkie stipulated. "Let us not, therefore, fall into the partisan error of opposing things just for the sake of opposition." The "loyal opposition" speech sounded a note whose admonition would be welcome today. "Ours must not be an opposition against—it must be an opposition for—an opposition for a strong America." Willkie's paean to constructive bipartisanship occasioned the greatest tsunami of laudatory telegrams ever received by a defeated candidate.

As the months ahead revealed, the success of FDR's wartime presidency and the design for the postwar world owed Willkie an incommensurable debt. "Under any other leadership but his," the columnist Walter Lippmann wrote, "the Republican party would have turned its back upon Great Britain, causing all who still resisted Hitler to feel that they were abandoned." The postelection Willkie-FDR pas de deux commenced immediately. James Roosevelt recalled hearing "great bursts of laughter" as Willkie and FDR met in the Oval Office the January evening before his father's third inauguration. The GOP leader announced his intention to fly to England on a personal fact-finding mission soon thereafter. Willkie insisted the trip was his own idea. Justice Felix Frankfurter and the publisher Harold Guinzberg claimed they planted the idea with Irita Van Doren at a cocktail party as a way for Willkie to arm himself against the isolationists with firsthand information about the war. The Luces, the Cowleses of the Des Moines *Register*, and the owners of the *Herald Tribune* encouraged Willkie, one of them making the significant point that neither the venerable Senator William Borah nor the scholarly Senator Charles McNary, both senior members of the Foreign Relations Committee, had ever left the United States. Wise in the ways of Washington, Joe Martin saw Oval Office machinations: "Roosevelt just trying to win you over." Martin warned that the trip "won't be well received by the Republicans."

Willkie (assisted by Harry Hopkins, FDR's resident eyes) conferred with Churchill and the British political class, made a Dublin side trip to meet Prime Minister Eamon de Valera, then flew home via Lisbon aboard the *Dixie Clipper* on February 5. But back home his fellow Republicans were uniting to oppose FDR's lend-lease legislation, which was designed to shore up hard-pressed British defenses with vast shipments of war matériel. Taft, Landon, Hoover, and Vandenberg closed ranks with Lindbergh of America First, Colonel McCormick of the *Chicago Tribune*, and Roy Howard of the Scripps-Howard chain and called for Willkie to be read out of the party. Landon was certain Willkie could never have been nominated at Philadelphia "had he revealed [his war bias]."

When FDR signed the lend-lease bill into law in early March 1941, he had Willkie to thank for the bravura performance before the divided Senate Foreign Relations Committee and the ex-candidate's steeply rising public esteem. According to the Gallup poll, the favorable press generated by the Senate committee appearance tipped public opinion in favor of the bill's passage. Revising the Neutrality Act was FDR's next challenge, a necessary sequel to lend-lease that entailed a bare-knuckles fight with the isolationists and their antiwar allies. Willkie meanwhile had returned to the practice of law as senior partner in the New York firm of Miller, Owen, Otis & Bailey, soon renamed to reflect his presence. Anti-Semitism as an isolationist ploy to thwart the neutering of the Neutrality Act brought him loping back into the fray. When a special subcommittee of the Senate Interstate Commerce Committee, headed by Gerald Nye, South Dakota's celebrated munitions industry sleuth, conducted two weeks of hearings into the Hollywood film industry, Willkie appeared before it to raise questions about the committee's sinister motives. Nye, a Neutrality Act architect, and his colleagues claimed to be concerned that "Hollywood" was trying to make the nation "punch drunk with propaganda to push her into war."

Colonel Lindbergh's America First Committee speech that September in Des Moines, Iowa, electrified the simmering accusations of a Jewish prowar conspiracy. With deft timing, FDR delayed informing the nation until the evening of Lindbergh's address that the U.S. Navy was under orders to "shoot on sight" German and Italian ships as a result of the U-boat torpedoing of the destroyer *Greer*. Urging Americans not to allow "the natural passions and prejudices of other peoples to lead our country into war," Lindbergh admonished American Jews to take no part in appeals to war, "for they will be among the first to feel its consequences." The country read Willkie's response a day later, unequivocally deploring "the most un-American talk made in my time by any person of national reputation." The Republican Party was compelled to distance itself from Lindbergh and the American First Committee, an image imperative depriving respectable noninterventionism of its most potent popular asset. At the beginning of October 1941, Willkie told a select audience at the Waldorf-Astoria that the Neutrality Act had lost its rationale in the present state of international affairs. Three days later, again with deft timing, FDR sent his revision message to Congress. The president's statement to the press complimented his partner in internationalism: "The Leader of the Republican Party himself—Mr. Wendell Willkie," who in word and deed demonstrated the American meaning of patriotism "by rising above partisanship and rallying to the common cause."

Asked where his party was heading, Willkie gave a *Detroit News* reporter a piece of his mind at the end of the year. "Look," he said, speaking of the hard-core isolationists, "if we go back, it will be so far back that neither you nor I nor anyone in this room can be a party to it. It will be way back. We can never let that happen." He had just come from a historic National Republican Committee meeting in Chicago in which after caustic words with Robert Taft, he successfully pushed the repudiation of the doctrine of isolationism. The new GOP document was enough to make Hoover and Landon rub their eyes. "We realize that after this war," Willkie's text read, "the responsibility of the nation will not be circumscribed within the territorial limits of the United States; that our nation has an obligation to assist in bringing about understanding, comity, and cooperation among the nations of the world." The implicit foreign policy bipartisanship of the document affirmed by the national committee in Chicago would emerge as controlling postwar doctrine, notably exemplified by Arthur Vandenberg's senatorial support of President Truman's foreign policy. Joseph Martin eventually judged this to be "Wendell Willkie's monument." In tipping the Republican Party off its solid isolationist base, Willkie started it down a curious evolutionary path into the "American Century" Henry Luce and the internationalists envisioned for it.

Willkie's standing with the public was excellent. A Gallup poll found that many Americans expected him to succeed FDR in 1944. Although GOP opinions about the party leader remained mixed, a December 1941 national survey of party leadership showed Willkie the overwhelming favorite for 1944. Viewed cynically, FDR's mid-October invitation to Willkie to join his administration may have been a brilliant maneuver to decapitate the opposition. FDR stipulated that the unprecedented arrangement "didn't mean that [Willkie] was to give up any of his partisan ideology." Given the political synergy between the two leaders and the grave situation abroad, an arrangement tantamount to coalition government arguably advanced the finest conceptions of leadership worthy of a great Republic. In less than six weeks America was to be traumatized by Pearl Harbor. Close advisers were opposed, however, and Willkie himself already had another fact-finding mission in mind as an alternative. FDR embraced the plan and proposed the title of ambassador-at-large, which Willkie graciously declined. Meantime the columnist Drew Pearson spoke for a fusion of powerful New York interests (David Dubinsky's ILGWU, Frank Altschul of Lazard Frères, FDR quietly) urging Willkie to run against Dewey for the governorship. Instead, on August 26, 1942, the head of the Republican Party flew off on a trip around the world. Joe Martin advised against it, as Willkie would be absent during the midterm elections campaign.

The trip around the world was an extraordinary odyssey. One of the first production models of the massive B-24, the *Gulliver* (on loan from the U.S. Army Air Corps with a six-man military crew), touched down in Cairo, Tripoli, Beirut, Damascus, Baghdad, Tehran, Istanbul, and Moscow, with its final stops in China, before returning to the United States on October 14. Willkie discussed military tactics at El Alamein with General Montgomery. He expressed deep misgivings to French naval officers in Alexandria about his government's dealings with Vichy's Admiral Darlan. Two separate delegations, one of Jews, the other of Muslims, pressed their cases with him in Jerusalem for the better part of a day. In Damascus, as guest of the leader of the Free French, he reminded General de Gaulle that Syria was not part of the French Empire but a mandated territory under international protection. Companion Gardner Cowles arranged a diversion of dancing girls in Baghdad who turned out to be prostitutes at a local establishment. The boy shah of Iran (placed on the Peacock Throne by the British after his father had revealed Axis sympathies) was overjoyed to have his first plane ride in Willkie's B-24. The Turkish stopover elicited special praise because his hosts made a point of showing Willkie local schools and institutions serving common folk. Conversely, Egypt's British overlords, imperturbably on display at Cairo's rambling Shepherd Hotel, appalled him. "Rudyard Kipling, untainted even with the liberalism of Cecil Rhodes," Willkie snapped.

The mission's two weeks in Stalin's Russia and two in Chiang Kai-shek's China were geopolitical priorities. Willkie decided that the Soviet system was functioning well under the circumstances. Stalin was the soul of convivial frankness during Willkie's two Kremlin visits. The Russian people were under strict orders to make themselves available to the distinguished visitor, who good-naturedly debated the virtues of communism and capitalism at the drop of a hat. Willkie impetuously spoke on the record to deplore the Allies' failure to launch the long-awaited second front, an indiscretion that caused FDR to downplay the value of Willkie's mission in the press. October in China was notable for Willkie's controversial assertion in Chungking that "colonial days are past" and that the Atlantic Charter portended "an end to the empire of nations over nations" (which provoked a famous rebuttal from Churchill). China was also notable for the special chemistry that developed between Willkie and Madame Chiang Kai-shek. The verbally fluent Wellesley-educated member of the Soong family dynasty extended herself to cultivate her influential American visitor "so essentially human that anything written down would not express the welcome felt in our hearts for him."

The American visitor allowed himself to soft-pedal the corrupt inefficiency of her husband's regime. General Joseph Stilwell and diplomat John Paton Davies noted that that "Little Sister," Madame Chiang, "accomplished one of her easiest conquests" in the utterly captivated world traveler. Only half-jokingly Willkie invited her to board the *Gulliver* from the tarmac and return with him to the United States. She came several months later to win arms, money, and hegemony for the Kuomintang. Her speech to both houses of Congress—she was only the second woman in history accorded the honor—was deemed a grand success. Willkie and Chiang resumed their amorous friendship at the Waldorf-Astoria, and her coverage in *Time* and *Life* furthered an image of Asian modernity, anticommunism, and business opportunities.

Roosevelt confided to Dean Acheson that he had been ready to offer Willkie the post of secretary of state. But the congeniality that had marked their Hyde Park meeting shortly before Willkie's world trip was conspicuously absent when FDR received Willkie in the White House on October 26. FDR was upset by Willkie's national radio address scheduled only days before the midterm congressional elections. Thirty-six million heard Willkie's "Report to the People" over four radio networks. Clare Boothe Luce touted it as the message "of a global Abraham Lincoln." William Allen White concurred, and the *Christian Science Monitor* hailed the new Marco Polo of international relations. Willkie's absence from the fall electioneering had raised criticisms among the party regulars, but the net GOP gain of forty-four House seats and eight in the Senate may have had some connection to his heralded return. Thomas Dewey, Willkie's least-liked opponent, was elected governor of New York, and Earl Warren, a Willkie sympathizer, captured the California statehouse. Taft and Vandenberg publicly withdrew from candidacies for the 1944 nomination.

Willkie and Irita Van Doren wrote *One World*, the narrative of the global circuit, in two months. By the time the book appeared at the beginning of April 1943, its principal author enjoyed more popularity than any other political leader in the country except the president. Walter Lippmann praised *One World* in *Foreign Affairs* magazine as "one of the hardest blows ever struck against the intellectual and moral isolationism of the American people." But what made the book distinctive was Willike's prescient twinning of America's inescapable involvement in the future affairs of the world with the just and necessary death of colonialism and race prejudice. The book cast the issue in vibrant terms:

> [T]hese newly awakened people will be followers of some extremist leader in this generation if their new hunger for education and opportunity [goes unanswered]. . . . If we had left the olive groves and the cotton fields and the oil wells of this region alone, we might not have had to worry. . . . But we have not left them alone. We have sent our ideas and our ideals, . . . our engineers and our businessmen, and our pilots and our soldiers into the Middle East; and we cannot escape the result. . . . If we fail to help reform, the result will be of necessity either the complete withdrawal of outside powers with a complete loss of democratic influence or complete military occupation and control of the countries by those outside powers.

Willkie foresaw the postwar promise and peril for the United States as a beacon of democracy in a world of decaying empires, rising expectations, vast oil deposits, and flammable Islam.

Much of the GOP congressional leadership and those speaking for the regulars might have applied Clare Luce's favorite neologism, "globaloney," to their leader by the fall of 1943. They were growing wary of a leader who no longer thought or spoke in their language. Even Henry Luce had been made nervous by Willkie's bounding liberalism.

Undaunted, Willkie announced his presidential campaign on February 2, 1944. His civil rights credibility was unmatched among blacks and Jews. He was awarded the 1942 American Hebrew Medal for defense of the film industry from senatorial inquisitors and his exposé of religious bigotry, "The Case Against Minorities" in the spring 1942 issue of the *Saturday Review of Literature*. He pledged to appoint a person of color to his cabinet or to the Supreme Court and to use the full power of his office to end institutionalized racism. Two years earlier he had become the first party leader to address the annual convention of the NAACP. Willkie had found on the world trip that "the maladjustments of races in America came up frequently." He wrote prescriptively about the problem in his last collection of essays, *An American Program*, and in "Citizens of Negro Blood," an article appearing in *Collier's* the day before he died. He embraced the Negro Double V agenda (victory abroad, victory at home), and he traveled twice to Hollywood with NAACP executive secretary Walter White in 1941 and July 1942 in his capacity as chairman of the 20th Century-Fox board of directors to mobilize the film industry for a more positive presentation of blacks in film.

He won the New Hampshire primary in mid-March and believed he retained the loyalty of the party machines in New York, Ohio, Illinois, Indiana, and Pennsylvania. The ironic reality was that he was now even more a man without a party than in those heady five days in Philadelphia in 1940. Willkie crashed in the Wisconsin primary in April. He terminated his presidential campaign and went home to Fifth Avenue. The Republican Arrangements Committee invited Herbert Hoover to address the national convention in Chicago, but it offered Willkie merely a seat among "honored guests."

In early July his old adversary Harold Ickes asked Willkie to join him for dinner with publisher Gardner Cowles at the Ambassador Hotel. FDR wanted to know, Ickes confided, "if you would accept if he nominated you for vice president on the Democratic ticket." That FDR really supposed he could convince the big-city bosses to accept an unpredictable Willkie over the progressive vagaries of Henry Wallace was certainly the audacity of hope. Once more, though, Willkie thought he had a better idea when he discussed FDR's offer with presidential speechwriter Sam Rosenman the next day at the St. Regis. Declining the president's proposition, the defeated GOP ex-leader revealed a plan for a third political party. FDR's reaction was enthusiastic, as Rosenman recalled, to the third-party gambit, a new party alignment to be formed after the 1944 election: "From the liberals of both parties, Willkie and I together can form a new, really liberal party in America." Three rounds of correspondence ensued, the last letter on August 21 from FDR reconfirming their plans to meet after the November elections.

Willkie entered Manhattan's Lenox Hill Hospital suffering from acute arrhythmia. The prognosis was guardedly positive. But there was to be no resumption of third-party planning with FDR. There were only notes for a book on race in the world with Walter White. Henry Wallace was dropped from the Democratic vice presidential ticket for the Missouri haberdasher Harry S. Truman. Thomas Dewey headed into a heated presidential campaign contest with FDR. Willkie died on the morning of October 8 at age fifty-four. "It's all over. He went very fast," a friend announced to the reporters waiting in the hospital lobby.

When news of his death reached the White House that day, the waspish Harry Hopkins upset Roosevelt by making a derisory remark. "Don't you ever say anything like that around here again," FDR exploded. "Don't even *think* it. You of all people ought to know that we might not have had Lend Lease or Selective Service or a lot of other things if it hadn't been for Wendell Willkie. He was a godsend to this country when we needed him most." Wendell Lewis Willkie was certainly one of the most unexpected, if not unlikely, presidential candidates from a major national party, more unexpected than William Jennings Bryan and only somewhat less unlikely than Barack Hussein Obama.

"AM I A 'SCREWBALL,' OR AM I A PIONEER?"

Pauli Murray's Civil Rights Movement

Glenda Gilmore

SHE WAS THE GRANDDAUGHTER OF SLAVES, AN ORPHAN BROUGHT up by her schoolteacher aunt in the segregated South. She never won elective office. She never became famous. She never made enough money to stop worrying about making ends meet. What she did do, time and time again for more than two decades, was hurl herself against the implacable façade of racial oppression that everyone called Jim Crow. Each time she failed to achieve her immediate goal, but in the long run she forged the weapons that a younger generation of activists carried into the phase of the civil rights movement that began in the mid-1950s.

Pauli Murray perfected two characteristics of leadership: indomitable persistence and relentless self-invention. She saw Jim Crow as an enemy to be attacked from every side. When, in 1939, a direct effort to end educational segregation at the University of North Carolina didn't work, she adopted Mahatma Gandhi's tactics and refused to move to the back of a Greyhound bus in Virginia. When she went to jail for that, she emerged to work with an organization that was dedicated to eliminating sharecropping, the system of economic exploitation that kept most southern African Americans in poverty. When a Virginia sharecropper found himself convicted of murdering his landlord in what appeared to be a case of self-defense, she went on a national speaking tour to raise awareness of how the poll tax and race hatred kept black people from serving on juries. During World War II she led the first organized sit-in movement in Washington, D.C., seventeen years before the Greensboro, North Carolina, sit-ins riveted national attention.

Not content to remain a perennial plaintiff, Murray became a lawyer to fight inequality. After the civil rights victories of the 1950s and 1960s, she helped found the National Organization for Women to extend those rights to women. Finally, when she was sixty-three years old, she sought the help of a higher power. She attended seminary and became one of the first ordained women priests in the Episcopal Church. Pauli Murray was the first black woman Episcopal priest. Pauli Murray was the first gay black woman Episcopal priest.

Despite the fact that Murray was one of the preeminent civil rights leaders of the twentieth century, most people have never heard of her. She achieved her leadership role and her success in subverting white supremacy by learning from her failures and capitalizing on the most incremental successes. Operating outside familiar organizational frameworks, such as the National Association for the Advancement of Colored People, she staked out toeholds of authority. Her tactics ranged from letters to the editor to her restaurant "stool-sitting technique" to writing social protest poetry to cultivating friendships with powerful people, such as Eleanor Roosevelt. Never an insider, Murray used her outsider status to make herself a thorn in the side of segregation and political oppression.

For those excluded from full democracy, public leadership not only involves untraditional activities but takes untraditional shapes. Sometimes shape-shifting black women leaders deliberately made themselves invisible; at other times they adopted middle-class trappings so as not to draw the attention of those who would thwart them. They took on the protective camouflage of black women's civic organizations, they organized inside their communities, and they ultimately protested injustice in the streets.

Murray pursued a more public role than did most of her peers, and she paid a high price. She made her life one long public campaign against injustice. That meant that she scrambled to earn a living, sacrificed her hope to become an accomplished poet, and struggled to come to terms with her sexuality. But Murray had no choice other than the one she made. She was born to fight white supremacy. She had the organizational abilities of a successful field marshal, the endurance of a marathoner, and the courage of her convictions. Even though the world offered no place for her, she repeatedly made a place for herself in it. As difficult as it was to speak out for what was right, Murray compulsively did so.

All her life she struggled to persuade people to listen to her. A five-foot-one-inch hundred-pound boyish-looking black woman, she was often overlooked by powerful white figures and African Americans, who often turned to leaders who were part of the establishment. Certainly her failures burdened her. For example, when Murray and her fellow Howard University students organized sit-ins at segregated restaurants in the nation's capital in 1943, she complained to March on Washington Movement organizer A. Philip Randolph about the lack of participation by adult black Washington residents in the protest. He told her patiently that "a mass movement" didn't develop by recruiting leaders to join it . . . "competency and conviction grow out of the movement. They are seldom brought to it." Murray's competency and convictions grew out of her one-woman civil rights movement. No one endowed her with authority; she seized it. Convinced in her heart that she deserved equal treatment, she never lost an opportunity to demand it. When she failed, she did not stop; she simply revised her tactics.

WHEN PAULI MURRAY launched a one-woman war against segregation at the University of North Carolina in 1938, she never imagined that the struggle for school integration would culminate a decade and a half later in *Brown v. Board of Education.* She wanted to enter UNC's Department of Social Work and earn an M.A. at once. Germany's treatment of Jews had already sparked a protest against the way that white southerners treated black southerners. The U.S. Supreme Court had just agreed to hear the NAACP-sponsored case of Lloyd Lionel Gaines, who had sued to enter the University of Missouri's law school. Aware of the significance of the historical moment, Murray thought she stood a chance of being admitted to the South's best graduate program on race relations.

Moreover, few people—white or black—had deeper ties to the all-white university. Pauli Murray was the great-great-granddaughter of James Strudwick Smith, one of antebellum North Carolina's foremost white men and a trustee of the University of North Carolina. In the early 1840s his sons, Sidney, a lawyer, and Frank, a doctor, graduated from UNC. One night Sidney forced his way into their slave's cabin and raped her. Frank heard her screams, jumped on his brother, and beat him savagely, crippling him for life. Nine months later in 1844 the slave, Harriet, gave birth to a baby girl, Cornelia Smith. The white Smiths left small plots of land to their black relatives and the bulk of their estate to the University of North Carolina. Cornelia Smith was Pauli Murray's grandmother.

Murray was born in 1910 in Baltimore, Maryland, but when her mother died, she went to live with another of Cornelia's children, Pauline Fitzgerald Dame, in Durham, North Carolina. Murray called Dame Mother, and Dame legally adopted her in 1919. In 1910s and 1920s Durham, Dame was a much-respected elementary school teacher. The family lived among those Murray termed the "respectable poor." Segregation was ubiquitous for Murray. "It's something you simply grow up with," she recalled. "It's not something that you suddenly experience." Twenty-year-old Murray protested even then: She rode her bicycle all over Durham rather than take her seat at the rear of the bus. Murray loathed Jim Crow as much for its repression of the soul as for its repression of the body.

When she graduated from Durham's Hillside High School, her class prophecy predicted that she would study law. But Murray was sure of only one thing: "I hated segregation so that all I wanted to do was to get away from segregation." She left for New York and entered Hunter College. Graduating in 1933, Murray emerged into a city in the grip of the Great Depression and into a Harlem alive with radical politics and the arts. She hustled about putting together part-time jobs and writing. For a few months Murray on a scholarship attended New York's Brookwood Labor College, where she learned radical politics and organizing. She landed a Works Progress Administration job teaching adult education and briefly joined a dissident Communist sect, the Communist Party Opposition (CPO).

In November 1938 Murray stood at a crossroads. Disillusioned with the CPO, increasingly antifascist, and homesick, Murray thought that the time was ripe to challenge segregation. She pointed to "the inescapable parallel between Nazi treatment of Jews in Germany and the repression of Negroes in the American South." Murray mused: "It seems to me that the testing ground of democracy and Christianity in the United States is in the South."

Murray sent her application to UNC on the day that the U.S. Supreme Court heard the NAACP's Missouri case. The UNC dean who answered her letter replied to "Mr." Murray, signing his letter "Cordially yours." But by the time the application arrived a few days later, someone had typed on the printed form, "Race——" and "Religion——." Murray knew she had a fight on her hands. She saw herself as a perfect plaintiff and hoped that the NAACP would take her case.

UNC rejected Murray's application on December 12, the day *after* the Supreme Court ruled that Lloyd Gaines must be admitted to the University of Missouri Law School. Apparently, the admissions office at UNC remained ignorant of the ruling because it stated flatly that "members of your race are not admitted to the university." Murray wrote to the university's president, Frank Porter Graham, noting that the rejection was illegal. "How much longer, Dr. Graham," Murray asked, "is the South going to withhold elementary human rights from its black citizens? How can Negroes, the economic backbone of the South for centuries, defend our institutions against the threats of Fascism and barbarism if we too are treated the same as the Jews of Germany?"

Murray threatened Graham with a lawsuit at the same time that she asked if she could meet with him over the upcoming Christmas holidays. He declined. Pauli Murray never made idle threats; as soon as she finished her letter to Graham, she engaged two black lawyers in nearby Durham who had previously tried to help a black North Carolinian enroll at the university. With her official rejection in hand, it was time to ask the NAACP to represent her.

In subsequent weeks Murray corresponded with President Graham, wrote a letter to the student newspaper, published a poem in the campus magazine, and sent press releases about her case to black newspapers around the nation. She pleaded to meet with anyone associated with the university so that there could be "a give-and-take process where prejudices are openly aired and accounted for."

When President Franklin Delano Roosevelt spoke at UNC in December 1938, Murray listened to the address by radio in New York. He accepted an honorary UNC degree from President Graham and warned his audience that "many other democracies look to us for leadership that world democracy may survive." His point was not to urge his audience to fight fascism abroad; rather, he wanted them to fight inequities in the U.S. South. "I am speaking not of the external policies of the United States," Roosevelt said; rather "I would emphasize the maintenance of successful democracy at home." The irony of the president of the United States making such a speech before a segregated audience of twelve thousand was not lost on Murray.

She seized the moment to publish an open letter to him in the black press. "I am a Negro," Murray wrote to FDR, "the most oppressed, most misunderstood and most neglected section of your population." Had he, she asked, "raised your voice loud enough against the burning of our people?" Did he mean it when he called UNC a place where "Americans [could] . . . support a liberal philosophy based on democracy?" Murray asked. "Or, does it mean that everything you said has no meaning for us as colored?" She told the president: "We are as much political refugees from the South as any of the Jews in Germany."

It might have been enough for most people to lecture the president of the United States and then distribute copies of the letter widely to the black press, but that wasn't enough for Pauli Murray. She sent a copy of the letter to Eleanor Roosevelt, along with a personal note asking the first lady to get the president to help her desegregate UNC. While Murray got a form letter from FDR, ER answered her personally, beginning a friendship and collaboration on civil rights issues that spanned decades. "I understand perfectly," ER told Murray. "But great changes come slowly," she said. "I think they are coming, however, and sometimes it is better to fight hard with conciliatory methods." ER cautioned: "The South is changing, but don't push too fast."

Despite all this action on the ground, the NAACP still had not formally agreed to represent her. Roy Wilkins, a NAACP official, saw Murray as a loose cannon. He objected to her public campaign and letters to university officials and observed that "in the present delicate situation following the University of Missouri decision, Miss Murray's letters are, to say the least, not diplomatic." He "strongly" opposed taking the case. Sometime in mid-February 1939 NAACP attorney Thurgood Marshall mentioned to Murray that her case suffered because she was not currently a resident of North Carolina. At the end of the month he called her into his office and told her he could not take the case. "I tried to argue with Mr. Marshall that if the state permitted nonresident white students to attend its educational institutions, it had a similar obligation under the Fourteenth Amendment to admit Negroes," Murray recalled. Moreover, Murray protested that her "ancestral home was there" and that she was an heir to North Carolina property. Pauli Murray was the ur–North Carolinian, descended from six generations of white and black residents.

But there was more. Marshall told her that she was "too maverick" and might not be "Simon-pure enough" to be an NAACP plaintiff. Her public letters branded her as a maverick, but Murray never understood Marshall's "Simon-pure" comment. Perhaps Marshall knew of her brief past membership in the Communist Party Opposition. The NAACP could never risk representing a Red or even a pinkish plaintiff, even one who had renounced communism.

But Thurgood Marshall may have told Pauli Murray something far more personal: that the NAACP could not represent her because she did not conform to feminine standards. Murray was a tiny woman who often dressed as a man and lived with women. At the time she worked for the WPA, Murray had been arrested and taken to Bellevue Hospital when the police found her hysterical on the streets of New York, beside herself after a lover's quarrel with a woman. The moment represented a sexual identity crisis for Murray. She transferred from Bellevue to a private psychiatric hospital, where she told doctors that she thought she was a "pseudo-hermaphrodite." Since she appeared to be a woman, she asked for an operation to find her male sex organs, but the doctors refused. In the late 1930s, two decades before the word existed, Murray thought that she was a transsexual person.

Murray didn't understand homosexuality, and science didn't either. In the months after the NAACP refused to take her case, she sought help at a psychiatric clinic. Doctors there told her that her problem originated from her refusal to submit to authority. Real women accepted things as they were. But Murray had the great good sense to ignore such drivel. "If it is a question of race conflict, submission to authority, being hemmed in by restrictions, why is it I am proud of my Negro blood?" she wondered. "I do submit to authority as far as I am able, until I am proven wrong, or my point of view is accepted." She finally decided that "psychiatric treatment is not what I need." Murray's brief membership in the CPO and her sexual identity crisis, on the record because of her arrest and commitment to Bellevue, left trails like coiled snakes that hissed for the rest of her life. She called the NAACP's rejection her "greatest disappointment" and decided that she could not afford to pursue the case privately.

A few months later, in 1940, Murray found work at an organization dedicated to economic justice for southern sharecroppers, most of whom were African Americans. Murray organized an awareness campaign called National Sharecroppers Week (NSW). She savored the sweetness of seeing her name appear on the NSW letterhead with board members Frank Porter Graham and Roy Wilkins. She dreamed up a student essay contest on "A Proposed Solution to the Sharecropper Problem" and convinced editors at the *Nation* to publish the winning essay. With typical boldness, Murray wrote to Eleanor Roosevelt, met with her in Manhattan, and secured ER's promise to serve as contest judge and speaker at the NSW dinner.

Over the next decades Murray and Roosevelt cultivated a friendship based on their differences—"race," age, and temperament—rather than on their similarities. ER used Murray to hear what "Negroes" were thinking, and Murray used ER to tell the administration what "Negroes" were thinking. ER used Murray to divine the future, but Murray used ER to realize her future. ER warned Murray to slow down and criticized her methods; Murray warned ER to speed up and criticized her methods. Murray wrote the longer letters, but ER always responded and sometimes invited Murray to the White House. Each woman recognized and treasured the other's spirit.

In the spring of 1940 Murray set out from New York to spend Easter in Durham with her mother, Pauline Dame. She took along Adelene McBean, nicknamed Mac, "a peppery, self-assertive young woman of West Indian parentage." Mac simply "could not believe that there were such things as real segregation laws in the South." Instead, she figured that "American Negroes were just too timid" to challenge custom. Murray worried that McBean would raise a ruckus when the Greyhound bus turned segregated somewhere south of Washington, D.C.

Murray had been studying Gandhian techniques of nonviolence and took reading material with her. She reasoned that Indians constituted a majority in their own country, while the "Am. Negro" constituted a minority surrounded by white people. She admired the Indians for a "willingness to sacrifice . . . to change heart of the enemy" and contrasted their activism with white people's criticism that African Americans "move too fast, upset friendly relations between the races." While the Indians made up a "well disciplined movement," Murray lamented that African Americans suffered from the lack of a grassroots movement. They counted instead on a "legalistic movement" headed by the "NAACP—through court tests." She set out for home armed with nonviolent ideas, but they took her only as far as Virginia.

"TO MRS. PAULINE DAME . . . EASTER GREETINGS. ARRESTED. PETERSBURG WARRANT GREYHOUND BUS. DON'T WORRY. CONTACT WALTER WHITE," read the (collect) telegram that Murray sent on March 23, 1940. A year shy of seventy and still teaching elementary school, Dame had barely recovered from the intensity of Murray's campaign to integrate UNC, but she wired back: "HOPE YOU OK DID AS REQUESTED WIRE ME YOUR NEEDS." Dame's message beamed like a ray of sunshine through the bars of the Petersburg, Virginia, city jail. Murray's coworkers back in New York contacted Roy Wilkins of the NAACP, and he mobilized the local chapter in nearby Richmond.

How had Murray gone from reading about Gandhi's nonviolent protest tactics one minute to staging her own act of civil disobedience the next? When the women changed to segregated buses in Richmond, they had to take seats at the back of an old vehicle. On the short ride from Richmond to Petersburg, McBean complained that her side ached from being thrown against the wheel well. Jim Crow's seating plan lacked place cards. Black passengers had to fill the bus from the back, leaving a row between them and the white passengers, who took the front seats. In other words, the "front" and "back" of the bus were relative concepts. Looking forward, Murray saw "several white passengers sitting alone on two-seat rows," and "two empty seats . . . just behind the driver's seat." If two white children, currently seated toward the middle of the bus, moved up to the empty row behind the driver, the demarcation line would advance, and Murray and McBean could move out of their row. Murray went up to the front, explained McBean's discomfort, and asked the driver if he would reseat the children. The driver pushed her backward and yelled, "Get out of my face and go back and take your seat." She asked again. She then appealed to the mother of the children, who refused to reseat her children.

When they stopped in Petersburg, Jim Crow seating reshuffled as a large group of African Americans waited to board the bus. Trying to guess where the color line would fall, Murray and McBean moved up to the third row from the back, but that seat was broken. They moved up one more row, "behind all the white passengers," but leaving behind the empty row with the broken seat. The driver mounted the steps, spied them there, and "growled . . . 'You'll have to move back!'" It was then that Murray snapped.

The image of her grandfather, a black Union veteran who had fought at the battle of Petersburg, appeared before her, and she "let go a machine gun fire of legal questions." The driver simply threatened to call the police. Murray threatened to call the NAACP and invoked "the 14th amendment, the Constitution and the Supreme Court of the United States." There! Murray thought. That would "fix him!" It didn't. When two policemen boarded the bus, McBean yelled, "You needn't think that your big brass buttons and your shiny bullets are going to scare me, because I have rights, they're substantial, and I'm sitting on them." The police officers admitted that they couldn't act unless the driver swore out a warrant.

Murray and McBean decided to use "Mahatma Gandhi's technique" and "just sat—and sat." A crowd of white men gathered outside the bus. Finally the bus driver returned with a warrant but hesitated and fixed the broken seat. The women moved back, but now McBean demanded an apology from the driver, who "mumbled something" about wanting "everybody to have a square deal." Then he distributed "witness cards" to the white, but not the black, passengers. Murray protested. The driver alighted and returned with the officers, who finally arrested the women for "creating a disturbance" and violating Virginia's segregation laws.

After Murray and McBean had spent the night in the Petersburg City Jail, the jailer allowed Murray to send telegrams, including the one to Dame and another to her sister in Washington, instructing her to contact Eleanor Roosevelt and the NAACP. On Easter Sunday 1940 two NAACP lawyers arrived at the jail after Thurgood Marshall assured them that the organization would foot the bill. They reported that "the ladies DO NOT want bail."

Murray and McBean saw themselves as political prisoners. Murray meditated on "the ways of Hitlerism and their American facsimile." She vowed that they would "go all the way to and from the Supreme Court and back again, if necessary." Marshall assured them that "two of the N.A.A.C.P.'s best lawyers were in charge of the case." For her part, Eleanor Roosevelt contacted the governor of Virginia, who told her that "Miss Murray was unwise not to comply with the law." Three days later a judge found them guilty of "creating a disturbance, disorderly conduct, and violation of Virginia segregation law." He allowed that "this is not the worst case of its kind." He fined Murray and McBean five dollars each plus costs. They appealed. The jailing of the women made front-page news in black newspapers across the country.

The black newspaper in Durham announced that the women signified "the beginning of a new type of leadership—a leadership that will not cringe and crawl on its belly merely because it happens to be faced with prison bars in its fight for the right." Murray and McBean lost their appeal and hoped that the NAACP would take the case up to the Supreme Court. The organization did not, perhaps because the state dropped the charges on violating the segregation laws to strip the case of its significance but retained the disorderly conduct charge. However, the NAACP probably remained reluctant to put Murray in the limelight. She had been dressed as a boy on the trip, and eyewitnesses might testify to that, allowing her sexuality to undermine her yet again. The NAACP's failure to appeal made Murray feel "particularly badly, because they led us to believe that the case had such far-reaching implications they were going to see it through." Crushed, the two women refused to pay the fine and packed their bags to report to the Petersburg City Jail to serve thirty-day sentences for disorderly conduct.

Murray used her month in jail to situate their experience within Gandhi's teachings. "Law is a tedious method of fighting social issues," she reflected. Serving her sentence constituted "civil disobedience," and she decided that African Americans must mount a direct action movement to complement the NAACP's litigation strategy. She argued that even "a Supreme Court ruling on segregation will not be enforced," and state segregation laws would stand "unless some 'civil disobedience' movement is started and catches the imagination of the Negro masses." Murray joined "Gandhi's movement" in 1940 because of "its possibilities for American minority and labor action."

Public notice as a cross-dressing woman might have cooked Murray's goose with the NAACP, but at the same time, her sexuality became a source of strength for her. Early in the 1930s she had tried to deny it by marrying briefly, then tried to persuade a doctor to find the male sex organs that she imagined she possessed, but by 1940 she had begun to embrace her differences. Her sexuality had limited her because "this conflict rises up to knock me down at every apex I reach in my career." She remained constantly on guard and lamented: "I'm exposed to any enemy or person who may or may not want to hurt me." As her religious faith grew, she became increasingly comfortable with the idea that she was a lesbian. Six months after the Petersburg incident, she told herself: "It is dangerous for you to think too much about your weakness. . . . The great secret . . . is not to think of yourself, of your courage or of your despair, of your strength or your weakness, but of Him for whom you journey. . . . He cannot show you a task without making you capable of fulfilling it."

Murray's refusal to abide by segregation custom and law, her practice of nonviolent direct action, her decision to serve her prison sentence, and her determination to link her individual oppression to that of her people represent strategies that were to make Rosa Parks and Martin Luther King, Jr., icons of the civil rights movement fifteen years later. Six years after Murray's arrest, the Supreme Court heard an almost identical case. In 1944, Irene Morgan of Baltimore had refused to move to the back of a Greyhound bus after it crossed the Virginia line. This time the only charge was violating the Virginia segregation statute. In 1946, in *Morgan v. Virginia*, the U.S. Supreme Court found that forcing interstate passengers to abide by Virginia segregation law put an "unconstitutional burden on interstate commerce." Murray must have smiled as she clipped the story of the Court's decision.

Months after her Petersburg arrest, Murray became an advocate for another black defendant in Virginia. By December 1940 sharecropper Odell Waller was facing execution for the murder of his white landlord. Waller admitted that he shot Oscar Davis but maintained that it was self-defense because he thought that Davis was going to shoot him first. The factual issue at trial came down to whether the crime was self-defense and manslaughter or premeditated murder, which could carry the death sentence. The all-white jury found Waller guilty of premeditated murder and sentenced him to death.

Pauli Murray became a special field agent on the Waller case for the socialist Workers Defense League, which helped Waller appeal. The WDL fought to reduce Waller's crime to manslaughter and save his life. It employed a critique of sharecropping, the poll tax, and discriminatory jury selection. Payment of the poll tax was a requirement for jury service, and poor African Americans could not afford to pay a poll tax, a pointless gesture since they weren't allowed to vote. Mostly well-off whites paid the poll tax; hence they made up the jury pools. Since only whites had heard Waller's case, he had been deprived of a jury of his peers.

The Waller case nestled within a discourse that Murray had helped craft during National Sharecroppers Week a year earlier. Sharecropping's exploitative nature might have seemed an esoteric exercise to the student competitor in Murray's contest who wrote: "Great Uncle Sam cannot allow such conditions." Now the case brought democracy, slavery, plunder, and destruction before the American public, and a man's life hung in the balance.

Without Murray and the WDL, Waller would have been executed at once. In November 1940, six weeks after his conviction, Murray visited Richmond to organize local support from the black ministers' alliance. To her horror, she found herself following silver-tongued Howard law professor Leon Ransom. She described the moment: "I get out two words and then I just burst into tears and stand there and just utterly collapse in tears trying to tell the story of this young sharecropper." But the response was "like a miracle." The ministers felt so sorry for her and Waller that they gave generously. Professor Ransom even invited her to apply to Howard Law School. Composure regained, Murray saucily replied, "Give me a fellowship and I will."

The appeal rested on whether Waller's attorney had committed an error at trial by omitting the all-white jury issue. The Virginia Supreme Court refused to recognize error. The attorneys twice appealed to the U.S. Supreme Court, which both times refused to hear the case. From November 1940 through June 1942 they won three stays of execution.

Meanwhile Murray took the case to the court of public opinion. She traveled nationwide with Odell's mother, Annie, to publicize her son's plight. Mother Waller and Murray made an unlikely but effective pair. "Annie Waller is an old woman. . . . Pauli Murray is the Negro of the new South, full of the problems of her people and an earnest student of their background," wrote journalist Murray Kempton. He continued: "The long, steady growth of the Negro race towards a full share of the benefits of emancipation is symbolized in the aspirations of young women like Pauli Murray."

On tour with Mother Waller, Murray left her boyish cross-dressing persona behind. A white reporter for the *Los Angeles Daily News* described one meeting: "I heard Pauli Murray, a slim, lissome and almost exquisitely pretty colored girl, talk to a handful of perspiring people about the conditions of sharecroppers, black and white in the South. It was one of the best addresses I had heard anywhere in recent years. . . . Frankly, I thought of Joan of Arc as she spoke. . . . I pictured her not only as the champion of her own people . . . but as their emissary to the rest of us." Murray garnered endorsements for Waller's defense from civil rights leader A. Philip Randolph, NAACP founder Mary White Ovington, educator John Dewey, and a score of other liberals. Dewey and Randolph argued: "In 1856, Dred Scott became a symbol for the abolition of slavery. Today another unknown Negro, Odell Waller, like that runaway slave, has in our time become the rallying point for those who would abolish the poll tax and the injustices of the sharecropper system."

Murray completed the Waller tour in the summer of 1941 and told herself, "[I]f we lose this young man's life, I'm going to study law." The case remained on appeal, but by now she had done all she could to publicize it. Early in September, Murray attended the latest Waller hearing before the Virginia Supreme Court and then entered Howard Law School. She was one of two women in the class and, at thirty, a bit older than most of her classmates. Her male classmates went off to war in the coming months, while she fought a domestic war against racial oppression.

Murray characterized the black liberation movement during World War II as "guerrilla-like warfare." She wrote to "Dear Brother Randolph," who led the March on Washington Movement (MOWM): "I've taken it upon myself to act as a 'little lieutenant' to the Commander of our new movement for Freedom." Throughout the war African Americans fought "America's second foe," racism, in the streets and in the press, through direct action and through the power of ideas in a series of protests that they called the Double V campaign.

During the war Murray became a public person, widely published and known to black leaders. In 1942 and 1943 she was devoted to A. Philip Randolph and the MOWM. When a black *Pittsburgh Courier* columnist criticized Randolph as a leader without a movement behind him, she pointed to herself as a member of the MOWM: "I am only representative of an increasing number of militant young Negroes. . . . If Randolph is a leader, it will be because these young Negroes make him a leader."

Murray saw the MOWM as the only vehicle for mass protest, and she acted on her conviction that ending segregation "demanded forceful action." During her first year in law school, racial incidents broke out all over the United States, and Randolph suggested a series of mass meetings "to protest . . . flagrant, outrageous and indefensible discriminations against the Negro." They would focus on reversing the Red Cross's decision to segregate the blood supply, desegregating the military, protecting black soldiers from southern mobs, and increasing black representation in federal government agencies. These strategies excited Murray, who grew increasingly angry in the first year of the war. "I too want to be a loyal citizen," Murray wrote, "I want something to believe in." But she cataloged the countless insults of segregation and asked, "Is this the brand of democracy we are asked to die for?"

At the close of Murray's first year at law school, the U.S. Supreme Court refused to grant a writ of certiorari in the Waller case. Just before the expiration of what seemed to be the last stay of execution, Randolph asked Murray to organize a delegation to meet with President Roosevelt. But no one at the White House would see them. Murray remembered the day as "one of unrelieved failure and humiliation." Finally, they returned to NAACP headquarters to await a call from Eleanor Roosevelt, who had been working all day to stop the execution. Eleanor's voice "trembled and almost broke": "I have done everything I can possibly do. I have interrupted the President twice." FDR told his wife that the matter was "not of the heart" but of the law. He could not pardon Waller. Randolph sighed. "The President and the Government of the United States have failed us." Waller died.

Murray organized a "silent parade . . . to mourn the death of sharecropper Odell Waller and to protest the poll tax which killed him." It was the only actual march that the March on Washington Movement ever made in the 1940s. One participant remembered Murray at a planning session: "I walked into this meeting . . . and heard this little small person with cropped hair, wearing these white sailor pants and standing on the table. She was on *fire*, talking about social injustice and Jim Crow." Five hundred people marched through midtown Manhattan to the sound of muffled drums. Young women, dressed in frilly white summer dresses, carried signs that shouted: JUSTICE AND MANHOOD: THE POLL TAX MUST GO.

As a member of the Washington MOWM chapter, Pauli Murray returned to law school ready to practice civil disobedience in the segregated capital. Ruth Powell, a Howard undergraduate from Massachusetts, inspired Murray's campaign. Powell went throughout Washington sitting in segregated restaurants—all by herself. No one ever served her. She had come to her singular sit-ins innocently enough, thinking that segregation did not apply to drugstore counters. Murray turned Powell's experiences into a movement by starting a mass action to "stool-sit."

She dispatched a questionnaire to students and faculty: "Am I a 'screwball,' or am I a pioneer? Do others think as I do on the perplexing problem of minority rights?" She discovered not only that there was no segregation law in Washington, but that an 1890s law on the books *prohibited* race discrimination. She taught nonviolent direct action techniques to scores of Howard undergraduates. She instructed those who sat in to respond to an order to move by asking why. When a manager explained that there were segregation laws or that the accommodation served only whites, the protester should again ask why. All the students she trained signed an "oath of nonviolence."

The action targeted the Little Palace Cafeteria, close to the Howard campus. Murray organized students into teams of four: Three students would go inside; one would stay outside to picket. In April 1943, after servers refused four groups of students, they took their empty trays to tables, pulled out books, and "assumed an attitude of concentrated study. Strict silence was maintained." The pickets marched outside, carrying such signs as WE DIE TOGETHER—WHY CAN'T WE EAT TOGETHER? Murray had lined up the Washington bureau reporters for the nation's black newspapers. After several days the owners capitulated. One can only imagine how the sit-in would have rocked the rest of the segregated South . . . if it had heard about it. They did not. While the black press broadcast it nationwide, the white press, even locally, ignored it.

The following April, Murray and the Howard students moved outside the Howard neighborhood with what they now called a civil rights campaign. Students signed a pledge to fight discrimination, promised to execute their "patriotic duty," and went through nonviolent direct action training. This time they targeted a national chain near Capitol Hill. Their signs asked: IS THIS HITLER'S WAY OR THE AMERICAN WAY? Murray exhorted them: "[N]o matter what happens to you temporarily, whether you are served in a restaurant, or go to prison, or get slapped down, the resources of human history are behind you and the future of human society is on your side." It took only twenty-four hours for forty-three students to desegregate the restaurant. A few weeks later Murray was graduated as valedictorian of her law school class and delivered her remarks standing in front of a huge bouquet of flowers sent by Eleanor Roosevelt.

Howard Law School's valedictorians traditionally attended Harvard Law School for graduate work. But Harvard responded to Murray's application this way: "Your picture and the salutation on your college transcript indicate that you are not of the sex entitled to be admitted." She felt the blow as sharply as she had when the University of North Carolina had written: "Members of your race are not admitted to the University." As she reached for her diploma, she already plotted a campaign against an evil she called Jane Crow.

World War II ended, and Murray earned her master's degree in law from Boalt Hall School of Law at the University of California, Berkeley. She spent the next few years practicing law in New York City. The Women's Division of Christian Service to the United Methodist Church retained her to compile a book on segregation laws in every state, hoping to encourage local Methodists to overturn them.

In early 1951, after two more Supreme Court decisions, the University of North Carolina decided to consider graduate and medical school applications "without regard to color or race." Murray celebrated by inquiring whether she could earn her doctorate in law there. UNC responded that it did not offer one. She realized that her 1938 application had contributed to the desegregation of public education. She saw herself as "part of a tradition of continuous struggle, lasting nearly twenty years, to open the doors of the state university to Negroes. . . . Each new attempt was linked with a previous effort. . . . Once begun, this debate would not be silenced until the system of enforced segregation was outlawed."

Pauli Murray lived a life filled to the brim in the following decades, working at Adlai Stevenson's law firm and finding a loving partner. She served on the Committee on Civil and Political Rights of the President's Commission on Women in 1962 and was a founding member of the National Organization for Women. When the March on Washington finally marched on August 28, 1963, Murray was there. She heard Martin Luther King, Jr., and celebrated at a downtown restaurant with a friend who had been in the Howard sit-ins. It was, she recalled, a cross between "a jubilee and Judgment Day." The next year Congress passed the Civil Rights Act of 1964, which outlawed discrimination based on race, color, religion, national origin, or sex in public accommodations, public facilities, and public education. It established the Equal Employment Opportunity Commission (EEOC) as its enforcement arm. Murray moved to Washington in 1966 to work as a consultant to the EEOC. She was nominated for general counsel, but her brief stint in the Communist Party Opposition in the 1930s cost her that opportunity.

In June 1973, Murray entered the General Theological Seminary in New York and joined the movement within the Episcopal Church to ordain women as priests. She had no way of knowing that this, her final civil rights movement, would succeed. She was sixty-three years old. During the three years that Murray attended seminary, the Episcopal Convention thrice rejected women's ordination. Murray stayed home rather than attend the fourth convention because she couldn't stand "the possibility of still another rejection in my life." She was praying alone when she got the news that the church would ordain women.

A few minutes later the rector of the Chapel of the Cross in Chapel Hill, North Carolina, phoned and invited her to celebrate her first Holy Eucharist as a priest in the church where her black and white ancestors had worshiped. Six weeks later, Murray walked down the short aisle, carrying her grandmother Cornelia Smith Fitzgerald's Bible. She marked the scripture reading with dried flowers from the bouquet that Eleanor Roosevelt had given her for her law school graduation. Murray took a long look at the balcony where her great-grandmother Harriet and her grandmother Cornelia had prayed as slaves. As she began her sermon, she gripped a lectern engraved with her white great-great-aunt Mary Smith's name. Murray felt as if "all of the strands of my life had come together." She later looked back on her one-woman civil rights movement with satisfaction. "In not a single one of these little campaigns was I victorious," she recalled. "In each case, I personally failed, but I have lived to see the thesis upon which I was operating vindicated," she said. "I've lived to see my lost causes found."

Leaders aren't just the few famous people who dominate the news or find their place in history books. They don't always represent the majority. They aren't always popular. They don't always win, and they aren't always remembered. Leaders such as Pauli Murray, brave and obscure men and women who act on their convictions even though they fail time and time again, sometimes change the course of history.

AR·2839
19 COLORADO 68

ROBERT KENNEDY
The Empathetic Leader

Evan Thomas

—

HE WAS SHY AND COULD BE MOROSE. SMALL AND SLOUCHY, HE RECOILED at backslapping. As a boy and as a young man he saw himself more as an acolyte than as a priest and operated for most of his life behind the throne. He could be mean or churlish, and he was often content to remain wordless. When he finally heard the applause, he was sure it was for his martyred brother.

Yet by accident, or fate, and through the force of his own will, Robert Kennedy became a leader for his time. By a kind of human alchemy, he was able to turn his fears and insecurities into leadership qualities—into empathy with the downtrodden and an impatient drive to better their lot. Even his inarticulateness became a virtue. Through his palpable yearning, his awkward yet fervent body language, he could reach dispossessed people who had trouble expressing their own hopes and fears. He became a kind of tribune for the voiceless. During the 1960s people were drawn to antiheroes in cinema and literature. They sensed in RFK a kind of brooding anger but also a vulnerability and sensitivity, a willingness to defy authority and take risks—to "dream of things that never were, and ask why not," in the phrase he borrowed from George Bernard Shaw.

A well-known cartoon from 1968 by Jules Feiffer shows RFK struggling to decide whether he is the "Good Bobby" or the "Bad Bobby," the protector of small children and poor blacks of his later years or the ruthless McCarthyite of his earlier years. Mythology notwithstanding, the progression from bad to good was not steady or linear. When he was the hard guy—"Ruthless Robert"—he was never so tough as he appeared, and when he emerged as a symbol of hope, he was not quite the figure of purity and innocence his followers wished him to be. He was intensely human. He was a creature of secrets and subterfuges at one level, yet he projected a kind of authenticity and sincerity that made him stand apart from, and above, the glad-handing politicians of his or any era. He was cunning but no phony. And he was willing to do what almost no politician, then or now, is willing to do: ask voters to make sacrifices for the greater good.

Robert Kennedy was born into a family that comes as close to American royalty as any. But there was nothing about his background that suggested that he was born to rule.

He was the third son and seventh child of Joseph and Rose Kennedy. His older siblings, Joe Jr., Jack, and Kathleen (known as Kick) were known as the golden trio. Attractive, athletic, charming, they were expected to succeed by their driven father, who announced on the birth of his eldest son that Joe Jr. would be president of the United States—and meant it. Robert, by contrast, was described by his father as "the runt." Little Bobby was small and uncoordinated and unhappy much of the time. His brother Jack called him Black Robert. In a more therapeutic age he would have been diagnosed as depressed. Robert's own description of himself as a boy verges on the pathetic: "What I remember most vividly about growing up was going to a lot of different schools, always having to make new friends, and that I was very awkward and dropped things and fell down all the time. I had to go to the hospital a few times for stitches in my head and my leg. And I was pretty quiet most of the time. And I didn't mind being alone."

He was, at the same time, desperate for attention. At the Kennedys' summer place in Hyannis Port, Massachusetts, Bobby was slow to learn to swim and fearful of the water. His brother Jack recalled how one day when the family was sailing off Cape Cod, Bobby threw himself off the boat into Nantucket Sound. His older brother Joe had to fish him out. "It showed a lot of guts or no sense at all, depending on how you looked at it," recalled Jack. At the Kennedy family dinner table, the "golden trio" sat at the head with their father, discussing world affairs. Bobby sat down at the other end of the table with his sisters, baby brother Teddy, his mother, and several nuns. Bobby was known as his mother's pet. He was the most pious of the children, an acolyte at church, especially considerate of aging clergy and the Kennedys' domestic staff. His mother, Rose, worried that he was "puny" and "girlish" and would turn out to be a sissy.

At Portsmouth Priory School, a Roman Catholic boarding school in Rhode Island, he was known as Mrs. Kennedy's little boy Bobby, according to his roommate, David Meehan. Young Robert felt tremendous pressure to catch up to his more successful siblings. In the spring of 1942, with his brothers headed off to the war as naval officers, Robert was caught cheating on an exam at Portsmouth and kicked out. He went to Milton Academy and on to Harvard and enlisted in the navy, but he could never match his brothers (who were engaged in their own mortal rivalry; after Jack became a hero by getting his PT boat cut in half by a Japanese destroyer, naval aviator Joe volunteered for a dangerous mission and was killed over the English Channel when his plane blew up). Failing his flight aptitude test, Robert served as an enlisted man on a destroyer—the *Joseph P. Kennedy*, named after his martyred brother Joe—scraping paint as he sailed around the peacetime Caribbean in 1946.

Robert yearned to get his father's attention. "I wish, Dad, that you would write me a letter as you used to Joe & Jack about what you think about the different political events and the war as I'd like to understand what's going on better than I do now," he wrote in 1945. He cast about for a role, for some way of proving himself worthy of the family name.

In the 1952 race for the U.S. Senate from Massachusetts, he found a useful niche in the shadow of his brothers. Stepping into the void left by Joe Jr.'s death, Jack had won a congressional seat in 1946 and was running against the incumbent, Henry Cabot Lodge. Father Joe needed someone to manage Jack's campaign, an enforcer who would do the hard and dirty work, who would dole out the cash where it mattered and chase off the hacks and old pols who hung around campaign headquarters with their hands out. Grudgingly at first, then with a kind of bird dog ferocity, Robert took on the role of brother protector.

He may have found some commonality with his father. "He hates like me," Joe Sr. reportedly said—in a way, a measure of respect. RFK developed a hard shell around his soft heart. He was curt and dismissive and ruthless when he had to be. Once, in a confrontation with the headquarters hangers-on, he shouted, "I don't want my brother to get mixed up with politicians!" The politicians felt the same way about Bobby. "The candidate's brother," as he was usually introduced, just shrugged. "I don't care if anyone around here likes me," he muttered, "as long as they like Jack."

The Kennedy brothers were a unique blend of old and new, heralds of the postwar generation that was changing American politics. Massachusetts Governor Paul Dever shrewdly described JFK as "the first Irish Brahmin" and Bobby as "the last Irish Puritan." Bobby proudly identified with the Irish and with the underdog. That was how he came to have his strange and regrettable association with Senator Joseph McCarthy, the Red-baiting demagogue whose congressional investigations terrorized government bureaucrats in the early 1950s. McCarthy was an old Kennedy family friend, a sometimes date of Bobby's sisters ("he kissed very hard," recalled Jean Kennedy Smith), and—to Bobby at least—a proud Irish tough guy who, as Bobby saw it, stood up to the pantywaist elitists in the State Department. At his father's recommendation, RFK signed on as a staff lawyer for McCarthy. That McCarthy was a fraud and a bully did not bother RFK, at least in the beginning. Kennedy did clash with McCarthy's henchman Roy Cohn, who called Kennedy a "rich bitch." The two nearly came to blows, and Kennedy eventually quit McCarthy's staff.

He remained a hard-charging lawyer for the Senate Permanent Subcommittee on Investigations, however, turning his prosecutorial attention to mobbed-up unions, particularly the Teamsters. Kennedy's investigation of mobsters like Momo "Sam" Giancana, the boss of the Chicago Mafia, has led to some psychohistorical theorizing. A onetime bootlegger, Kennedy's own father had some shadowy connections to organized crime, never fully proved but often speculated about. Certainly RFK was aware of the rumors. Was he playing with fire by going after the mob? Joe Sr. was furious when RFK told him of his intention to investigate organized crime. But young Kennedy went ahead, producing sensational televised hearings in the late 1950s that exposed nefarious ties between the Mafia and organized labor. Historian Doris Kearns Goodwin has speculated that some deeper Oedipal urge was driving RFK. Was he somehow trying to get even with the father who had ignored him and favored the more successful older sons? Kennedy's psyche was so complex that armchair psychologizing is intriguing but ultimately not determinative.

In any case, RFK never turned up any ties between his father and the mob (or, rather, links that were made public). And he continued to play his role as brother protector.

In December 1960, at the father's insistence, President-elect John F. Kennedy nominated his brother Robert to be attorney general of the United States. (Joe wanted Bobby to keep an eye on FBI Director J. Edgar Hoover. Joe knew that Hoover kept files, including one on a sexual affair between then Lieutenant John F. Kennedy and a woman suspected as a Nazi spy, Inga Arvad, during World War II.) Such nepotism would be unthinkable now, but RFK was easily confirmed by the Senate in February 1961.

Robert Kennedy turned out arguably to be the best attorney general in history. Certainly, his legacy on pressing for civil rights and prosecuting organized crime is unrivaled. The Deep South was still under the hold of Jim Crow in the early 1960s. The U.S. Supreme Court's order to desegregate schools "with all deliberate speed" had been met with massive resistance, and blacks were still, by state law, excluded from whites only restrooms and hotels and other public accommodations. The civil rights movement was rising but had still not aroused the national conscience. In the spring of 1961 a group of black and white activists calling themselves Freedom Riders began traveling on buses in the South to force federal intervention to uphold the law outlawing segregation in interstate commerce. The Freedom Riders were beaten bloody by white mobs (with local police standing by watching), and their bus was burned. The spectacle drew international attention—and brought shame on the United States just as the new president was preparing for a summit meeting with the Soviet Union's Nikita Khrushchev in Vienna in June. JFK was furious about the Freedom Riders. "Tell them to call it off!" the president angrily instructed his special assistant for civil rights, Harris Wofford. "Stop them! Get your friends off those buses!"

Robert Kennedy had dispatched one of his assistants, John Seigenthaler, to Alabama to meet with local officials and "hold their hands" to avoid violence. But when Seigenthaler himself was beaten over the head and hospitalized as he tried to rescue a black woman from the mob, RFK began to see things in a different light.

All through his life, Robert Kennedy was experiential. He went searching for new experiences, and he allowed himself to be moved and stirred and shaped by what he saw and heard and felt. He was open to change and very sensitive to unfairness and injustice. Kennedy himself began traveling to the South as attorney general, and what he experienced there, talking to everyone from segregationist police chiefs to poor children with distended bellies, profoundly influenced him. Not right away—he was impatient with angry young blacks and their leaders, including Martin Luther King, Jr., with whom he had an uneasy relationship—but slowly he came to appreciate what they were fighting for and, crucially, to identify with them. As time went on, he became the most important advocate in the Kennedy administration for not only enforcing the existing laws but changing them to outlaw segregation and discrimination everywhere.

Blessed with a shrewd sense of the possible and good political timing, Kennedy and his brother the president waited for the right moment, then pushed hard. The time came in June 1963. Governor George Wallace of Alabama was defying efforts to integrate the state university, and in Birmingham, Sheriff Eugene "Bull" Connor was turning fire hoses and police dogs on small black children marching for freedom. A new witness, the TV camera, was recording it all for the nation to see. On the warm June day that Wallace "stood in the schoolhouse door" to defy the U.S. Justice Department, RFK persuaded his brother to seize the moment and address the nation, calling for a federal civil rights bill to outlaw racial discrimination everywhere in the land. RFK saw the need, as his aide Burke Marshall put it, "to get at the heart of the matter."

In retrospect, JFK's speech, which launched the legislative effort that became the Civil Rights Act of 1964, was a stroke of great political courage, one that required real sacrifice. By siding with the civil rights movement, President Kennedy was in effect writing off the base of his own political party. The Democrats would never carry the Solid South again. Southern state and local leaders, who all were, in 1960, Democrats, within a generation or less became almost entirely Republican. Most of Kennedy's political advisers were well aware of the political risk involved. In the internal deliberations preceding President Kennedy's speech, "every single person who spoke about it in the White House—every one of them—was against President Kennedy sending up that bill, against making it a moral issue," Marshall recalled. The "conclusive voice within the government" was Robert Kennedy's. "He urged it, he felt it, he understood it. And he prevailed."

In the South "Bobby" became a curse word. RFK was also scorned as "Raul" (after Raúl Castro, the Cuban dictator's younger brother). When the attorney general went south to speak in the autumn of 1963, President Kennedy, in the wry, slightly mocking tone that the Kennedys used with one another, urged his brother to come back soon—or not at all.

While the attorney general was bringing federal law enforcement to bear in the cause of civil rights, he was also attacking the mob. Fearing corruption of his own agents, the FBI's J. Edgar Hoover had always been reluctant to take on the Mafia. But Kennedy ordered the bureau into action, investigating, wiretapping, shadowing, and, where possible, bringing cases against mob bosses. The biggest of these and the target of the most Justice Department attention was Momo Giancana, boss of Chicago.

In Kennedyland, things are rarely as simple as they seem. In February 1962 the attorney general was informed by the director of the FBI that the president of the United States had been sleeping with a girlfriend of the most powerful figure in the Mafia. Giancana's moll was a woman named Judith Exner. JFK had encountered her during his Senate years, while palling around in Las Vegas with Frank Sinatra, the singer who allowed himself to become too close to gangsters. The Judith Exner affair, one of many for the eternally priapic president, continued into the White House. The FBI had learned of it through wiretaps on Giancana. Hoover reveled in such items of potential blackmail, which gave him a kind of job insurance and power over his nominal bosses.

To complicate matters further, Giancana had been hired by the CIA to try to assassinate Cuba's Fidel Castro. The mob hit on Castro, a hated and feared figure in the fervid Cold War era, never happened (or even came close). But Giancana's multiple ties to the administration created, at the very least, a political headache for RFK. The potential for scandal was enormous, even at a time when the press was relatively more docile and did not write about the sex lives of politicians or probe too deeply into the CIA.

Still, Kennedy continued to press the FBI to investigate Giancana, to shadow the mob boss. On tapes of secret FBI bugs planted in his Chicago headquarters, Giancana was heard to complain that the constant pressure and scrutiny from the feds made him feel as if he were living "in Russia." Deputized by his brother to oversee CIA covert action against Cuba, RFK also pressed hard to overthrow or kill Castro, alienating many spooks with his meddling in CIA matters.

Robert Kennedy had created a host of enemies. When his brother Jack was slain by an assassin's bullet on November 22, 1963, Kennedy immediately feared an act of retribution. From his house, Hickory Hill, in McLean, Virginia, he called his informants in Chicago to ask if the mob had killed his brother, and he called an informant in a CIA safe house in Washington to ask if the anti-Castro Cubans had turned on the president. He asked about the Teamsters' Jimmy Hoffa, and he directly asked the director of the CIA, John McCone, if there had been any CIA involvement. He did all this on that bright November afternoon before he went to Andrews Air Force Base to greet the coffin returning from Dallas, and to the day he died he was never satisfied with the answer that Lee Harvey Oswald had been a lone gunman, that there was no conspiracy behind him.

After his brother's death Robert Kennedy sank into darkness. Many years later, recalling the weeks and months after the assassination, John Seigenthaler described Kennedy as a "man on a rack." He seemed tortured, haunted. He began to waste away, disappearing into his brother's black overcoat and bomber jacket, which he wore like a hair shirt. (Sailing on a yacht off the coast of Maine, RFK watched in horror as the bomber jacket blew over the side. Like the little boy who had been rescued by his older brother, he dived in after it and nearly drowned of exposure before he was fished out of the water, holding the jacket.) His humor, always sardonic, turned black. "Been to any good funerals lately?" he would ask. He began driving his convertible, too fast, at night, often to Arlington Cemetery. He would climb over the wall and sit by his brother's grave until dawn. For a time he lost his faith. On the night of his brother's death, as a friend closed the door to the Lincoln Bedroom, where Robert had gone to sleep (or tried to), the friend heard Robert's voice cry out, "Why, God?"

In March 1964, Robert accompanied the president's widow, Jacqueline, to the island of Antigua, where they stayed with other houseguests at the home of Mrs. Paul Mellon. Jackie gave RFK a copy of Edith Hamilton's *The Greek Way*, and Kennedy spent most of the next several days in the cool dark of his room, lost to the world. He read of the House of Atreus, doomed to repeat the sins of their fathers; of overweening pride that brings men low; of fatal hubris. He felt that the great Greek poets and playwrights were speaking to him, about his own family and the curse of pride. He memorized Aeschylus:

All arrogance will reap a harvest rich in tears
God calls men to a heavy reckoning
For overweening pride.

"In agony learn wisdom!" cries the herald in Aeschylus's *Prometheus Bound.* Kennedy tried to. Slowly and painfully he pulled himself out of his depression. Though never much of a student, he began reading Shakespeare and Camus, marking up the texts of the books, which he carried in his pocket or briefcase. He forged a crude existential philosophy, a conviction that yes, man is doomed, but that is no excuse to give up. Rather the opposite. Man must get up every day and challenge the fates to give meaning to existence.

He willed himself back into public life. In the summer of 1964 he decided to resign as attorney general (he had almost stopped going to the office) and run for the U.S. Senate from New York.

Though Kennedy had known great power as his brother's unofficial deputy president, he had always worked behind the scenes. He had been a shrewd consigliere. "Thank God for Bobby," JFK had said to his aide Dave Powers after the Cuban missile crisis in October 1962. It had been RFK, more than any other in the so-called Ex Com of top advisers who worked with the president during those perilous thirteen days, who understood how to mix public firmness with private conciliation toward the Soviets. The communication between JFK and RFK had been almost nonverbal. "They hardly had to speak with each other. They understood each other from half a word," recalled British diplomat and philosopher Isaiah Berlin. "There was a kind of constant, telepathic contact between them."

But now Kennedy had to take the public stage, to speak out, to ask for votes. The family expectation—Kennedys are *winners*—hung over him. After JFK had been elected president, he had given his brother a cigarette case with the half-joking inscription "When I'm through, how about you?" But the younger brother felt weak, unsure, unsteady—unready, perhaps never ready. Two months into the campaign, looking out a hotel room window at a vast crowd assembled in downtown Buffalo, he said, mournfully, "They're here for Jack." RFK continued to mope, muttering about doom, until a campaign aide, Paul Corbin, grabbed him and said, "Get out of this mysticism. Get out of your daze. . . . God damn, Bob, be yourself. Get a hold of yourself. You're real. Your brother is dead."

Kennedy was swept into office on the tailwind of LBJ's 1964 landslide (he badly trailed LBJ's vote total in New York, galling to RFK, who loathed Johnson as a usurper). Kennedy did not turn out to be much of a senator in the conventional sense. "He was in the Senate, but not of it," recalled Majority Leader Mike Mansfield. He was not nearly as effective at working the cloakroom or tending to his home state base as his little brother, Edward (who, in the jokey way of the Kennedys, gave RFK a book, entitled *What I Know About New York Politics*, with the pages left blank). But he was, in his own way, a visionary leader. Sensing the rising despair of the inner city, he created a model for urban redevelopment in the Bedford Stuyvesant Restoration Corporation. Wary of straight welfare payments, he emphasized jobs as a way to restore the dignity of young black men who felt they had none. He was able to reach out to black voters in ways that most white politicians could not—by not just pretending to listen but by conveying, almost ineffably, his empathy. Sonny Carson, a black activist, recalled watching RFK walk into a local church. "Man, it was like the Pope walked in," said Carson. "There was a strangeness that caused blacks to love him. He was the younger brother full of pain."

In June 1966, Kennedy was invited to South Africa, to address the students who were agitating against apartheid. It was a very low time in South Africa. Most of the world had turned away from the plight of the country's oppressed black majority. But Kennedy went, spinning out his existentialist credo, at once melancholy and hopeful, high-minded but direct. "Each time a man stands up for an ideal, or acts to improve the lot of others, or strikes out against injustice, he sends forth a tiny ripple of hope, and crossing each other from a million different centers of energy and daring, these ripples build a current that can sweep down the mightiest walls of oppression and resistance . . ." said Kennedy, in his reedy but urgent voice, in his Day of Affirmation speech at Cape Town University. When he finished, there was silence. Like a child, recalled Margaret Marshall, his student leader host, he looked around him, "as if to say, was the speech okay?" Then, with a rush, a roar of applause crashed over him. For the next three days, he traveled about the country, often stopping to address impromptu crowds while standing on the roof of his car. Blacks, banned from touching whites in South Africa, reached out to hold his hand. Later Marshall recalled his impact: "He reminded us—me—that we were not alone. . . . We all had felt alienated. . . . He reset the moral compass, not so much by attacking apartheid, but by simply talking justice and freedom and dignity—words that none of us had heard in, it seemed like, an eternity. He didn't go through the white liberals, he connected straight—by standing on a car. Nobody had done that. How simple it was! He was not afraid."

At home students were increasingly agitating to protest against the Vietnam War, taking over school buildings and shutting down campuses. By the long hot summer of 1967, race riots were erupting in cities from coast to coast, so severe in Detroit that army paratroopers were called in to stop the sniping. Kennedy began touring the country, meeting with Hispanic migrant workers, destitute Native Americans on reservations, and blacks living in rural poverty. His daughter Kathleen recalled him bursting into the family dining room at Hickory Hill, back from a tour of the Mississippi Delta. "In Mississippi, a whole family lives in a shack the size of this room," he announced to his nine children, ages two to fifteen. "The children are covered with sores and their tummies stick out because they have no food. Do you know how lucky you are? Do you *know* how *lucky* you are? Do something for your country."

As the Vietnam War dragged on and deepened, Kennedy had been slowly transformed from a hawk to an outspoken dove. By the winter of 1968 he was under growing pressure to challenge President Johnson for the Democratic Party nomination. Kennedy loathed Johnson and wanted him out of office. But he hesitated to run against his old rival. In tense conversations with his advisers, he worried that his candidacy would badly split the Democratic Party and elect a Republican—Richard Nixon—in November. He may, at some level, have feared for his own safety. He was an obvious target for assassination, though whenever he was made aware of a threat against him, his instinct was to defy it and stick to any public speaking plans.

Kennedy was furious when he saw someone at a rally hold up a poster that read KENNEDY: HAWK, DOVE—OR CHICKEN? When an aide laughed at the sign, Kennedy sharply told him, "It's not funny." But he continued to agonize. At a dinner with his wife, Ethel, and friends at Hickory Hill in January, he said, "I think if I run I will go a long way toward proving everything that everybody who doesn't like me has said about me . . . that I'm just a selfish, ambitious little SOB that can't wait to get his hands on the White House."

And yet . . . it was Robert Kennedy who liked to quote Dante that "the hottest places in Hell are reserved for those who, in a time of great moral crisis, maintain their neutrality." In snowy New Hampshire, Senator Eugene McCarthy, running as a peace candidate, almost defeated LBJ in the traditional nation's first primary.

On March 16, 1968, Robert Kennedy declared his candidacy for the Democratic nomination. The day after, he flew to Kansas State University to deliver a long-scheduled lecture. The KSU field house was packed with fifteen thousand students, some of them actually hanging from the rafters, waving signs like KISS ME, BOBBY. His voice flat and stammering, his right leg shaking, Kennedy began tentatively but then cut loose, jamming his fist in the air while pounding out an antiwar diatribe. When he was done, "the field house sounded as though it was inside Niagra Falls; it was like a soundtrack gone haywire," recorded journalist Jack Newfield. After a similarly raucous event at his next stop, before seventeen thousand at the University of Kansas, Stanley Tretick, a photographer for *Look* magazine, gawked at the hysteria and exclaimed, "This is Kansas, fucking Kansas! He's going all the fucking way!"

RFK knew better. The party establishment was against him. "Who else could have brought together Big Business, Big Labor, and the South?" Kennedy boasted self-mockingly to a speechwriter, Milton Gwirtzman. "And the Jews," added Gwirtzman. Kennedy was slow to find his voice. At first his speeches were too hot, then too cool—too much like his brother's. At the end of March, Kennedy received an enormous boost when LBJ, who was having nightmares about RFK's deposing him, announced that he would not seek reelection. But Johnson made clear that the party machinery would work to elect Vice President Hubert Humphrey, not Kennedy. In a casual conversation with Gene McCarthy, Johnson avoided saying anything about Kennedy. Instead, he drew his hand across his throat, in a cutting gesture. Johnson began feeding bits of gossip about Kennedy to investigative reporters, including hints of Kennedy's involvement in the Castro assassination plots and his role as attorney general in wiretapping Martin Luther King.

On April 4, only five days after Johnson dropped out of the race, Kennedy and the entire nation were jolted when a gunman shot and killed Martin Luther King as he stood on a motel balcony in Memphis.

Kennedy was on the way to a rally in the inner city in Indianapolis, where he was campaigning in the Indiana primary. The local police told him they could not guarantee his safety in the ghetto and peeled away. Kennedy went on. Standing on a flatbed truck, his hands thrust into the pockets of his brother's black overcoat as he hunched over in the wind and cold, he told the crowd, most of whom were still unaware in that pre-CNN age, that King was dead. There was an audible gasp. But Kennedy continued:

> For those of you who are black and are tempted to be filled with hatred and distrust at the injustice of such an act, I can only say that I feel in my own heart the same kind of feeling. I had a member of my family killed. . . .
>
> My favorite poet was Aeschylus. He wrote, "In our sleep, pain which cannot forget falls drop by drop upon the heart until, in our own despair, against our will, comes wisdom through the awful grace of God."
>
> What we need in the United States is not division; what we need in the United States is not hatred; what we need in the United States is not violence or lawlessness; but love and wisdom, and compassion toward one another, and a feeling of justice toward those who still suffer within our country, whether they be white or they be black.
>
> So I shall ask you tonight to return home, to say a prayer for the family of Martin Luther King, that's true, but most importantly to say a prayer for our own country, which all of us love—a prayer for understanding and that compassion of which I spoke. . . .
>
> Let us dedicate ourselves to what the Greeks wrote so many years ago; to tame the savageness of man and to make gentle the life of the world.
>
> Let us dedicate ourselves to that, and say a prayer for our country and our people.

The inner cities blew up on the night King died: riots in 110 cities, thirty-nine deaths, more than twenty-five hundred injured. But Indianapolis stayed calm.

King's assassination seemed to make Kennedy even more willful about ignoring threats against his own life. In Lansing, Michigan, one week after King was shot to death, police informed Kennedy's staff that a man had been seen on a rooftop holding a gun. Fred Dutton, Kennedy's closest aide, pulled the blinds down in RFK's hotel room. "Don't close them," Kennedy instructed. "If they're going to shoot, they'll shoot." Kennedy told Dutton, "We're not going to start ducking now." In his daybook, he quoted Camus: "Knowing that you are going to die is nothing."

For the first three weeks of April, Kennedy crisscrossed the nation, drawing huge throngs, trying to prove his popularity to the bosses who controlled the Democratic National Convention. "The crowds were savage," recalled John Bartlow Martin, who traveled with Kennedy as an adviser. "They pulled his cufflinks off, tore at his clothes, tore ours. In bigger towns, with bigger crowds, it was frightening." In Kalamazoo, Michigan, a housewife reached into the car and calmly removed Kennedy's right shoe, which she displayed to reporters as a trophy of war. One overheated woman yanked Kennedy's head down by the tie; another pulled him out of the car altogether, breaking his tooth on the curb. Kennedy's shyness would seize him at the beginning of a motorcade or mass rally. He would grimace, tight-lipped, before plunging into a crowd, as if he were diving into icy water. As the crowd closed around him, he would let his body go limp. "It was like he wasn't there," observed Peter Fishbein, a young aide who traveled with the candidate. "His stare was vacant." Once, when their car was nearly rolled over by a wildly impassioned crowd in California, Fishbein looked at Kennedy, who was limply waving and looking away. "Even for him, it could be scary," said Fishbein.

Viewed several decades later, the films and photographs of Robert Kennedy's eighty-eight-day campaign seem feverish, almost hysterical. Not just the jumpers and screamers waving signs that said BOBBY IS SEXY, BOBBY IS GROOVY, I LOVE YOU, BOBBY, but the farmers and workers and housewives who closed in on him, clutching at him, pulling him from his car and—twice—stealing the shoes off his feet. They came out, at first, to cheer the myth of Camelot restored. They saw, instead, a raw, somewhat reticent young man struggling to be honest with them and with himself. His speeches were effective not so much for their words, which, when scripted, were usually bland, or their delivery, which was often flat or awkward, as for something more ineffable: the emanations of compassion and understanding that he conveyed. Inarticulate but urgent and sincere, Kennedy could reach poor and dispossessed people who themselves had difficulty articulating their needs and anxieties. People loved him even though he challenged, even baited them to overcome their fears and narrow self-interests. He embarrassed middle-class college students, whose support he desperately wanted, by belittling their draft deferments, pointing out that the casualties in Vietnam were disproportionately suffered by minorities and the poor.

On April 26, Kennedy spoke to an audience of medical students and doctors at the University of Indiana. His hands were shaking as he gripped the podium. His knuckles shone white, and his fingers nervously played along the fluted pedestal. The students, almost all white and middle class, looking forward to their prosperous careers, challenged Kennedy on his plan to provide more health care for the poor. "Where are you going to get all the money from for these federally subsidized programs you're talking about?" one of the students asked.

"From you," Kennedy replied. There were boos and hisses, but Kennedy hung in, quoting Camus on the duty to reduce the number of children who suffer: "If you do not do this, who will do this?" Just as a few in the crowd began to clap, Kennedy taunted them some more: "You sit here as white medical students while black people carry the burden of the fighting in Vietnam." By the time he was done Kennedy had won grudging but respectful applause.

John Bartlow Martin, a Hoosier himself, watched with fascination as Kennedy stumped around the mostly conservative state: "He went yammering around Indiana about the poor whites of Appalachia and the starving Indians who committed suicide on the reservations and the jobless Negroes in the distant great cities, and half the Hoosiers didn't have any idea what he was talking about; but he plodded ahead stubbornly, making them listen, maybe even making some of them care, by the sheer power of his own caring. Indiana people are not generous or sympathetic; they are hard and hardhearted, not warm and generous; but he must have touched something in them, pushed a button somewhere. He alone did it."

Some of Kennedy's appeal was a matter of body language, of tone. One is struck, listening to scratchy recordings of Kennedy's speeches, how deeply mournful he sounded. Martin described Kennedy's strangely captivating aura of frailty, urgency, and humility: "He always looked so alone, standing up by himself on the lid of the trunk of the convertible— so alone, vulnerable, so fragile, you feared he might break. He was thin. He did not chop the air with his hand as his brother Jack had; instead he had a little gesture with his right hand, his fist closed, the thumb sticking up a little, and he would jab it to make a point. When he got applause, he did not smile at the crowd, pleased; instead he looked down, down at the ground or at his speech, and waited til they finished, then went on. He could take a bland generality and deliver it with such a depth of feeling that it cut like a knife. Everything he said had an edge to it."

Kennedy won the Indiana primary on May 7, then Nebraska, an even more conservative state, a week later. (There were far fewer primaries in those days; Kennedy ran in only a half dozen.) But in Oregon on May 28 he lost to McCarthy. Kennedy was too hot, too edgy for some voters, who associated him with riots and blood feuds. (Oregon is "one giant suburb," Kennedy fretted to a newsman on the plane to Portland. "It's all white Protestants. There's nothing for me to grab a hold of.")

Kennedy's last week of campaigning in California was a blur of motorcades and stifling auditoriums, screaming teenyboppers and little black schoolchildren, gaily running beside Kennedy's car. In Watts, Los Angeles Mayor Sam Yorty refused to provide police protection (Yorty regarded RFK as a subversive), so a militant group called Sons of Watts escorted Kennedy's car through the ghetto. In Chinatown in San Francisco, a loud popping car sent Ethel Kennedy diving to the bottom of the car. Kennedy, standing on the hood, remained upright, but his knees buckled. The loud bangs were only firecrackers. In San Diego that night Kennedy, exhausted, sick, stopped in mid-speech to go offstage and vomit. He returned to the ballroom and finished, as he always did, by paraphrasing Shaw: "*Some men see things as they are, and ask why. I dream of things that never were and say why not.*"

The next day Kennedy won the California primary over McCarthy by 46 to 42 percent. "We are a great country, an unselfish country, and a compassionate country," he told the sweltering crowd in the Ambassador Hotel shortly before midnight. "So my thanks to all of you,"—he wound up—"and now it's on to Chicago, and let's win there."

Kennedy was supposed to exit through the ballroom doors, but the crowd was so heavy that his bodyguard, Bill Barry, veered in a different direction, escorted by the hotel maître d' though a back entrance into the kitchen corridor. Members of the kitchen staff reached out to shake the candidate's hand, but as they did, a mentally deranged drifter named Sirhan Sirhan stepped out and shot Kennedy in the head with a snub-nosed pistol. There were screams and a struggle. Back in the ballroom "an awful sound" rolled "like a moan," recalled Jack Newfield. A woman screamed uncontrollably, "No, God, no. It's happened again."

Robert Kennedy was no Jack Kennedy—or Martin Luther King. He lacked the rhetorical force and commanding presence to be a conventionally gifted leader. But in his time he was a force in part because of the qualities that were *not* presidential, at least in the way most politicians wish to project. John Bartlow Martin captured the ineffable differences between JFK and RFK: "Jack Kennedy was more the politician, saying things publicly that he privately scoffed at. Robert Kennedy was more himself. Jack gave the impression of decisive leadership, the man with all the answers. Robert seemed more hesitant, less sure he was right, more tentative, more questioning, and completely honest about it. Leadership he showed; but it had a different quality of searching for answers to hard questions in company with his bewildered audience, trying to work things out with their help."

It is far from clear that Kennedy would have won the Democratic nomination. Humphrey had the support of organized labor, still a great force in the party, and most of the big party bosses. Even if nominated, Kennedy might have lost to Nixon in the fall. The nation was fearful in 1968, and Kennedy's heat and passion may have been too much for Nixon's "Silent Majority."

It is also difficult to say whether Kennedy would have been an effective president. He would have tried hard to disengage from Vietnam, perhaps saving thousands of lives (America lost another thirty thousand soldiers after Nixon was elected). Without question, Kennedy would have tried to face the problems of race and poverty. But those were, and are, bedeviling problems, and Kennedy might have found himself mired in interest group politics as he tried to push legislation on Capitol Hill. Kennedy's ruthless streak did not just vanish amid the hearts and flowers of 1968. He had a secretive side, and it's possible he would have resorted to subterfuge and dirty tricks against his foes—wiretapping at home and covert action abroad.

But it is more likely that Kennedy would have displayed a style of leadership that has almost vanished from modern politics. He would have been honest with voters about the sacrifices they needed to make. He would have offered more than lip service to the need for the country to face up to its problems. He believed fervently in public service, and he would have set a personal example while impatiently goading the young to honor their personal commitment to change. He might have failed, but he would have failed trying honestly and with all his heart.

When Robert helped design JFK's grave, he disagreed with his brother's widow. RFK wanted a plain white cross. Jackie wanted something far grander, more elegant, and she prevailed. Today, from the hillside at Arlington Cemetery, you can see all of the federal city stretched before JFK's memorial, with its eternal flame and sweeping curve of marble engraved with the words of Kennedy's inaugural address: "Let the word go forth from this time and place. . . ."

To find Robert Kennedy's grave, you must wander down a narrow alley shielded by trees. On a block of marble are carved some fragments of speeches he wrote, mournfully quoting Aeschylus. His body lies under a small, plain white cross, inscribed only with his name and the years of his birth and death. The effect is a little lonely. You wonder about the frightened small boy who almost became a great man, and where he might have led us had he lived.

FURTHER READING

GEORGE WASHINGTON: The General

Flexnor, James Thomas. *Washington in the American Revolution, 1775-1783.* Boston: Little, Brown, 1967.

Higginbotham, Don. *George Washington: Uniting a Nation.* Lanham, Md.: Bowman and Littlefield, 2002.

Jones, Robert. *George Washington: Ordinary Man, Extraordinary Leader.* New York: Fordham University Press, 2002.

Kwasny, Mark. *Washington's Partisan War, 1775-1783.* Kent, Ohio: Kent State University Press, 1996.

Lengel, Edward G. *General George Washington: A Military Life.* New York: Random House, 2005.

CHARLES FINNEY: Prophet of Social Reform

Charles Finney's collected works, including his 1868 *Memoirs* and all his published sermons can be found online at www.gospeltruth.net. The Gospel Truth Ministries' Web site also contains a nineteenth-century biography of Finney: Robert Samuel Fletcher, *History of Oberlin College from Its Foundation Through the Civil War*; and "Reminiscences: Personal Remarks Made at a Memorial Service July 28, 1876, to Honor Charles Finney," plus other material on Finney.

RECENT BIOGRAPHIES

Hambrick-Stowe, Charles E. *Charles Finney and the Spirit of American Evangelism.* Grand Rapids, Mich.: W. B. Eerdmans Publishing Co., 1996.

Hardman, Keith. *Charles Grandison Finney, 1792–1875: Revivalist and Reformer.* Syracuse, N.Y.: Syracuse University Press, 1988.

OTHER SOURCES

Barnes, Gilbert Hobbs. *The Anti-Slavery Impulse, 1830–1844.* American Historical Association. New York: D. Appleton-Century Co., 1933.

Cole, Charles C. *The Social Ideas of the Northern Evangelists, 1826–1860.* New York: Columbia University Press, 1954.

Cross, Whitney R. *The Burned-over District: The Social and Intellectual History of Enthusiastic Religion in Western New York, 1800–1850.* New York: Harper and Row, 1968 [1950].

Johnson, Paul E. *A Shopkeeper's Millennium: Society and Revivals in Rochester, New York 1815–1837.* New York: Hill and Wang, 1978.

McLoughlin, William G., Jr. *Revivals, Awakenings and Reform.* Chicago: University of Chicago Press, 1980.

Miller, Perry. *The Life of the Mind in America: From the Revolution to the Civil War.* New York: Harcourt, Brace and World, 1965.

Ryan, Mary P. *Cradle of the Middle Class: The Family in Oneida County, 1790–1865.* New York: Cambridge University Press, 1981.

Thomas, Benjamin Platt. *Theodore Weld: Crusader for Freedom.* New Brunswick, N.J.: Rutgers University Press, 1950.

PRESIDENT ULYSSES GRANT AND THE BATTLE FOR EQUALITY

I am grateful to my friend Sidney Blumenthal for many hours of conversation on the politics of the Civil War era and for allowing me to see his continuing work in progress on the subject, which was especially instructive about Grant's life before the Civil War.

SELECT BIBLIOGRAPHY

Bunting, Josiah, III. *Ulysses S. Grant.* New York: Times Books, 2004.

Current, Richard N. *Arguing with Historians: Essays on the Historical and the Unhistorical.* Middletown, Conn.: Wesleyan University Press, 1987.

Foner, Eric. *Reconstruction: America's Unfinished Revolution.* New York: Harper & Row, 1988.

Grant, Ulysses S. *Personal Memoirs of U. S. Grant.* New York: C. L. Webster & Co., 1885–86. 2 vols.

Hesseltine, William Best. *Ulysses Grant, Politician.* New York: F. Ungar Publishing Co., 1935.

McFeely, William S. *Grant: A Biography.* New York: Norton, 1981.

Simpson, Brooks D. *Let Us Have Peace: Ulysses S. Grant and the Politics of War and Reconstruction, 1861–1868.* Chapel Hill: University of North Carolina Press, 1991.

———. *The Reconstruction Presidents.* Lawrence: University Press of Kansas, 1998.

Smith, Jean Edward. *Grant.* New York: Simon & Schuster, 2001.

Waugh, Joan. *U. S. Grant: American Hero, American Myth.* Chapel Hill: University of North Carolina Press, 2009.

J. PIERPONT MORGAN: He Knew He Was Right

Adams, Charles Francis, Jr. Massachusetts Historical Society, Charles Francis Adams II Papers—"Memorabilia."

Adams, Henry. *The Education of Henry Adams.* New York: Library of America, 1983 [1918].

———. *The Letters of Henry Adams,* ed. J. C. Levenson, Ernest Samuels, et al. Cambridge, Mass.: Belknap Press of Harvard University Press, 1982–88. 6 vols.

Emerson, Ralph Waldo. *The Letters of Ralph Waldo Emerson,* ed. Ralph L. Rusk. New York: Columbia University Press, 1939. 6 vols.

Friedman, Milton, and Anna Schwartz. *A Monetary History of the United States 1867–1960.* Princeton, N.J.: Princeton University Press, 1963.

Galbraith, John Kenneth. *Money.* Boston: Houghton Mifflin Co., 1975.

Morgan Grenfell Company Archives, London.

Shakespeare, William. *Twelfth Night.*

Smalley, George W. *Anglo-American Memories.* New York: G. P. Putnam's Sons, 1912.

Woolf, Virginia. *Roger Fry.* New York: Harcourt Brace Jovanovich, 1968 [1940].

CHIEF JOSEPH AND THE CHALLENGE OF INDIAN LEADERSHIP

Hampton, Bruce. *Children of Grace: The Nez Perce War of 1877.* Lincoln: University of Nebraska Press, 2002.

Josephy, Alvin M. *The Nez Perce Indians and the Opening of the Northwest.* New Haven, Conn.: Yale University Press, 1965.

McWhorter, Lucullus Virgil. *Yellow Wolf: His Own Story.* Caldwell, Idaho: Caxton Printers, 1940.

Thompson, Scott M. *I Will Tell of My War Story: A Pictorial Account of the Nez Perce War.* Seattle: University of Washington Press, 2000.

West, Elliott. *The Last Indian War: The Nez Perce Story.* New York: Oxford University Press, 2009.

WHEN PRESIDENTS BECOME WEAK

Cooper, John Milton. *Woodrow Wilson: A Biography.* New York: Alfred Knopf, 2009.

Dallek, Robert. *Flawed Giant: Lyndon Johnson and His Times, 1961–1973.* New York: Oxford University Press, 1998.

———. *Nixon and Kissinger: Partners in Power.* New York: HarperCollins, 2007.

Kennedy, David. *Freedom from Fear: The American People in Depression and War, 1929–1945.* New York: Oxford University Press, 1999.

McCullough, David. *Harry Truman.* New York: Simon & Schuster, 1992.

Stueck, William. *The Korean War: An International History.* Princeton, N.J.: Princeton University Press, 1995.

THE PHENOMENON: W. E. B. DuBois

DuBois, W. E. B. *Black Reconstruction in America, 1860–1880. An Essay Toward a History of the Part Which Black People Played in the Attempt to Reconstruct Democracy in America.* New York: Harcourt Brace, 1935.

———. *Dusk of Dawn: An Essay Toward an Autobiography of a Race Concept.* New York: Harcourt Brace, 1940.

———. *The Souls of Black Folk.* Chicago: A. C. McClurg & Co., 1903.

———. *The Writings of W. E. B. DuBois.* New York: Crowell, 1975.

Ferris, William H. *The African Abroad: or, His Evolution in Western Civilization: Tracing His Development Under a Caucasian Milieu.* New Haven, Conn.: Tuttle, Morehouse & Taylor, 1913.

Lewis, David Levering. *W. E. B. DuBois: Biography of a Race, 1868–1919.* New York: Holt, 1993.

———. *W. E. B. DuBois: The Fight for Equality and the American Century, 1919–1963.* New York: Holt, 2000.

Painter, Nell Irvin. *Creating Black Americans: African American History and Its Meanings, 1619 to the Present.* New York: Oxford University Press, 2006.

Tolney, Stewart E., and E. M. Beck. "Racial Violence and Black Migration in the American South, 1910–1930." *American Sociological Review*, vol. 57, no. 1 (February 1992).

MR. McGRAW

Alexander, Charles C. *John McGraw.* New York: Viking, 1988.

Deford, Frank. *The Old Ball Game.* New York: Atlantic Monthly Press, 2005.

Greenberg, Eric Rolfe. *The Celebrant.* Lincoln: University of Nebraska Press, 1983.

Pietrusza, David. *Rothstein.* New York: Carroll & Graf Publishers, 2003.

Ritter, Lawrence S. *The Glory of Their Times.* New York: Macmillan, 1966.

HOOVER AND ROOSEVELT: Two Approaches to Leadership

Bernanke, Ben S. *Essays on the Great Depression.* Princeton, N.J.: Princeton University Press, 2000.

Freidel, Frank. *Franklin D. Roosevelt: A Rendezvous with Destiny.* Boston: Little, Brown, 1990.

Kennedy, David M. *Freedom from Fear: The American People in Depression and War, 1929–1945.* New York: Oxford University Press, 1999.

Leuchtenburg, William E. *Herbert Hoover.* New York: Times Books, 2009.

Rauchway, Eric. *The Great Depression and the New Deal: A Very Short Introduction.* New York: Oxford University Press, 2008.

Schlesinger, Arthur M., Jr. *The Age of Roosevelt.* Boston: Little, Brown, 1956–60. 3 vols.

THE QUALITIES OF LEADERSHIP:
Dwight D. Eisenhower as Warrior and President

Ambrose, Stephen E. *The Supreme Commander: The War Years of General Dwight S. Eisenhower.* Garden City, N.Y.: Doubleday, 1970.

———. *Eisenhower the President.* New York: Simon & Schuster, 1984.

Barber, James David. *The Presidential Character: Predicting Performance in the White House,* 2d ed. Englewood Cliffs, N.J.: Prentice Hall, 1977.

Burns, James MacGregor. *Leadership.* New York: Harper & Row, 1978.

Cartwright, Dorwin, and Alvin Zander, eds. *Group Dynamics: Research and Theory.* New York: Harper & Row, 1968.

Chandler, Alfred D., Jr., ed. *The Papers of Dwight David Eisenhower.* Baltimore: Johns Hopkins Press, 1970–2001. 21 vols.

Eisenhower, Dwight D. *Crusade in Europe.* Garden City, N.Y.: Doubleday, 1948.

———. *The White House Years.* Garden City, N.Y.: Doubleday, 1963, 1965. 2 vols.

Ferrell, Robert H., ed. *The Eisenhower Diaries.* New York: Norton, 1981.

Greenstein, Fred I. *The Hidden-Hand Presidency: Eisenhower as Leader.* New York: Basic Books, 1982.

Parsons, Talcott, and Robert F. Bales. *Family, Socialization, and Interaction Process.* New York: Free Press, 1955.

THE IMPLAUSIBLE WENDELL WILLKIE: Leadership Ahead of Its Time

Brands, H. W. *The Traitor to His Class: The Privileged Life and Radical Presidency of Franklin Delano Roosevelt.* New York: Doubleday, 2008.

Halberstam, David. *The Powers that Be.* Urbana-Champaign: University of Illinois Press, 1975.

Hofstadter, Richard. *The American Political Tradition and the Men Who Made It.* New York: Vintage, 1989 [1948].

Johnson, Donald Bruce. *The Republican Party and Wendell Willkie.* Urbana: University of Illinois Press, 1960.

Madison, James H., ed. *Wendell Willkie: Hoosier Internationalist.* Bloomington: Indiana University Press, 1992.

Neal, Steve. *Dark Horse: A Biography of Wendell Willkie.* Lawrence: Kansas University Press, 1984.

Parmet, Herbert S., and Marie B. Hecht. *Never Again: A President Runs for a Third Term.* New York: Macmillan, 1968.

Peters, Charles. *Five Days in Philadelphia.* New York: Public Affairs, 2005.

Root, Oren. *Persons and Persuasions.* New York: Norton, 1974.

Stone, Irving. *They Also Ran.* New York: Doubleday, 1945.

White, Walter, *A Man Called White: The Autobiography of Walter White.* New York: Viking, 1948.

Willkie, Wendell L. *Free Enterprise: The Philosophy of Wendell L. Willkie as Found in His Speeches, Messages and Other Papers.* Washington, D.C.: National Home Library Assoc., 1940.

———. *One World,* intro. Donald Bruce Johnson. (University of Indiana Press, 1943.) New York.: Simon & Schuster, 1966 [1943].

———. *An American Program.* New York: Simon & Schuster, 1944.

"AM I A 'SCREWBALL,' OR AM I A PIONEER?": Pauli Murray's Civil Rights Movement

Gilmore, Glenda Elizabeth. *Defying Dixie: The Radical Roots of Civil Rights, 1919–1950.* New York: Norton, 2008.

Murray, Pauli. *Proud Shoes: The Story of an American Family.* New York: Harper & Row, 1978 [1956].

———. *Song in a Weary Throat: An American Pilgrimage.* New York: Harper & Row, 1987.

Scott, Anne Firor. *Pauli Murray and Carolina Ware: Forty Years of Letters in*

Black and White. Chapel Hill: University of North Carolina Press, 2006.

White, Deborah Gray. *Too Heavy a Load: Black Women in Defense of Themselves, 1894–1994.* New York: Norton, 1999.

ROBERT KENNEDY: The Empathetic Leader

Beran, Michael Knox. *The Last Patrician: Bobby Kennedy and the End of American Aristocracy.* New York: St. Martin's, 1998.

Newfield, Jack. *Robert Kennedy: A Memoir.* New York: Dutton, 1969.

Schlesinger, Arthur, Jr. *Robert Kennedy and His Times.* Boston: Houghton Mifflin, 1978.

Stein, Jean, and George Plimpton. *American Journey: The Times of Robert Kennedy.* New York: Harcourt Brace Jovanovich, 1970.

Wills, Garry. *The Kennedy Imprisonment: A Meditation on Power.* Boston: Little, Brown, 1981.

Witcover, Jules. *85 Days: The Last Campaign of Robert Kennedy.* New York: Putnam, 1969.

Wofford, Harris. *Of Kennedys and Kings: Making Sense of the Sixties.* New York: Farrar, Straus & Giroux, 1980.

ON THE CONTRIBUTORS

Kevin Baker, novelist and journalist, is the author of the *City of Fire* trilogy, comprising the historical novels *Dreamland*, *Paradise Alley*, and *Strivers Row*. *Paradise Alley* earned Baker the 2003 James Fenimore Cooper Prize for Best Historical Fiction from the Society of American Historians.

Alan Brinkley is the Allan Nevins Professor of History at Columbia University. His first book, *Voices of Protest: Huey Long, Father Coughlin, and the Great Depression*, won the National Book Award. He is also the author of *The End of Reform: New Deal Liberalism in Recession and War*; *Liberalism and Its Discontents*; *Franklin Delano Roosevelt*; and *The Publisher: Henry Luce and His American Century*.

Robert Dallek is professor emeritus at UCLA and since his retirement has also taught at Oxford University, the University of Texas, Boston University, Dartmouth College, and Stanford University. He is the author of *An Unfinished Life: John F. Kennedy, 1917–1963*, as well as biographies of Lyndon Johnson and Harry Truman.

Frances FitzGerald, noted writer and journalist, is the author of *Fire in the Lake: The Vietnamese and the Americans in Vietnam*, winner of the Pulitzer Prize and the National Book Award. She is also the author of *Way Out There in the Blue: Reagan, Star Wars and the End of the Cold War*. She is a regular contributor to the *New Yorker* and *New York Review of Books*.

Thomas Fleming is the author of more than forty nonfiction and fiction titles, including *Washington's Secret War: The Hidden History of Valley Forge* and *The Officers' Wives*. He was recently awarded the Richard Hughes Award for Lifetime Achievement from the New Jersey State Historical Commission. His most recent book is *The Intimate Lives of the Founding Fathers*.

Glenda E. Gilmore is the Peter V. and C. Vann Woodward Professor of History, African American Studies, and American Studies at Yale University and earned her Ph.D. at the University of North Carolina at Chapel Hill. Her most recent book, *Defying Dixie: The Radical Roots of Civil Rights, 1919–1950*, was one of the American Library Association's Notable Books of 2008 and the *Washington Post*'s Best Books of 2008. Her first book, *Gender and Jim Crow: Women and the Politics of White Supremacy in North Carolina, 1886–1920,* published in 1996, won the Frederick Jackson Turner Award, the James A. Rawley Prize, the Julia Cherry Spruill Prize, and the Heyman Prize.

ANNETTE GORDON-REED is professor of law at Harvard Law School, professor of history at Harvard University, and the Carol K. Pforzheimer Professor at the Radcliffe Institute for Advanced Study. Her most recent book, *The Hemingses of Monticello: An American Family,* was awarded the Pulitzer Prize, the National Book Award, the Society for Historians of the Early American Republic Book Award, and the Frederick Douglass Book Prize among others. She is also the recipient of the 2009 National Humanities Medal. She is the author of *Thomas Jefferson and Sally Hemings: An American Controversy*; *Race on Trial: Law and Justice in American History*; and *Andrew Johnson: The 17th President, 1865–1869.*

WALTER ISAACSON is the president and CEO of the Aspen Institute, a nonpartisan educational and policy studies institute based in Washington, D.C. Isaacson is also the chairman of the board of Teach for America and the U.S.-Palestinian Partnership. He has been the chairman and CEO of CNN and the editor of *Time* magazine. Isaacson is the author of *Einstein: His Life and Universe*; *Benjamin Franklin: An American Life*; and *Kissinger: A Biography*; and coauthor, with Evan Thomas, of *The Wise Men: Six Friends and the World They Made.*

DAVID KENNEDY is the Donald J. McLachlan Professor of History, emeritus, at Stanford University. He is the winner of the Pulitzer Prize, Francis Parkman Prize, Ambassador's Prize, and California Gold Medal for Literature, all for *Freedom from Fear: The American People in Depression and War, 1929–1945.* Other noted works include *Birth Control in America: The Career of Margaret Sanger* and *Over Here: The First World War and American Society.*

DAVID LEVERING LEWIS is the Julius Silver University Professor and Professor of History at New York University. He is twice winner of the Pulitzer Prize for his two volumes on the life of W. E. B. DuBois, which also received the Bancroft Prize and the Francis Parkman Prize. His other books include *When Harlem Was in Vogue*; *Race to Fashoda*; and *God's Crucible: Islam and the Making of Europe, 570–1215.*

JEAN STROUSE is the Sue Ann and John Weinberg Director of the Dorothy and Lewis B. Cullman Center for Scholars and Writers at the New York Public

Library. An occasional contributor to *The New Yorker*, the *New York Times*, the *New York Review of Books*, and *Slate*, she is the author of *Alice James: A Biography*, which won the Bancroft Prize, and *Morgan: American Financier*.

Evan Thomas is the assistant managing editor at *Newsweek* and the Ferris Professor of Journalism at Princeton University. He is the author of *Robert Kennedy: His Life*; *The Very Best Men: The Early Years of the CIA*; *The Man to See: The Life of Edward Bennett Williams*; and *The Wise Men: Six Friends and the World They Made* (with Walter Isaacson). His most recent book is *The War Lovers: Roosevelt, Lodge, Hearst, and the Rush to Empire, 1898*. Thomas has won numerous journalism awards, including the National Magazine Award in 1998 for *Newsweek*'s coverage of the Monica Lewinsky scandal.

Elliott West is the Alumni Distinguished Professor of History at the University of Arkansas. He is the author of *The Contested Plains: Indians, Goldseekers, and the Rush to Colorado*, which received the Francis Parkman Prize from the Society of American Historians and the PEN Center Award. His most recent book is *The Last Indian War: The Nez Perce Story*.

Sean Wilentz is the Sidney and Ruth Lapidus Professor in the American Revolutionary Era at Princeton University. He is the author of *Chants Democratic: New York City and the Rise of the American Working Class, 1788–1850*; *The Rise of American Democracy: Jefferson to Lincoln*, which won the Bancroft Prize; and *The Age of Reagan: A History, 1974–2008*. Wilentz also writes about American music, for which he has received a Grammy nomination, and he is the historian in residence at Bob Dylan's official Web site. His most recent book is *Bob Dylan in America*.

INDEX

Note: Page numbers in *italics* indicate an illustration; page numbers in **boldface** indicate the primary discussion of the individual.